THE BUFFET

A BUSINESS PARABLE

50 Lessons on Leadership & Success
from the World's Greatest All-You-Can-Eat Place

DAN TECK

DandiLove Unlimited

DandiLove Unlimited, Portland, OR
© 2026 Dan Teck

This is a work of fiction. Names, characters, places, events, and incidents are either products of the author's imagination or are used fictitiously. Any resemblance to actual persons, living or dead, or to actual events or locales, is entirely coincidental.

The information contained in this book is provided for general educational and inspirational purposes only. It is not intended as a substitute for professional advice, including but not limited to financial, business, medical, psychological, or legal advice. Readers should consult qualified professionals for guidance specific to their own circumstances. Neither the author nor the publisher assumes any responsibility for any loss, injury, or adverse consequences that may result from the use or application of the ideas contained herein.

Printed in the United States of America
ISBN: 978-1-953766-05-2
Library of Congress Control Number: 2026900105

www.danteckauthor.com

To Jodi,
with eternal love and gratitude for sharing the buffet of life.

And to you, reader,
because without you, these are just words filling up my head and my hard
drive. May you take what appeals to you, leave the rest, savor each bite,
and walk away nourished. And may you use that nourishment to help you
live your dreams and empower others to live theirs.

Contents

Introduction

Seven years ago, I got an opportunity that changed everything.

It all started on a typical Monday afternoon in mid-December. I was sitting in my cubicle, my eyes bleary from staring at spreadsheets, when a hard tap on my shoulder jolted me out of my half-stupor. I spun around in my swivel chair and stared up at my boss.

"Got a minute?" she asked.

My heart sank. "Look, if this is about the Jenkins account," I stammered, "I can assure you—"

She held up her hand. "Relax."

Which is what they always say before delivering bad news, like…no, she wouldn't fire me, not right before Christmas. Would she?

"Actually," she said, peering down at me with her icy-blue eyes, "I've got an offer."

Like a severance offer, I assumed. Don't cry, I told myself. And don't accept the first offer. You can still talk to HR and maybe negotiate a deal—accept a pay cut or something like that. It's not necessarily over. Just breathe.

She wheeled over a chair from the empty cubicle next to mine, sat down across from me, and flashed a quick smile—or at least as close to one as I'd ever seen her attempt. And it might have just been my imagination, but I thought I detected a sinister curl to her lip right before she continued speaking. "We'd like you to set up a new office—all new employees, all new equipment, all new everything. You'd have complete control over day-to-day operations and would receive a substantial raise. Also, the company would provide a car and apartment during your time there." She named a town I'd never heard of, then held up her long, bony index finger. "Your sole responsibility would be to make the branch profitable by the end of next year."

She leaned back and spread her hands in front of her as if stretching out an accordion. "Think of it as an experiment in scalability. If it works, the company plans to open branches all over the country—perhaps even internationally—with you at the helm. But to test the model's viability, we have to start with one branch."

I hadn't realized I'd been holding my breath until I released a noisy exhale. So, I wasn't being fired after all—hallelujah! But this offer seemed too good to be true. What was the catch?

As if she could read my mind, my boss leaned forward and continued. "However, if you fail, the branch would be shut down, anyone you hired would be let go, and your position with the company would be terminated."

I gulped.

She stood and returned the chair to the neighboring cubicle. "Think it over—but not for too long. I have to tell corporate at their weekly meeting, so I'll need your answer by Friday." And then, with a perfunctory pat on the shoulder, she walked off and left me to my thoughts.

If she'd asked a few years earlier, I wouldn't have even considered accepting the offer. Back then, I'd been happy, secure, and surrounded by loved ones. Why give that up to move someplace where I didn't know a single person? (I had to look up the town just to see where it was: basically, far away in the middle of nowhere.)

But now, things were different. Over the past few years, most of my family and friends had moved away. My new neighbor was driving me nuts with his motorcycle-repair business. (Early Saturday morning seemed to be his preferred time for revving.) And I was newly single— and not by choice. (Well, by *Maya's* choice.)

I was ready for a change. And that raise sure sounded nice.

Then again, I didn't know the first thing about how to set up an office. I'd never done anything like that. I'm not sure why I even got offered the position. It was just a matter of time until they realized I had no idea what I was doing and had totally botched the project. Or maybe they already knew and were just looking for someone guaranteed to fail so they could write off the expenses and get some sort of tax break. In any case, I'd be lucky to even make it a year before I got fired.

Sure, my current position wasn't exactly enriching (in any sense), but I was getting by just fine. And my retirement fund was off to a nice start. (Decades away from being cashed in, but at least heading in the right direction.) I knew what I was doing, and I was comfortable—two things I definitely wouldn't be able to say about the new position.

My boss was right—it made sense to take some time to think it over. There were a lot of factors to consider. I figured I should probably make a list of pros and cons, discuss it with friends and maybe even a life coach or career counselor, and then sleep on it to see if things felt different in the morning. And even then, I would have to…

No! This was exactly the sort of thing Maya always complained about. "You're not decisive enough! That's why you'll always be stuck in that dead-end job. I need someone who's willing to take chances—a go-getter!"

Well, I'd show her who was going places! I would turn that new office into an empire, and then she'd be begging me to take her back.

Before I could talk myself out of it, I marched into my boss's office and accepted the offer. And then I promptly ran to the bathroom and threw up.

As I knelt on the hard, cold tiles, depositing wave after wave of my lunchtime burrito into the toilet, one thought kept pounding in my brain:

What have I done?

* * *

The next three weeks passed in a blur. I worked straight through Christmas and New Year's in a haze of packing, planning, and panic—tying up loose ends, filling out paperwork, and training my replacement. During all this time, however, I received absolutely no guidance for the next stage of the operation. My boss said the company wanted to encourage innovation, not create a cookie-cutter franchise. Her only piece of advice felt more like an ominous admonition: "Write down everything you learn: the good stuff, the bad stuff, even the complete failures. That way you'll know better for next time, and the company can benefit from your mistakes."

Mistakes? Failures? It's almost like she expected me to crash and burn—reawakening my fears that this whole ordeal was some kind of elaborate tax-write-off scheme with me as the fall guy. I studied my boss's expression for some clue, but I couldn't get a read on her. She just stared down at me with that maddeningly inscrutable look on her face as she handed me a notebook. "Write it all in here."

The notebook had a single word on the cover: *Lessons*. When I flipped through the pages, I saw that they were all blank. A surge of heat shot into my forehead. Really?! A *blank* book?! What good would *that* do me? I was getting ready to embark on the biggest challenge of my life. They should've been giving *me* lessons—preparing me for the next steps—not expecting *me* to teach them! I was just about to give my boss a piece of my mind—to teach *her* a lesson about how to treat your employees—but she'd already turned and walked away.

And that was the last I saw of her.

That night, I went home and kept doing exactly what I'd been doing almost every moment when I wasn't at work: packing. And by "packing," I mean getting rid of almost everything I owned: selling, donating, recycling, or throwing out anything that wouldn't fit into two suitcases and a carry-on bag. And before I knew it—just one week into the new year—I was handing over those two suitcases to the woman at baggage check-in, carrying my remaining bag onto the plane, and flying toward the next chapter of my life.

* * *

After we touched down and disembarked, I walked to the baggage carousel and picked up my suitcases. (Thankfully, they arrived safely— not that it would've been hard to replace everything: a few changes of clothes, toiletries, and a couple of books—including my boss's gift of the *Lessons* notebook.) I stepped away from the carousel and looked around the waiting area, half expecting to see a familiar face or maybe even a driver holding a sign with my name on it.

No one.

And that's when it hit me: I really was on my own.

Taking a deep breath, I picked up my bags, walked outside, and caught a cab to my new home.

As promised, the apartment came fully furnished. And the company had provided a car: on the kitchen counter were the keys to a fairly new-looking sedan, which was waiting for me in the complex's parking lot. Granted, it was all rather generic—the car, the furniture, the apartment complex—more like a hotel than a home. In fact, I strongly suspect that it had once been a hotel, converted to residential housing with minimal effort. But I didn't mind. It was safe. It was clean. And for now, it was mine. I didn't need high-class accommodations or personalized décor. I just needed a place to sleep. And almost as soon as I'd lugged my bags inside, that's just what I did: I collapsed onto the queen-sized bed, with my clothes and the bedspread still on, and didn't wake up until almost twelve hours later.

The next morning, I headed straight to the new office—which, like my apartment and car, was provided by the company—and took the first steps toward building a thriving, profitable branch.

Supposedly.

It was January 9—already a full week into my one-year ultimatum. By New Year's Eve, I'd be profitable or I'd be unemployed, so I knew I had to get moving and set up the office. Instead, I spent the week planning, pondering, and spinning my wheels. Nonetheless, I stayed busy from dawn to dusk. At night, I'd heat up a microwave dinner, watch TV, and fall into deep, dreamless sleep. And in the morning, I'd get up and start the process all over again—until Saturday arrived and I finally took a day off to rest, finish unpacking, and check out the area.

Despite the winter chill, the sun was out, so I decided to walk into town. It felt good to get outside and stretch my legs. Other than that, though, the walk was fairly uninspiring. I passed some more apartment complexes and a few townhouses before the residential area gave way to businesses—mostly the same chain stores I knew from my previous town (and the one before that and the one before that). But that suited me just fine. After all, I'd only be there a year, so I didn't really feel like acquainting myself with an entirely different set of dining and retail options. The situation was already new enough; it was nice to have something familiar in the midst of the upheaval.

After walking for a few miles, I was more than ready for one of those familiar eateries. But the strip mall I was passing didn't have anything I recognized. Then I spotted a promising sign, tucked between a nail salon and a discount shoe store. Dark green letters on a white background: *The Buffet.*

Sounded good to me. In fact, that was just what I needed—a generic place where I wouldn't stand out or feel like a loser for eating alone. The door said *Hours of Operation: Mon–Sat, 12–2 p.m.* I looked at my watch: 12:14. Perfect. I'd have plenty of time to eat, do a bit more exploring, and then head home while it was still light out.

I pushed open the glass door and walked inside.

1. Choices

At first glance, the buffet didn't look particularly impressive: a small entryway with a narrow bench, a coat rack, and just enough room for the cashier plus the five or six people ahead of me. I took it as a good sign that the place wasn't empty, although this was hardly the kind of lunch-hour rush you'd see in a town's hottest restaurant. But that was fine with me. I didn't need a hot restaurant, just a hot meal.

The closest thing to a theme seemed to be "no frills." No decorations, no list of specials, no host, hostess, or maître d'. And the closest thing they had to a menu was a sign that said *All You Can Eat*, followed by a mid-range price—more expensive than a fast-food joint but less than a fancy restaurant. Not exactly a bargain, but it seemed reasonable. Besides, after my vigorous walk and a week of meager meals, I'd worked up an appetite, so I planned to get my money's worth.

When I reached the front of the line, I paid the cashier, took a tray from the stack, loaded it up with a plate, napkins, and utensils, and made my way into the buffet to see what looked good.

Within moments, I was flooded with disappointment. This wasn't a proper buffet; it was just a glorified salad bar—and not even that glorified: just basic lettuce, carrots, cucumbers, tomatoes, and a few other options that didn't look particularly appealing. It's not like it cost a fortune, but for what I'd paid, I expected something a bit more substantial—a hot, hearty meal that would fill me up for the rest of the day. Was it too late to get my money back? I didn't think they offered refunds, and anyway, did I really want to be "that guy"—especially in my first week in town?

I'd already made up my mind that this would be my one and only time here, so I decided to make the most of it. If nothing else, I could pig out on lettuce and hope to find somewhere better for dinner—or just have an extra frozen meal when I got home.

Fortunately, as I pushed my tray farther along the three metal rails it rested on, the offerings started to look a bit more promising. There were actually more types of lettuce than I'd realized at first: red leaf, green leaf, iceberg, butter, romaine, and a bunch that I didn't even recognize—plus a wide selection of other green leafy vegetables: spinach, kale, and others that I wasn't brave enough to try just then.

Just beyond the predictable carrots, cucumbers, and tomatoes, they offered mushrooms, celery, red onions, radishes, avocados, artichoke hearts, and bell peppers in a range of colors.

Still browsing the options before I started taking anything, I made my way to the end of the buffet…only to realize it wasn't the end at all—it continued around a corner I hadn't noticed before, which led to a much bigger room. That's where they seemed to keep the less common ingredients: raw beets, grilled beets, pickled beets, pickled cucumbers, pickled onions, caramelized onions, grilled onions, grilled zucchini, grilled corn, grilled peppers, sun-dried tomatoes, and a whole array of vegetables I'd never even seen.

Next to the veggies sat bowls of walnuts, almonds, cashews, peanuts, pecans, pistachios, sesame seeds, pumpkin seeds, sunflower seeds, and a wide variety of other seeds and nuts I couldn't identify. (Part of the buffet's no-frills policy seemed to be a lack of labels: you either knew what something was or you didn't.)

Just beyond that I found a selection of beans: black beans, kidney beans, pinto beans, green beans, garbanzo beans, lentils, and much more—some of them fresh, some of them cooked, and some of them seasoned with spices and vinegar (or so I assumed, based on the pickly smell).

The next area featured a colorful display of fruits—a mix of dried and fresh. Some seemed obvious (raisins, apples, oranges, bananas, melons), but there were also many that I'd never thought of putting on salad: apricots, cranberries, kiwis, peaches, plums, pears, papayas, mangoes, watermelons, and a full-color spectrum of berries. The olives alone required over a dozen containers to accommodate all the varieties.

The next station was filled with dozens of salad toppings—including croutons, baked pita chips, hummus, guacamole, parsley, basil, mint, and the last thing I expected to see in an unassuming, no-frills buffet: edible flowers.

After that, I wasn't entirely surprised to see a huge display case dedicated to dressings. Clearly, I'd underestimated this place. This was no ordinary salad bar.

But just when I thought I'd seen it all, I noticed a stairway at the end of the room. I walked down the short flight, and what I saw at the bottom almost made me fall on the floor: a room about ten times the size of the salad room, loaded wall-to-wall with a full selection of appetizers, entrées, desserts, soups, side dishes, beverages, and more—including a whole station dedicated to baked potatoes, another one for pasta, a grill for do-it-yourself paninis, one for crepes, one for pancakes, and one I knew I'd be visiting: a Belgian waffle iron, along with batter and every imaginable topping.

This was the most elaborate buffet I'd ever seen in my life! But then I noticed something even more mind boggling: between the buffet displays, open doors led to even more rooms. I wandered through one and then another…and another and another and another. The main level had looked pretty big, but this downstairs area seemed endless. It must've been at least a city block long and wide. No, *ten* city blocks, if not more. It just went on and on.

As best as I could tell, most rooms were dedicated to a particular type of cuisine—almost every one I could imagine: Chinese, Japanese, French, Spanish, Italian, Indian, Vietnamese, Thai, Middle Eastern, Ethiopian, West African, South African, Moroccan, Mexican, Cuban, Fusion…the buffet just kept going, and the options just kept coming.

I walked through one room after another as if in a trance—until a screech of feedback jolted me back to my senses (and practically scared me out of my skin), followed by an announcement from an overhead speaker: "Attention, buffet customers. We are now closed. Please bring your tray to the nearest cleaning station and exit the building. Thank you for dining with us. We hope to see you again."

Closed?! I looked at my watch—sure enough, it was exactly two. How could that be? I hadn't even seen every room yet! I needed more time!

I looked forlornly at my tray. Aside from the plate, napkin, and utensils I'd taken when I first arrived, it was still empty. I'd been here almost two hours and hadn't taken a single bite of food or even a glass of water, much less eaten a meal. I'd gotten so lost in the maze of options that I'd forgotten why I'd come here in the first place: to eat! But now it was too late.

I followed the crowd of diners—all of whom, aside from myself, were just finishing their meals—dropped off my clean tray with their dirty ones, and made my way out the door.

I walked home just like I'd walked through the buffet: in a stupor. Except this time, instead of admiring a bounty of food options, I berated myself with every step. I was such an idiot! I'd wasted time, I'd wasted money, and I'd wasted a great opportunity. What was my problem?

It would've been bad enough if this sort of thing had only happened once, but it wasn't just today. I'd been doing basically the same thing all week. I'd had *one* job to do at work—set up the office—and I hadn't done it. Sure, every day I'd set off with the intention to do it, but I soon grew overwhelmed with all the choices:

- What type of furniture should I get (standing desks, ergonomic chairs, or traditional workstations)?
- How should I lay out the office (cubicles, open floor plan, numerous small offices)?
- What kind of lighting should I use (fluorescent, LED lamps, or mostly natural lighting)?
- How should I decorate it (generic paintings, motivational posters, plants, sculptures)?
- What kind of computers should I get (desktop, laptop, mini)?
- What supplies did I need (staplers, pens, whiteboards, or something more high-tech)?
- What amenities should I offer (break room, water cooler, vending machines, exercise equipment, nap room, ping-pong tables or other games)?

The questions were endless, and so were the options. And nothing seemed straightforward. Even the most innocuous-seeming question— *What kind of desks should I buy?*—opened up a whole can of worms, requiring personal considerations, business considerations, and even some soul-searching. What kind of office did I want to create? Should it be fun, out of the box, and stimulating—the kind of place that inspired creativity and made talented people actually want to come to work and stay with the company? Or should it be more serious, straightforward, and results oriented—a no-nonsense environment where professionals could do their work without distractions or juvenile zaniness? What kind of company did I want this to be? What kind of a person did I want to be? What truly matters? Why am I here? Who am I?

As my business considerations spiraled into existential angst, I'd inevitably collapse onto the floor (since the office didn't have any chairs—because I hadn't ordered them), shut my laptop (which usually had at least a dozen tabs open—displaying mountains of office-supply options), and fight the urge to run away, pull out my hair, or cry.

My "solution" was to examine the problem: feeling overwhelmed by all the choices. So when I eventually reopened my computer, I'd look up information about how to make choices—and end up watching videos, taking self-assessment quizzes, and reading articles about decision fatigue, analysis paralysis, FOMO, iterative decision making, maximizers and satisficers (yes, that's an actual word), and why offering six jars of jam is better than twenty-four.

By the end of the week, I'd learned a lot. And it was rather fascinating. And eye opening. And fun. But I still hadn't picked out a chair.

So, when the weekend rolled around, all I wanted was some lunch and a couple of hours to forget my problems. But this crazy buffet shoved it all right back in my face. Except now I supposedly knew better, which just made me berate myself even more for making the same dumb mistake.

Yes, of course it would've made sense to just eat *something* at the buffet. Or, since I hadn't eaten there, it would've made sense to go to one of the restaurants I passed along the way home. But I was so wrapped up in my thoughts about what had just happened—at the buffet and at work the previous week—that this didn't even occur to me. I walked almost blindly but somehow made it home, where I stuck a frozen burrito into the microwave. And as I waited for it to heat up, I made three decisions:

1. I was going to stop beating myself up for not making a choice—at work or at the buffet. After all, it made sense to take some time to get the lay of the land, familiarize myself with the possibilities, and weigh my options. It was the responsible thing to do. However, enough was enough. It was time to decide, act, and move on.

2. With that in mind, I resolved that the following Saturday, I would go back to the buffet, spend fifteen minutes exploring the options, and then pick something and eat it. Yes, I knew my selection might not be the best food in the entire buffet. And no, fifteen minutes wouldn't be nearly enough time to see everything they offered, but it would be enough time to find something that looked appealing. And if I didn't like it, I could always go back and get something else.

3. In the meantime, I'd do something similar at work: I'd spend one day on each decision (e.g., office furniture)—researching, weighing the options, etc.—and then by the end of the day, make a decision. So by the end of the week, I would have made decisions in five major areas and would be able to move forward with the next steps. And, as with my buffet selections, if my first choices didn't work out, I could always trade them in for something better. But I had to start somewhere. Besides, my boss didn't say the new branch had to be the best office ever; she simply said it needed to be profitable by the end of the year. And that goal did not depend on finding the perfect chair.

The microwave's beep jolted me out of my reverie, but I already felt better—and ready to eat. I took my burrito to the kitchen table, sat down (fortunately, as I've mentioned, the place came furnished, so unlike work, I actually had a table and chair here), and enjoyed my good-enough-for-now lunch.

When I was done eating, I went to my bedroom, pulled out my *Lessons* notebook, opened it to the first page, and wrote my first words in it:

Lesson #1:
You have almost endless options but limited time.
Choose something, or you'll be left unsatisfied.

2. Trust

That week at work, I kept my promise: each day, I made at least one decision—and acted on it. I ordered basic office supplies, LED light bulbs, and furniture—nothing fancy, but certainly good enough to get the branch up and running. And by the end of the week, I was well on my way to having a functional office set up.

Then, on Saturday, I set out to keep my other promise: to make a decision at the buffet—and act on it. In other words, choose a meal and eat it.

After a brisk walk there, I arrived just as the doors were opening. Like the previous week, the line moved quickly, so it didn't take long for me to pay, grab a tray, and load it with a plate, a glass, napkins, and utensils. Now the only thing missing was the food.

I glanced at my watch—12:15. Perfect. I'd given myself fifteen minutes to browse the options before choosing a meal, so my deadline was 12:30. Plenty of time to explore but also plenty of time to eat before the buffet's two p.m. closing time.

To make sure I stuck to the plan, I'd made a deal with myself: no choice, no lunch. Period. No stopping at another restaurant. No frozen burrito when I got home. No cold Chinese leftovers from the fridge. Not a bite before dinner. And no dinner before six.

It might sound harsh—especially because I'd intentionally skipped breakfast that morning—but the past week had reminded me that to get things done, I needed three things: decisions, deadlines, and consequences. It's like my old manager once told me: without a deadline, a goal is just a dream—and without consequences, a deadline is meaningless. My grumbling stomach reminded me that this choice would not be meaningless.

Determined not to repeat last week's lunchless fiasco, I steadied my tray before me and strode intrepidly into the culinary jungle.

As I explored room after room, surrounded by delectable dishes and tantalizing smells, I remembered just how miraculous the buffet was. But

I also remembered its two major shortcomings: no maps and no labels. With all these rooms (dozens, if not hundreds), how could anyone find their way around? And even if you did know where you were going, without labels, how could you know what the foods were—and which ones you might like? It was a total crapshoot.

At least with typical restaurants, the menus described the foods, or at least named them, and a server could always explain or suggest something. But at the buffet, you were on your own—here's a tray; good luck. It was downright rude. And it was getting under my skin.

But it didn't take me long to realize why: I wasn't really mad at the buffet; I was mad at my company.

True to their word, they'd sent me out here all by myself and offered absolutely no guidance. Yes, I understood the rationale behind it: They didn't want a franchise. They didn't want someone to simply copy the home office, having the same successes but making the same mistakes. They wanted originality. They wanted innovation.

Well, that all sounded great in theory—no micromanaging, no limits on creativity. But in reality it felt like I'd been dropped into the wilderness with nothing but a workspace and an ultimatum: fend for myself or fail.

Sure, I'd been making decisions by myself all week. But it would've been so much easier if they'd just told me what was the best equipment and the most effective office set-up. After all, they'd been doing this for years. Would it be so terrible to give me the benefit of their experience? Hopefully I'd gotten good furniture, lights, and supplies, but how was I to know?

Now, on my alleged day off, I was in the same situation: all on my own with absolutely no guidance.

I glanced at my watch again—12:26. Egad! Only four minutes left until I'd be condemned to an afternoon of hunger. I had to choose something…fast! I looked around and, to my horror, realized that I'd wandered into a room full of totally unfamiliar food. My heart raced and my head spun. What was all this stuff? Without labels, how would I know what to eat (or even *consider* eating)? How would I know if it was something I wanted? How could I choose?

No sooner had I asked the question than the answer came to me: the same way I'd chosen the office supplies—by trusting myself. I couldn't depend on someone else to tell me what chairs to buy—or what food to eat. But I didn't need anyone else for this. I could rely on my own senses. Did it look good? Smell good? Taste good? In short, *did I want it?* That's all that mattered here—not what someone else might think I should do. And right now, I knew what I wanted: *to eat!*

Among this vast array of unidentified cuisine, one dish kept catching my eye: a hearty-looking stew that seemed to be loaded with veggies. No matter how many other foods I looked at, this one kept drawing me back. I took a few steps closer and inhaled the warm, comforting aroma. Knowing I'd found a winner, I scooped a generous serving onto my plate…moments before my watch flipped over to 12:30.

Catching my breath and wiping the sweat out of my eyes, I examined the nick-of-time meal: a mouth-watering blend of what I *think* were chickpeas, zucchini, and carrots in an earthy sauce topped with fresh herbs (possibly cilantro, but I'm not exactly a foodie, so don't take my word for it).

Whatever it was, it smelled amazing and looked appetizing, healthy, and just different enough from my usual fare to make it interesting. (Although, with all due respect to the buffet, just about anything would look interesting next to my typical weekday meals: frozen burritos and microwave dinners.) And hey, even if this stew wasn't the best meal in the entire place, it was infinitely better than what I'd had last time: nothing.

I found an empty table, set down my mystery meal, and dug in.

It tasted every bit as delicious as I'd hoped, although not all the ingredients were what I'd expected. Those "carrots" turned out to be sweet potatoes (or maybe yams—I never could tell the difference). And there was something sweet that I couldn't quite place (maybe apricots?) as well as a tangy flavor (lemon juice? orange zest? apple cider vinegar?) that gave it an invigorating *zing*. But even without knowing the meal's name or ingredients, I liked it.

And as a bonus, the satisfying meal also came with the satisfaction of knowing I'd made the decision myself—I'd trusted my gut, just like I'd done with the office chairs, desks, and lights. And just like the previous week, I headed home with a valuable take-away—not leftover food, but a lesson that would serve me long after lunch.

Lesson #2:
Guidance can help—but first and foremost, trust
your senses, trust your gut, trust yourself.

3. What Are You Looking For?

After I went home and wrote down that second lesson, I didn't just close my notebook and forget what I'd learned. I took it to heart. And in the coming days, I let it guide my decisions—from how I decorated the break room to which laptops I ordered for my future employees. And soon it felt like a little seed inside me was taking root—a growing confidence that came from trusting myself.

However, as soon as I started to feel stronger about myself, everything around me started to go wrong. First, when the man came to deliver the laptops I'd ordered, he brought desktops—complete with big, clunky monitors, the likes of which I hadn't seen in decades. Then my car wouldn't start, so I had to get it towed to the shop. (So much for the "reliable" company car!) Of course, the problem turned out to be much bigger (and, not surprisingly, more expensive) than they'd originally estimated, and it took two days to fix. Then, when I finally got the car back, I drove to the office only to learn that some genius on the top floor had left the window open overnight—in the middle of a snowstorm!—and the pipes froze…and then burst, which meant the whole building had to be shut down and repaired.

So, basically, the entire week was shot.

When Saturday rolled around, I decided to pretend the week had never happened and give myself a fresh start ("Shake the Etch A Sketch," as Maya says). So I started the day the same way I'd started the previous two Saturdays: by walking to the buffet.

The recent snow was mostly melted by then, and I figured a nice brisk walk would clear my head and help me move forward. Instead, I just kept dwelling on the past week. How could people be so incompetent? I'd clearly marked *Laptop* on my order and confirmed it twice before I checked out. And what was the deal with the car? I'd only been here three weeks—hadn't someone inspected it before they left it with me? And was it really that big a problem, or was the mechanic scamming me? And then the whole thing with the frozen pipes—so unnecessary, so stupid! Who leaves a window open in winter? Even if they didn't care about the pipes (or the heating bill), just think about the lost time and income. Maybe they were on a fixed salary and got paid whether they worked or not, but I was on a profit-or-perish plan, and my countdown clock was ticking! A lost week meant 2% of my precious twelve-month window was gone forever with nothing to show for it. These fools could be costing me my future!

Every step I took seemed to reinforce the messages of the past week: people were idiots, and the world was going down the drain…and trying to take me with it! And it wasn't just the past week; it was everything I saw during the walk: Why was there a lone boot on the sidewalk? Did it just fall off someone's foot? And then did they just keep walking through the snow with one boot and one sock…and not notice until they got home? Also, the sidewalk was half-covered with litter that didn't look accidental—a crumpled-up napkin, an empty soda can, a plastic bag— which was doubly inexcusable, given that there were garbage cans every few blocks! And how come some patches of snow still hadn't been shoveled? It was storekeepers' responsibility to tend to the sidewalk in front of their shops. Even if they were lazy or didn't care about how it affected pedestrians (such as me!), it was a lawsuit waiting to happen— one slip and someone could sue them right back to the Stone Age.

I figured that things would get better once I reached the buffet, but the annoyances just kept piling up, starting from the moment I walked in. The line was longer than it had been before, and it was barely moving—which was crazy because, really, what did the cashier have to do? There was only one option and one price, so what was the holdup?

When I finally paid and started exploring the food options, everything looked strange, off-putting, unidentifiable, or inedible. I just wanted a hot, hearty meal, but I had to walk past row after row of what I can only assume were fruits: Durian? Rambutan? Persimmon? Dragon fruit? I couldn't even tell you for sure because, as I've mentioned, they refused to use any freaking labels!

And it wasn't just the food or the buffet itself that annoyed me. The customers seemed to be doing everything in their power to create a miserable experience for everyone there. Every other table seemed to have a screaming baby or three. There was also a table of rowdy teenagers—shouting, rough-housing, and throwing wadded-up napkins at each other. And, as if the noise weren't bad enough, everyone I got close to had unbearable B.O.

Worst of all were the people who didn't clean up after themselves. Didn't they know they had to bus their own table? That was the buffet's policy—part of the self-serve experience, which was how they kept their prices down. So these people who abandoned their trays on their tables were forcing everyone else to pick up their mess…and pick up the bill!

As I walked through room after room, everything I saw annoyed me. I started keeping a running total of all the problems—the rude customers, the unappealing food, and the buffet's inherent shortcomings—and was soon well into high double digits. Although it brought me no joy, it became a sort of game: "Find the Next Problem!"

I became so focused on the task at hand—scanning the room for flaws and then tallying them—that I didn't notice the man standing directly in front of me until he tapped me on the shoulder, smiled, and asked, "What are you looking for?"

I was so startled that I'm not even sure how I responded. I think I muttered something about "just browsing" or "seeing what looks good." And although the man smiled and offered a parting pleasantry as he walked away, I felt guilty—because I'd lied to him. I wasn't looking for something I liked; I was looking for what I *didn't* like. And, not surprisingly, I was finding it.

But how was this helping me? Clearly, it wasn't, so why was I doing it? I guess I'd just gotten in the habit over the past week, with everything going wrong. But even with all the mishaps, I could've just as easily looked for something better…and found it.

Sure, the wrong computers were delivered, but it worked out fine. They brought the right ones the next day, and to apologize for their mistake, they gave me a free six-month warranty instead of the usual fourteen days. And everything else I'd ordered had arrived promptly and correctly.

And yes, I'd had car problems. But the mechanic fixed it, and now the car was running better than ever. And for the two days they'd been working on it, they loaned me a fully electric car, which I'd always wanted to try. (Turns out, it was super easy to drive and never needed recharging.) And because the company was footing the bill, it didn't cost me a dime.

Now, looking around the buffet, I had to admit that the vast majority of the diners were polite and conscientious. And because the buffet was so big, if I did end up sitting near someone who created a disturbance, I could simply get up and move. After all, there were dozens of rooms with available tables and nearly endless food options—most of which looked great. So why was I focusing on the food I *didn't* want instead of what I *did* want?

So, what did I want?

I didn't have an exact meal in mind, but I knew I wanted something hot and hearty. And tasty, of course. Looking around, I saw row after row of options that would more than fit the bill.

I followed my nose into a room filled with the unmistakable aroma of curry. Yes, I could definitely go for something with a bit of kick. And the buffet had plenty of options that looked (and smelled) like they'd satisfy my spice craving. Their spread was more extensive and appealing than any Indian restaurant I'd ever been to. They had chana masala, dal makhani, baingan bharta, aloo gobi, aloo matar, veg biryani, pav bhaji, masala dosa, and dozens of other meals—including my all-time favorite: aloo saag. And it looked absolutely amazing.

Yes!

Why mess around? I'd wasted more than enough time looking for things I didn't like and didn't want. It was time to bring out the big guns. This is what I wanted. I'd found it (surprisingly quickly and easily, once I'd stopped playing my "Find the Next Problem" game), and now I was taking it.

I scooped out a hearty serving of the aloo saag—along with a side of basmati rice, two pieces of naan, a samosa, and a dollop of tamarind sauce—and found a quiet table where I could savor my meal. And savor it I did. The flavor surpassed my expectations (second only to the homemade version by Maya's mom), and with every bite, I could feel the food nourishing me on a deep level. Not only did it give me pleasure in the moment and the health benefits of the fresh veggies, but it also shifted my attitude in a way that I could carry well beyond the buffet.

Right then and there, I made a pact with myself: I was now officially done focusing on what I didn't want—at the buffet, at work, and throughout my life. I wasn't being naïve. I knew I'd still face occasional setbacks, but I also knew I was strong enough to handle them and get back on track—quickly and perhaps better than ever. And no matter what happened, I would start off by looking for what I wanted...and feeling confident that I'd get it.

Lesson #3:
You find what you look for, so look for what you want to find.

4. Help

In just three visits, the buffet had given me more than just great food—it had taught me about making choices, trusting myself, and focusing on what I want (instead of what I don't want). This was clearly somewhere worth going back to, so I decided to make it a weekly ritual to eat lunch there every Saturday.

I also decided that, just like I'd done the first three weeks, I would always walk there and leave my phone at home. Between staring at computers at work, TV at home, and my phone whenever I needed to check Maya's social media updates (numerous times per day), I figured I could use a few hours of physical movement and non-screen time each week. And who knows—maybe looking away from screens helped me notice lessons I might have otherwise missed.

Whatever the reason, going there made me feel better, and that's what ultimately mattered.

After my latest positive shift at the buffet, I was able to enjoy the rest of my weekend and start the new workweek feeling upbeat, optimistic, and confident. Yes, I knew I had challenges ahead of me, but now I wasn't focusing on the problems; I was looking for solutions.

The first solution I tackled was connecting all the laptops I'd just bought. I'd never done anything like this before, but I was willing to learn. Besides, as branch manager of a technology company, I figured I should know how to do this kind of stuff. So I fired up the laptops, rolled up my sleeves, and dove in.

It didn't take me long to realize why my old office had a full-time network administrator who handled this stuff. The more I looked into it, the more complex it seemed to grow. There were so many factors to consider: platform, mobile accessibility, updates, analytics, accountability, and above all, security. If I made one mistake, the whole office could end up infected with viruses. How had Khalil made this all look so easy? (I asked the question rhetorically, but the answer immediately came to me: years of training and decades of experience.)

After two days I hadn't made any progress, so I decided to set the project aside. I wasn't giving up; I was simply shifting to a different area for the time being. After all, there were lots of projects to take care of, so as long as I moved forward, that's what counted.

I decided to focus on another essential task: setting up an accounting and bookkeeping system. Again, I knew this was something we'd need. Again, it was new to me. And again, it didn't take long for me to realize how complex it was—and to appreciate Glenna, the CPA who handled my old office's bookkeeping. I'd never even heard of half the terms mentioned in the so-called beginner's training I tried to work my way through: Accrual accounting method? Bank reconciliation? Capex? And all the software options that were supposed to simplify the process just made it feel more overwhelming.

After two more days of unsuccessful struggling on unfamiliar ground, I once again shifted my focus. This time I decided on something basic: writing a business plan. I knew this was important, perhaps even essential. After all, I was now running a business, and we needed a plan. But after a day of trying to come up with market analysis, operations plans, and financial projections, all I'd written was a one-line executive summary: *Become profitable by the end of the year.* A great intention—but how would this happen? And how would I set up the computer network that would help us become profitable? And how would I set up the bookkeeping system so I'd even know whether we actually were profitable?

By the end of the week, I had lots of questions and very few answers. I didn't know how to move forward with the business. I didn't know whether I'd gotten myself in hopelessly over my head. I didn't know what I was doing.

But after all that time spent out of my comfort zone, I did know what I needed at that moment: comfort. Specifically, comfort food. Which for me meant one thing: Belgian waffles. And I knew just where to find them.

Saturday morning I headed to the buffet on a mission. Ever since my first time there, I'd had my eye on their waffle iron. In fact, it was much more than just an iron—it was an entire station. They had fruit, syrup, powdered sugar, and a whole array of other options I never would've thought of as toppings but which looked delicious. As I walked to the buffet, I could practically taste the delicacies that awaited me. And I could practically feel the much-needed comfort the meal would provide.

I picked up my pace.

When I got to the buffet, I knew exactly where to go. Despite the confusing layout, lack of a discernible system, and seemingly endless rooms, I remembered the way to the waffle station. I'd seen it on all three of my previous visits, and I'd made a mental note of its location, knowing that the day would come when I'd need to find my way back. Well, that day had arrived. And my memory served me well: within minutes, I found my way to the waffle room and walked straight to an entire table filled with…soup.

Lots of soup. Every type of soup imaginable. And nothing but soup. Which was all fine and good (after all, most of it looked delicious), but there was one problem: it wasn't waffles.

Was I in the wrong room? I spun around, studying my surroundings. No, this was definitely the place—same decorations, same doors, same copper pipe with that weird red valve just under the ceiling. So where were the waffles? Had they moved them? I looked in the adjoining rooms. Still no waffles. Instead, there was bread, desserts, and salads— which I *know* used to be near the entrance.

My mind reeled as the situation became disturbingly clear: just when I'd started to learn my way around, they'd rearranged everything. How could they do this to me? This was pure madness! More than that, it was downright cruel.

To make matters worse, everyone else seemed to know exactly where they were going, what they were doing, and how to get what they wanted. I felt like I was in the middle of a well-choreographed dance performance, but I'd missed all the rehearsals and didn't know any of the steps.

All at once, the scales fell from my eyes, and I saw the buffet for what it truly was: a confusing labyrinth that overwhelms you with pretentious foods and turns even the smallest matter (getting a freaking waffle!) into a major ordeal. What did I ever see in this place? Why had I vowed to come here every Saturday? Would it really matter if I broke my personal promise? It's not like I'd signed a contract or anything. I could just walk out right now and never come back and no one would even notice—and I'd probably be better off. Maybe I should ditch my tray and go to another restaurant. Surely there was a waffle house somewhere in this town. But even if there was, how would I find it? Thanks to my stupid ritual, I'd left my phone back at the apartment, and I still didn't know my way around the area.

It was time to face the facts: I was lost and had no idea what I was doing.

What *was* I doing? Everything was falling apart. I had no business being here in this town where I didn't know anyone and no one knew me, trying to accomplish something I'd never done, without any training or guidance about how to proceed. I never should've been offered this position, and I certainly shouldn't have accepted. Maya was right—I wasn't a successful go-getter. I was a loser, a fraud, and an impostor—and not a very good one at that! I wasn't fooling anyone. Maybe it was time to pack up, go home, and submit my resignation.

I was about two seconds from dropping my tray, collapsing onto the buffet floor, and weeping. But just then, I saw something that looked like manna from heaven: a waffle!

It was drifting past, practically right under my nose, carried by a woman with wire-framed glasses, a messy ponytail, and clearly impeccable culinary taste. Before I realized what I was doing, I tapped her shoulder. "Excuse me, where did you get that?"

Based on her startled expression, I probably looked a bit crazed, but she quickly softened and smiled. "Oh, yeah—they rearranged everything this week. Now the waffles are right next to the…" She pointed to the nearest door and gestured vaguely. "Why don't I just show you?"

"Thank you so much," I said, my body flooding with relief as I followed her into the next room. Suddenly, instead of being on the verge of weeping from misery, I felt like weeping from joy. "I've been wandering around for—"

"No worries." The woman cut me off with a wave of her hand. "I've been coming here for years, and I never would've found anything if someone hadn't helped me. I'm glad I get to pay it forward." She led me around a corner. "Voila!" She gestured toward a table that had everything I'd been looking for and more: half a dozen waffle irons, vats of batter, and a glorious display of every imaginable topping. There was maple syrup, fruit syrup, chocolate syrup, caramel sauce, nut butters, powdered sugar, cinnamon, creamy spreads, and a wide variety of fresh fruits, including strawberries, bananas, blueberries, and raspberries that looked like they'd been picked just minutes earlier. The whole display was magnificent—a banquet fit for angels. Gourmet angels with down-home tastes, that is.

"Bon appétit!" the woman said. She turned to walk away but then stopped abruptly. "Oh! Just one more thing. If you're looking for maple syrup, go for the white pitcher—that's the good stuff. The silver one is just artificial sweetener."

And with that, she disappeared into the crowd, leaving me with a solution not only to my waffle problem but also my work problems. It was so obvious now. Finding the waffles had been so much easier when someone guided me—someone who had experience, someone who knew where she was going and how to get there, someone who could relate to my problem and also solve it. Wouldn't the same thing be true at work? Why had I been trying to figure it all out and do everything by myself? Surely there were plenty of people who could show me the ropes, point me in the right direction, and help me get there.

I ladled out a serving of batter into the waffle iron, closed the lid, set the timer, and pondered my situation. Yes, I'd had the best intentions when I'd tried to set up the network, create a bookkeeping system, and write a business plan, but there was no reason for me to do all this on my own. This was never supposed to be a one-man operation. I was a branch manager, not a solopreneur. And even if I could figure it all out, I wouldn't do it nearly as efficiently or as well as a trained, experienced professional. Hiring competent employees would multiply my impact, fill the gaps in my abilities, and save me a ton of time. Asking for help didn't mean I wasn't trusting myself; it just meant that two heads are better than one—especially if one of those heads had years of training and experience.

I was pulled out of my thoughts by the iron's soft *ding* sound, indicating that the waffle was ready. As I transferred it onto my plate, I made a decision: First thing Monday morning, I was going to start looking for an assistant. Someone with experience setting up a new office. Someone who could guide me through the process. Someone who knew what the heck they were doing.

But first, it was time to load up my waffle and pour on some maple syrup—the good stuff from the white pitcher.

Lesson #4:
You don't have to go it alone. Help is available; you just have to ask.

5. Structure

Realizing that I didn't have to go it alone, I advertised for an assistant manager—preferably, someone with experience running an office who was willing to build a new branch from the ground up. I was soon flooded with résumés, but one of the applicants seemed head and shoulders above the rest: Laney. She had everything I was looking for: an MBA, years of managerial experience, and (as far as I could tell from her cover letter) a great attitude regarding the challenge ahead.

I interviewed her on Monday, hired her on Tuesday, filled out her paperwork on Wednesday, showed her around the office on Thursday, and got into my first fight with her on Friday.

Well, maybe *fight* is too strong a word for it. Disagreement. Strong disagreement. Fundamental disagreement.

It was about the direction of the company. The vibe of the company. The underlying philosophy of the company. More specifically, it was about org charts. In a nutshell: she thought we needed one; I didn't.

I said that dictating an organizational structure would make the office a stuffy, rigid, and unfun place to work. It would rob employees of their creativity, their spontaneity, their ability to innovate and collaborate. And it would make work feel like, well…*work*.

She said that without structure, the operation would be sheer chaos. Employees would be lost, confused, and stressed. And so would we.

I said I wasn't on some big power trip, and I didn't want to set up a hierarchy that put me above everyone else. I wanted us all to be in it together—not to turn the office into some kind of medieval fiefdom where I was the lord and overseer.

She said it *was* my responsibility to oversee everyone. I needed to keep tabs on everyone and not be out of the loop. I needed to know what was happening in my own office. That was my job.

I said I could do that without a structure.

She said a structure would make it easier. And it didn't have to be a rigid hierarchy. We could create a flat structure, a circular structure, a fluid structure, a decentralized structure, or a hybrid structure that pulled elements from different approaches.

I said she wasn't hearing me—I didn't want any structure at all.

She said to take the weekend to think it over.

I said I would.

And then I went home, thought it over, and decided that I wished I'd never hired her in the first place.

By the time I woke up the next morning, however, all thoughts of work were out of my head. It was already late, my belly was grumbling, and I was only focused on one thing: lunch.

I reached the buffet at exactly noon and loaded up my tray with the first things that looked good: a big bowl of pasta, a side salad, and a slice of peach pie. Then I found a spot at the nearest table and dug in.

As expected, the food was delicious. But after a few bites, something made my stomach turn. No, it wasn't my meal. It was the meal of the young boy at the table next to me. Like me, he was eating a bowl of pasta, which, like mine, looked delicious. What made me sick is what he was doing to it: scooping in a big spoonful of mustard.

And he didn't stop there. After spreading the mustard around, he dumped in a bowl of applesauce. And then it just got worse: he stirred the applesauce around and then poured in half a glass of soda.

Did anybody else see this? I looked at the people next to the kid: a slightly younger boy (maybe three or four years old), a teenage girl, and a woman who I assumed was their mother. None of them were paying any attention to the food-mixing boy. The woman was reading a book, the girl was wearing headphones and scrolling through her phone, and the younger boy was absorbed in eating his lunch—that is, until the slightly older boy (who, based on his appearance, seemed to be his brother) started dumping food in there too. He poured soup over his brother's peanut butter and jelly sandwich. Then he dumped the drenched sandwich into the boy's juice and poured that over his would-be dessert: a piece of chocolate cake.

The younger boy put down his spoon, glared at his brother, and started to shake—seemingly crying without a sound. But still, neither the girl nor the woman intervened or even looked up. And the older boy kept right on doing what he was doing: taking every food, beverage, and condiment within his reach and mixing them all together on his and his brother's plates.

All I'd wanted was to eat my lunch in peace—to enjoy my weekly treat without any drama. Instead, I spent the whole time debating whether or not I should go over and say something. After a while, though, the family got up and left, leaving the boy's creation behind on the table.

Joylessly, I finished my own meal. Rather than savoring my food, I was just trying to keep it down while fighting the urge to fixate on the abandoned plates.

When I got up to leave, I took one last look at them. The once colorful, varied meals had been reduced to nauseating, uniform blobs.

I knew it wasn't my business. They weren't my kids. Sure, it was harmless fun—for the older brother, anyway. And there were bigger problems in the world. But it really got under my skin.

I thought the mom should have told the older boy not to mix his foods like that—or at least not to do it to his brother's food. I thought of how the kid had taken at least half a dozen perfectly good foods and wasted them all. I thought I was going to hurl.

And then I thought, maybe Laney has a point.

Lesson #5:
Structure and hierarchies reduce chaos, confusion, and waste.

6. It Just Takes One

After I smoothed things over with Laney, we proceeded with her suggested org chart. By the time we finished, my head was swimming. And after a few days of trying to actually fill those positions, my head was drowning.

We'd decided to keep the team relatively small at first—approximately a dozen new hires—based on Laney's suggested motto: "Big enough to thrive, small enough to care." It seemed like the process would be straightforward enough. Nonetheless, it involved multiple steps: First, we figured out what positions we needed and how everyone would work together. Next, we wrote the job descriptions and posted them online. Then, we got into our second fight—this time about whether or not to use recruiting firms.

I thought it was a waste of money to give an agency 25% of an employee's salary; Laney thought the investment would pay for itself by helping us find higher-quality candidates. I said I'd consider it in the future and reminded her that, thanks to the hierarchy she'd practically insisted we set up, I had the final say. Then I spent the rest of the day apologizing for being unnecessarily heavy handed, trying to reassure her that I really did value her input.

If the hiring process was already causing such headaches with my one and only employee, how much worse would it get once we started filling the entire office? I soon found out: a lot worse.

The floodgates opened, and soon we were deluged by a sea of résumés, applications, and cover letters (a shockingly high percentage of which contained appalling grammar). An even higher percentage of the applicants were grossly unqualified (such as the aspiring system administrator who had no computer training or experience). And a few of the people weren't even applying to our company (the online equivalent of a wrong number).

This was the good part.

The bad part was that many of the applicants couldn't be instantly disqualified; they had sent their application to the right place, knew what job they were applying for, and knew how to use spell check. This meant that Laney and I had a lot of applications to read and a lot of decisions to make.

Even among those who'd survived the first round of cuts, there were still plenty of clunkers—people whose cover letters came across as arrogant, rude, random, overly personal, or overly long. (I'm sorry, but thirty-seven pages is not a cover letter; it's a novella.) And upon closer inspection, many of the remaining résumés contained (or *didn't* contain) concerning elements—if not exactly red flags then at least some yellow ones: job-hopping, unexplained employment gaps, irrelevant experience, or terrible formatting. (I know it shouldn't matter for most positions, but come on—how hard is it to master Heading 1, Heading 2, bold, and italics...especially if you're applying to be a designer? If they couldn't get *this* right, what else would they struggle with?) And then there were some applicants who didn't seem to have anything wrong with them but simply weren't the right fit for us.

The more time I spent with the applications, the more depressed I grew. How hard was it to find a decent candidate? It's not like I was looking for a Nobel laureate—just someone who knew how to update a website. (Or had basic qualifications for bookkeeping, tech support, sales, marketing, or whatever position they were applying for.)

Laney and I had initially set a goal that by the end of the week, we'd narrow down the pile to the top five candidates for each position. Then, the following week, we'd interview them and make our final decisions. It seemed like a reasonable plan at the time, given that we had dozens of applications for each position. In fact, I'd initially wondered how we would choose only five finalists per position. But after a few days of swimming in this sea of mediocrity (or worse), I began to despair of finding anyone worth interviewing, much less hiring.

By Friday afternoon, my head hurt more than it had all week, making it hard to even think, much less make important decisions. So I once again pulled rank and told Laney we were pushing back our top-five picks until Monday. I told her I needed to sleep on it. But what I really needed was to *eat* on it. I don't know why, but I felt sure the buffet would make everything clear.

Unfortunately, it just made everything worse.

I arrived at my usual time—noon on Saturday—and spent the next hour spiraling into a deeper and deeper funk. Everything I saw dragged me down. The appetizers looked unappetizing. The desserts seemed sickeningly sweet. And I could've sworn I saw moss growing on the pumpernickel loaves.

Had I deluded myself for the past month? Was the buffet not a magical oasis of culinary wonders but just an oversized, understaffed lunch joint that couldn't even keep its food fresh (and was possibly violating multiple health codes)? Seriously, how hard was it? I didn't expect gourmet cuisine, just a decent-tasting lunch that would fill me up and not make me puke.

I walked through room after room, and everywhere I looked, I saw another unsuitable option. Some of the food just looked gross. (Brussels sprouts in fennel sauce? No thank you!) Some of it looked dangerous. (Rotten strawberries, anyone?) But most of it looked decent but just wasn't what I wanted just then. Gazpacho soup? Looked good, but I felt like something hot. Miso soup? Not filling enough—with all that walking around, I'd worked up an appetite! Pizza? Too generic; I could get that anywhere.

After an hour of fruitless wandering (despite seeing many actual fruits—none of which looked appetizing), it looked like my lunch plan was turning into an epic fail. The buffet had let me down. I'd thought it would provide dozens—perhaps even hundreds—of appealing options. And it's not like I needed hundreds of meals or dozens or even two. I just needed one. Which didn't seem like too much to ask. Yet here I was, still walking around with an empty tray.

Until I saw the ratatouille.

Even from a distance, it looked good. Up close, it looked even better. And the smell was the best part of all—a mouth-watering blend of herbs, spices, onions, and garlic (which, now that I was single, I no longer needed to avoid).

Before I realized what I was doing, I loaded up my plate, found a free table, and chowed.

After a few bites, the knot in my stomach began to loosen and my brain kicked into gear for the first time in days. My epic fail had suddenly transformed into a success. It's not that this ratatouille was the end-all be-all of the culinary universe, but it was certainly more than good enough. It was delicious. It was satisfying. And it taught me just what I needed to know for the next week at work.

Lesson #6:
When you're faced with a problem, it doesn't matter how many bad options there are. You just need one viable solution.

7. Balance

On Monday morning I returned to work with a renewed sense of optimism about the hiring process. I could do this. After all, I didn't need to hire hundreds of people—just one per position. And I didn't have to find that person right away—just five people (or even three or four) who had potential. And I didn't have to do it alone—Laney would be with me the whole time, offering guidance, recommendations, and the wisdom of her expertise. I could do this. *We* could do this.

So, after we'd refilled our coffees and brought them into the conference room, Laney pulled her chair next to mine, tightened her already-tight ponytail, and opened the folder of remaining résumés. We hoped to find a few diamonds, even if they were still in the rough. And most of them were. (Rough, that is.) But by the end of the day, we'd managed to find a few for each position who might be polished into something valuable. You couldn't always tell on paper, though, Laney told me. I nodded my head like I knew, like I'd been through this process before. That's what the interviews are for, she said. Again I nodded, like I'd ever conducted an interview. And then, as if she could read my mind, she point-blank asked me: "You've conducted interviews before, right?"

I nodded again and said, "Absolutely." Which was true; I'd interviewed her. But for some unfathomable reason, I added, "plenty of times."

"Great! Then you can take the lead." She smiled. "I'll go make the calls and start setting them up for tomorrow. No time like the present, right? Or at least the near future." She picked up the résumés from the *Yes* pile, straightened them with an efficient tap against the table, and strode into her office before I could stop her, before I could tell her what I was thinking.

Which was: NO! WAIT! I don't know what I'm doing! I've never done anything like this! How should I act? What should I say? What should I ask the candidates? How do I make sure the process is friendly but also professional, ethical, and effective? How do I come across as a confident boss (or potential boss) without seeming arrogant? What if they can tell I don't know what I'm doing? How do I make the office seem like an appealing place to work? Above all, how do I find the right person for the job? If someone seems perfect, should I offer them a job on the spot? And what if they're terrible? How soon can I end the interview without being rude? Or should I not worry about being rude? But what if someone secretly records me saying something rude and it goes viral and then no one wants to work here and we lose all our customers before we even open the office?

I did some quick math. We had a dozen positions to fill and approximately five candidates for each spot. That was roughly sixty interviews! And if Laney set them all up for this week (which was her goal, which meant she would do it), that would be approximately fifteen per day—about one every half hour. Egad! What had I gotten myself into? I couldn't handle that—I'd be dead by the end of the first day. Or, if not, I'd probably wish I were.

My head started throbbing. This time it went way beyond my usual stress headaches. Was this what a stroke felt like? Or an aneurysm? Or just me facing up to the obvious truth: Maya was right—I wasn't a go-getter. I wasn't cut out to be a leader. Who was I kidding? But maybe there was still time to get out of it.

I ran into Laney's office to tell her not to make the calls after all; I'd changed my mind. But when I got there, she was already on the phone, smiling and giving me a thumbs up. "Great!" she said. "We'll see you at ten-thirty." She hung up and jotted something down in her planner. "That's three already for tomorrow morning. Looks like it'll be a full day."

I stifled a wince and forced a smile. "Great! Looking forward to it!"

I left the office early and spent the night trying to learn everything I could about the interview process, trying to convince myself that it would be fine, and trying not to slip into a full-blown panic attack.

As it turned out, the actual interviews were the easy part. Most of them flew by—a blur of forgettable faces, generic conversations, and overpriced outfits. But a few stood out—some of them because I couldn't wait to get them out of the office (such as the guy who insisted that the tech industry was a conspiracy of mind control and urged me to escape while I still could), and others because I couldn't wait to invite them back and start working together (such as the guy who'd sold his first app for seven figures). Assuming they wanted to work together, that is. Almost everyone had been reasonably polite, but who knows what they were really thinking. Maybe I'd made a fool out of myself without even realizing it and now they wouldn't work here if their lives depended on it.

Fortunately, Laney had been with me throughout each interview, and she assured me I'd conducted myself very professionally and hadn't said or done anything that would turn me into a meme-of-the-week pariah. She also agreed that we already had some potentially good fits: qualified candidates with compatible personalities and realistically ambitious career goals. By the end of the week, it looked like we had the makings of a solid team.

And that's when the head-throbbing resumed.

And so did the avalanche of questions. What do I do now? Should I hire the one who I get a good feeling from, even though they don't have the most experience? Or do I go with the one with spotless qualifications but that I don't feel drawn to, even though I can't put my finger on why? What if I make the wrong choice? What if I hire a dud and let a gem slip away? What if my hiring mistakes set the office on the road to irreversible ruin?

This time, the questions weren't just hypothetical or anticipatory. They had immediate (or almost-immediate) real-life consequences. Should I hire Candidate A or Candidate B? The answer could make or break careers—including my own. It could build the business—or wreck it. It could make me look like a top-notch manager—or just an idiot.

Suddenly, things were getting real.

By the time the week was over, some people would say I needed a drink. But I've never been a fan of alcohol. What I needed was something deeper. I needed a buffet.

I'd love to say that I felt better the moment I stepped into the buffet—that my head stopped aching, my worries lifted, and everything became instantly clear. But it was the opposite: my head hurt worse than it had all week, and I felt more confused than ever. After wandering in a daze for almost half an hour, I stopped right in the middle of the appetizers room and looked around, bewildered. What should I do? I felt paralyzed. I couldn't even decide what to eat for lunch—how was I going to decide on a team for work?

It's not that none of the candidates were good enough—many of them seemed excellent. Just like many of the foods around me looked excellent. But which one should I pick? And what if I made the wrong choice? What if I passed up something that looked good, decided to get it next time, and then found out it had been discontinued? I might not have a second chance—just like I might not have another chance to hire a great candidate if I passed on them now.

And how could I make sure everyone meshed together as a team? Everyone seemed so different. And a lot of the stand-out candidates were lacking in a key area: they had the training but not the experience, or vice versa. And several of the ones who seemed well rounded were socially awkward or just plain weird. (Like that guy who ended our interview by asking, "When you call you *you*, who's the you who calls you you?" That'll teach me to ask if they have any questions for me!) What if people's holes, flaws, and inadequacies became more and more glaring over time? Would one bad apple really ruin the whole bunch? Or did everyone have issues right from the start? No matter who I chose, the office could be doomed.

I knew I was spiraling and that if I didn't get a grip on myself, I'd end up missing out on a great lunch—and possibly blowing my chance at a great career. So, I took a deep breath and decided to bring out the big guns. I still didn't know what to do about work, but I did know what I should eat—my all-time favorite food: aloo saag. I'd already had it here, so I knew it was great, and I was in serious need of a surefire winner.

I found my way to the Indian-cuisine room and looked around for the saag. But before I could find it, something else caught my eye—an old favorite that I hadn't seen before at the buffet: thali.

Like the thalis I'd had before, this one came on a big silver tray with about half a dozen small silver bowls on top of it. Each bowl had a single ingredient or mini meal: rice, naan, dal, curries, chutneys, and even a rice pudding for dessert. It was easy, it was convenient, and it had everything I wanted on one tray. As I took my first bite, I was happy to find that it exceeded my expectations in terms of taste.

But it also did something more than that. It got me thinking: none of the individual components would have made a meal on its own. (At least not a satisfying one—unless you just can't get enough plain basmati rice.) But it didn't have to. No single ingredient had to be everything: sweet, savory, spicy, and satisfying. Together, though, they were all that and more—a full, balanced meal on one platter.

Just like no single candidate had to be everything. It was okay if some were a bit spicy, others a bit plain, some a bit more experienced, others young and eager. It was about the combination. It was about assembling a balanced team where each part complemented the others.

Maybe Brenda's calm presence at the front desk could balance Diego's gregariousness. Laney's pragmatism could balance Kareem's vision. Liam and Yasmin could bring in the customers, and Yun could keep them happy. And while Sofia, Keiko, and Tamika focused on their specialties—bookkeeping, design, and legal matters—Nora could hold everyone together in HR.

I exhaled. The pressure was off. It didn't all fall on one person. It didn't all fall on *me*! I could relax, enjoy the blend of talents and flavors, and savor the meal.

Lesson #7:
No single person needs to have every quality and fill every role. But together, a team can be balanced, complementary, and stronger than the sum of its parts.

8. Rejection

I hated being the bad guy. Not just the messenger or the bearer of bad news, but the actual *cause* of that bad news. The one who had to say, "We've decided to go in a different direction," which is obviously a euphemism for "You didn't get the job," which is obviously a euphemism for "You've been rejected."

All too often, I've been on the other side of these interactions. And every time, my mind quickly turns "You've been rejected" into "You're a reject." It turns "You're not right for the job" into "Something's wrong with you." And any attempts to soften the blow just make it worse. Like when they say, "It's not about you." Of course it's about me! *I'm* the one you're not hiring. The one you're firing. The one you're rejecting. The one you're dumping.

(Yes, even three months later, the Maya breakup still stung, which made me empathize that much more with the rejected candidates. Even if it was just about a job and not a life partner, I knew how much it hurt. And now I'd be the one delivering the blow. Again and again and again.)

Laney offered to make the calls—to break the news to the candidates we didn't select—and believe me, I was seriously tempted to take her up on the offer. But I felt strongly that, as branch manager, I should be the one. I needed to make the hard decisions and take on the unpleasant tasks that no one else wants to do. I needed to be the guy who says, "The buck stops here."

But I hated the buck. And I hated the calls. Every time I picked up the phone, the knot in my stomach tightened. And every time I had to break the disappointing news, it felt like another kick in the gut—like *I* was the one being rejected.

I especially hated it when they begged or bargained. "I'll work for a lower salary." "I'll work longer hours." "I'll come on board without pay for a trial period." "You don't have to pay me unless I get results." (Which hit a little too close to home—it was essentially what I was doing.)

Even worse than the bargainers were the sour-grape insulters. "Fine, I don't wanna work for your stupid company anyway." "The fact that you're not hiring me just proves what an idiot you are." "Good, because you were the worst interviewer I've ever met, so I'm sure you're an equally incompetent manager. Have fun failing." Or the response I heard several times that week: "Big mistake. Huge." They'd obviously forgotten they had to do something significant first—like develop a billion-dollar app—or they didn't have anything to rub in my face. Still, these weren't exactly fun calls.

And the absolute worst of all were the ones who tried to lay a guilt trip on me. "I'm a single mother; I need this job to feed my kids." "I just got laid off because my company downsized." "My wife is on disability, and if I don't get this job we'll be evicted from our home and our four-year-old son will have to give away his puppy, who's his only friend in the world." They made it seem like it was all my fault—which, in a way, it was. If I had selected them for the position, they'd be okay. But I hadn't. I'd rejected them. Because I'm a bad guy. *The* bad guy.

Ugh.

So, let's just say it was not a fun week. And by the time Saturday rolled around, I was more than ready to get away from the office, leave my phone at home, and stuff my face at the buffet.

The moment I stepped inside, I felt the boost in my mood—and my appetite. The amazing aromas beckoned me forward, and as I walked through room after room, I was once again amazed by how many lunch options looked delicious, nutritious, and wonderfully prepared. It would be a tough choice—but I wasn't complaining!

I was tempted to try the chili, which smelled amazing, but my stomach was a bit off (probably remnants of the stressful week of unpleasant calls), so I didn't want to push my luck with something spicy. That meant that curries were also out, at least for this week. I considered the wide array of pasta dishes, but I was already feeling a bit sluggish, so I wanted to go easy on the carbs. Unfortunately, that also meant taking a rain check on the fresh-baked breads, as enticing as their aromas may have been.

Not everything looked appealing, though. The lasagna crust was burnt. The gnocchi looked "nyucky." And I'm just not a big enough fan of cabbage to base a whole meal around it.

There were still plenty of great options, though. And as much as I would've loved to eat dozens of them, I knew I was just going to eat one lunch today. I eventually chose a vegetable kebab and a small salad with chick peas and artichoke hearts. Excellent selections, if I do say so myself. Every bite hit the spot.

That's not to say that many of the other options wouldn't have been good, however; they just weren't good for me on that day. Or maybe they would have been, but I couldn't eat them all. At least not in one day. It was nothing against the foods (well, most of them) and nothing against the chefs (for the most part). And certainly nothing personal. It was just lunch.

But how could I explain that to the chefs? What if the chef who made the chili had seen me pass it by and got upset—felt insulted, rejected? What if they confronted me: "Hey! You got a problem with my chili?" I'd have to tell them that nothing was wrong with the chili; it looked great. It's just that I didn't want anything spicy right now. It's not you; it's me.

Ditto for the ravioli, the bread, and even the cabbage. There's nothing wrong with it. Some people can't seem to get enough sauerkraut, coleslaw, and kimchi. But it's just not my thing.

Of course, if the chef asked me about the lasagna or the gnocchi, things could get a bit awkward. What if I pointed out the burns and they got mad—insulting me and yelling that I don't know the first thing about pasta? I'd try to tell them it wasn't the end of the world. There was probably a quick fix: just don't cook it quite as long. Maybe set a timer for the next batch; or if they already use a timer, set it for sooner. It didn't mean they were a bad chef. And it certainly didn't mean they were a bad person. They'd just overcooked some food.

As I imagined these hypothetical conversations with the "rejected" chefs, my mind naturally drifted to all the actual conversations I'd had recently with people who I actually had rejected. I almost wished they could be here with me now, walking past row after row of meals…and "rejecting" almost all of them—not because there was anything wrong with most of them but simply because they weren't the right fit right now. Just like most of the candidates. It didn't mean they were bad employees or bad people or that they wouldn't be a great fit at some other time or for some other company. But just not for me right now.

And I thought of how pointless it had been for the people to beg, bargain, or insult me. But I also thought of the one surprisingly positive rejection call I'd made. I'd started out with the usual knot in my stomach, which progressed to the usual kick-in-the-gut feeling at the moment I delivered the coup de grâce. I braced myself for backlash, but then something unexpected happened: instead of becoming bitter, angry, or desperate, the man thanked me for my time and asked me a question: *Why?* He wanted to know what had led to my decision and whether he could have done anything better—not so that he could try to change my mind but simply because he wanted to learn, grow, and prepare for future opportunities. He said he was completely open to honest feedback, so I told him the truth: he seemed like a wonderful candidate, but he'd been lacking in cloud technology training, which was essential for that position. Again, he thanked me for my time, told me he would get the training he needed, and invited me to contact him in the future if other opportunities arose that he was qualified for. And if that should happen, he'd certainly be among the first I would think of. Because he's not like my imaginary lasagna chef who insults me for giving honest feedback; he's like the (also imaginary) one who buys a timer, sets it for less time, and makes better lasagna in the future.

And while I couldn't have all these people (real or imaginary) with me just then, I could learn from them. Which is exactly what I did.

Lesson #8:
Rejections don't mean there's anything wrong with you, but they can provide opportunities for growth.

9. Second-Guessing

Well, we did it! We hired the staff. And although you never know until you actually get started, I felt like we had the makings of a really good team. And for the first time, I could actually see this plan succeeding—creating a profitable branch within a year—not as some distant dream or hypothetical scenario, but as a real-life experience in an actual office with actual people conducting actual business.

I couldn't have done it without Laney. First, she set up the remaining interviews. Some were part of what she called her "data-driven recruitment strategy." (I didn't even ask—for fear of looking stupid and for fear that my head would explode trying to follow her explanation. Anyway, she seemed to have it all under control with her ATS software. Again, I didn't ask.) She also made arrangements with the stragglers—people who had to reschedule or simply couldn't make it in the previous week. I wasn't sure if this was a red flag already. After all, if they really wanted the job, they would've made time, right? But Laney assured me that this might actually be a sign that they were essential in their current jobs and couldn't just skip out for an hour or two during a workday. Maybe these were the kind of conscientious, committed employees we did want.

But Laney's biggest help came when it was time to make the actual decisions. She reviewed all the candidates with me, discussed their perceived strengths and weaknesses, and helped me put together the best possible team—a well-balanced blend of training, experience, competence, confidence, vision, dedication, and a sprinkle of that X factor that we couldn't quite define but could certainly feel from several of the new hires. (Personality, I guess, but something more too—a certain *je ne sais quoi*, as Maya's dad used to say.)

She also figured out the budget, so when candidates negotiated about their starting salary, we knew when we had wiggle room, when we had to stand firm, and when we had to move on to our second choice (which happened with a couple of candidates who wouldn't budge).

And she said something I hadn't thought of but was so obvious once I heard it: the new people weren't going to start the following Monday (as I'd assumed they would) but two weeks later—to give them time to put in two weeks' notice and make necessary arrangements (which for Keiko, our blue-haired designer, included moving to be closer to work—how's that for commitment!).

That gave me and Laney two weeks to get our ducks in a row—to prepare for orientation, come up with a strategy and a schedule, and make sure we were ready to hit the ground running once the new hires arrived. But for the time being, all I had to do was relax, celebrate, and enjoy myself—which, on Saturday, meant lunch at the buffet.

I didn't let the overcast skies dampen my spirits or change my plans. I threw on a parka and set out for my weekly walk. Call me a creature of habit, but I'd already grown so fond of this routine that I refused to drive—just like I refused to bring my phone. This was my personal time: no work, no interruptions. Just me and my meal.

Sure enough, about halfway there, it started drizzling. But I honestly didn't mind. I put up my hood, picked up my pace a bit, and kept thinking of the celebratory lunch that awaited me. I deserved it. I'd reached a big milestone at work. I'd taken an important step toward my yearlong goal. And I was going to savor the moment…and the meal.

Before I left, I'd known exactly what I wanted: the falafel and hummus wrap plus peach pie and a shake. After the wet, chilly walk, though, I changed course and selected a hot cup of oolong tea, a hearty bowl of barley stew, and a big slice of multigrain toast for dunking. This might not sound like everyone's idea of a party, but for me it hit the spot—every bite, sip, and slurp was delicious and satisfying.

But somewhere between spoonfuls of stew and the last sip of tea, the second-guessing kicked in.

Should I have gotten something more festive after all? (Namely, just about anything else!) I mean, who eats barley stew at a party? Why didn't I go for one of my old favorites—or try something new that I'd had my eye on? After all, it's not like there was any shortage of amazing-looking hot meals there. It didn't even have to be unusual—even a slice of pizza would've been more festive. Or at least a mug of hot cocoa. What was wrong with me? Didn't I know how to have fun? To seize the moment? To set a positive tone? Who was going to follow a barley-eating, oolong-sipping would-be leader?

If this is what I chose for my celebratory meal, how could I trust *any* of my choices? Had I made mistakes with the new hires too? Maybe there'd been better candidates, but I just didn't give them enough time to apply. Or maybe I'd made my hiring decisions based on superficial reasons instead of looking at what really mattered. Maybe on some subconscious level, I didn't hire Owen simply because I didn't want someone with that name to be our director of finances. (Similarly, did I not hire Aiden for customer support simply because his name was *too* on the nose? Ditto for Brandon, who'd applied to be director of marketing.) Yes, Laney had guided me and reassured me that these were good decisions, but maybe I was wrong to listen to her. Maybe I'd been wrong to hire her in the first place. After all, only a few weeks in, she was already taking over what was supposed to be *my* office! Maybe I should fire her, tell all the new hires that I'd changed my mind, and start over from square one. And maybe I should ditch the barley stew and go back for some spring rolls. Or a samosa. Or those tasty-looking tamales. Or maybe I should've taken something from that amazing-looking spread of Peruvian dishes. I hadn't seen that before—maybe it was a one-off for this week only. What if I tried to get it next week but found out it had been discontinued? I might not have a second chance—just like I might not have another chance to hire a great candidate if I passed on them now.

I looked down at my bowl and saw that it was nearly empty. Only a corner of the toast remained. And my tea was finished. Where had it all gone?

I took a deep breath and remembered my original plan: to savor the meal. The meal that was right in front of me. Not spring rolls. Not samosas. Not tamales. The meal I *had* chosen.

I took another breath and another spoonful of the stew. It was no longer what I'd call "piping hot," but it was plenty warm enough to enjoy, which I did—mainly because it was mind-bogglingly delicious. (I don't know what they put in there—some kind of "Where have you been all my life?" spice combination.)

And then I dunked in the remaining bit of toast, soaked up the flavor, and thought of how amazing the buffet's homemade breads tasted. And I thought of how I had made a good choice after all. And although I tried not to think of work, I thought about the hiring choices I'd made.

Except this time I didn't get down on myself. I didn't feel a wave of buyer's remorse (or hirer's remorse). I didn't speculate about the ones who got away. (Not even Owen the accountant.) I simply acknowledged that I'd made the best choices I could. If they didn't turn out well, I could always make changes later, but I fully expected that they'd all be just fine.

Did I know there were many other options—at work and at the buffet—including some very appealing ones? Yes, of course. But I'd chosen the ones I'd chosen. And now all I had to do was exactly what I'd initially intended: relax, celebrate, and enjoy.

Lesson #9:
Make a decision and align with it.

10. Overcomplicated

"First time here, darlin'?" the cashier asked the man in front of me.

"How'd you know?" he asked.

"Well, our regulars don't usually look around for menus...'cause we don't have any!" Looking over the man's shoulder, the cashier winked at me.

And just like that, it was official: I'd only been coming to the buffet for two months, but I'd been ordained as a "regular." I wore the title with pride. I liked being an insider, a familiar face, someone in the know. It's hard to believe that not too long ago, I was in the same position as this first-timer, but now, as a buffet veteran, I could listen to his questions with good-natured amusement.

"So, how does this work?" he asked.

"Well, you pay me, then grab a tray, take whatever food you want, and eat it."

The cashier's straightforward explanation didn't seem like a head-scratcher, but the man literally scratched his head. "There's no host to take me to my table?"

"Sit wherever you want."

"And no one takes my order?"

"Nope. Self-serve."

"And after I take the food, do I have to weigh it?"

"Nope. Same price, no matter what it weighs."

"So I just pay you now and—"

"That's it—ya just pay up and chow down!" The cashier smiled again, but this time a hint of a sigh escaped her lips.

"Come on, buddy!" shouted someone in the growing line behind me. "I'm starvin' like Marvin—let's move it!"

I sympathized with the man's impatience but also felt bad for the guy in front of me. As a recent newbie, I knew how overwhelming the buffet could seem at first. Still, I had to admit that my amusement had taken several steps in the direction of exasperation.

Whether he'd been spurred on by the growing impatience behind him or had finally grasped the buffet's system, the man seemed ready to pay and move on. He counted out a few bills and coins and then looked up at the cashier. "I'm so sorry," he said. "I'm a bit short on cash. Do you take credit cards?"

"Credit, debit, checks, gift cards, digital wallet…whatever ya got."

He started to hand over a card, but then pulled it back. "Should I get a punch card first?" he asked. "In case I come back, so I can get a voucher or coupon or—"

"Nah, we don't do that. Same price for everyone." She tapped his card against her reader and handed it back with a smile. "Okay, you're all good to go, honey."

"So now I just—"

"Help yourself and enjoy!" She gestured to the stack of trays and the rows of food beyond it, then turned back to me. "Next!"

Within moments, I had paid, grabbed a tray, and loaded it up with a napkin, utensils, and a plate. Now the only question was what food to put on that plate. Or, more accurately, that was *my* only question. Clearly, the newbie still had many other questions. As I walked behind him, I watched him stop a fellow customer. "Excuse me, where do I pay if I want to go back for seconds?"

"No need to pay again," the customer replied. "Go back as many times as you want. The entrance fee covers everything—all you can eat."

"And do some foods cost more than others?"

"Nope. Same price for everything."

The newbie thanked the customer and then took a few more steps into the buffet, seemingly comfortable with the answer. But a few moments later, he stopped someone else. "Excuse me, how do I heat up the food?"

The man he'd stopped looked confused. "Heat it up?"

"Yeah, like if it's soup or something I want hot. Are there microwaves or something?"

"It's already hot—everything that's supposed to be, that is." The man laughed. "You don't have to heat it up; you just have to eat it up!"

The man he'd stopped gave the newbie a good-natured pat on the shoulder before walking away. At that point, though, I don't think I would've been so understanding. I mean, did this newbie seriously think the buffet made you cook your own food? And could he really not grasp the simplicity of their system? Pay once, take whatever you want, eat it. It's not rocket science, buddy. But he just wouldn't accept that it could really be that straightforward. As I walked away, I caught his final words to the next person he stopped—asking about the buffet's food-management system and whether he'd have to scan any bar codes to keep track of what he'd taken. All I could do was shake my head, grab some food, find a table, and get on with what I'd come here to do: eat my lunch.

As I ate my falafel sandwich—simple, straightforward, satisfying, and scrumptious—I contemplated the newbie. Why had he been so intent on overcomplicating such an obviously simple situation? There were enough genuinely complicated things in the world—like brain surgery, rocket science, and what I'd been doing all week: creating an onboarding program for a dozen new employees. It sure would be nice if my job could be as straightforward as my lunch, but at the office, I was managing a lot more than falafel and iced tea. I'd already written over a hundred pages explaining how each person's role supported the company's mission, and I'd barely scratched the surface of all I needed to cover. I'd hoped to have everything completed earlier in the week, but it was spiraling into a much bigger project than I'd expected. Which made sense because, unlike the buffet, my job actually was complicated!

But did it have to be?

Did I really need twenty pages to describe what the company did? We created technology that enhanced lives—why not just say that? Was it necessary to wax poetic about personal expression, or could I just tell them we didn't have a dress code? Did I really need to exhaustively cover every possible scenario that Tamika might encounter, or could I just say that her job was to make sure we did everything legally? Instead of presenting dozens of ways to do business, couldn't I just tell Yasmin and Liam that they were in charge of marketing and sales, respectively? And

Laney didn't need a big handbook; she already knew what her job was: to help me run the place!

Sure, business was complex, but it didn't have to be complicated. And neither did my explanation. It could be simple without being simplistic. It could be clear and concise without minimizing the importance of what we do. It could let everyone know the essence of their role while still leaving plenty of room for exploration and expansion. I didn't need the ultimate business guide, just a starting point.

I looked at my sandwich—a model of simplicity and elegance: falafel, lettuce, and hummus in a pita pocket. Basic yet delicious. So delicious, in fact, that I decided to go back for seconds—which, as the newbie now knew, I didn't have to pay extra for!

And as soon as I got back home, I pulled out my *Lessons* notebook, turned to the next blank page, and wrote my new three-word business mantra.

Lesson #10:
Don't overcomplicate it.

11. Boundaries

Monday was our first day with the entire team. And in keeping with my new mantra, I decided to scale back my initial onboarding plans and keep things simple: No multi-day extravaganza, off-site team-building exercises, elaborate presentations, or guest speakers. Just a casual meet-and-greet in the conference room—with plain old tea, coffee, water, fourteen name tags, and fourteen chairs: enough for me, Laney, and the twelve people we'd hired.

The two-hour session was just enough time for everyone to introduce themselves, talk about their background, and share a fun fact unrelated to work (which is how I learned that Tamika has lived in seven countries and that petite, unassuming Zoey has done three Tough Mudders—a fact that became more impressive after I learned what that was).

As planned, I kept my own remarks brief—sharing a bit about myself, the company, and our goals (although not my "profit-or-perish" wager, which I'd decided to keep to myself—no reason to worry the troops on the first day…or ever). I made sure to wrap things up by noon, but first I told them something I felt very strongly about: my open-door policy.

What I didn't mention is *why* I felt so strongly about this: I didn't want to be like my old boss. Every time I'd gone to her for help, her door was locked. She was always either on a call, working on a time-sensitive project, or just "busy"—although I could often see her through the plate-glass window, just staring into space. In her big, cushy office, behind her locked door. While we underlings were left to fend for ourselves.

Well, I would be a different kind of boss. I would actually support my staff. My door would always be open—figuratively and literally. I'd always be available to anyone who wanted to come in and talk—to discuss questions or concerns, to review their recent work or plan their next project, or just to shoot the breeze. I would be the boss who valued personal connections—and you can't have personal connections if you literally lock everyone out!

Despite my sincere invitation and my literally open door, only a handful of people stopped in to talk on Monday afternoon. Throughout Tuesday, however, the trickle grew into a small stream. And by Wednesday, I had a steady flow of people in and out of my office—sometimes one at a time, sometimes three or four at once, and sometimes so many that we could barely fit.

This trend continued through the end of the week. My office was hopping—every minute of every day! It was the place to be. It was the social hub of the branch. It was everything I'd hoped it would be: a place where employees felt comfortable. Where they knew they were welcomed. Where they knew they were safe to share, to be themselves, to be heard, to be seen, to be connected.

Throughout the day, people popped in to ask questions, swap stories about past work experiences, or compare outfits. Since I'd announced our lack of a dress code, the tech team had traded their suit jackets for hoodies and t-shirts with nerdy jokes (e.g., *I'm only here because the server is down*, *It works on MY computer*, or Nikhil's favorite: *Have you tried turning it off and then on again?*). Liam, on the other hand, still wore immaculate suits with matching pocket squares, saying he wouldn't be caught dead without one. And everyone loved Brenda's hand-knit cardigans.

By Friday afternoon, everyone in the office knew that it hadn't been just lip service—they really could come visit any time. More than that, they knew that their boss cared.

All in all, it was a great week. However, there was one minor problem: I hadn't gotten any work done.

Which wouldn't have been such a problem except that there was a *lot* of work to do. It turns out, getting a new branch up and running is a rather complex operation with a lot of steps—who knew?!—and, as branch manager, it was my job to coordinate all these steps. Hard to do when your office feels like Grand Central.

Not that I minded. I enjoyed having everyone hanging out, passing through, chatting, connecting. But I felt guilty that Laney had to pick up the slack for so much of what I should've been doing. After all, she was just one person and had enough on her own plate already without handling my tasks. I felt nervous about all the unfinished work that was piling up. Also, on a personal level, I was exhausted.

A few years earlier, our company had every employee take a personality test. Mine said I was something I'd never heard of—something that I didn't think was possible: a "social introvert." It sounded like an oxymoron. I'd thought that introverts were supposed to be antisocial. But the results page said that some introverts enjoy socializing—especially in small groups—but they still feel drained afterward and need time alone to recharge. That described me to a T!

It's not that I don't like people or that I don't value our connections. If anything, I value them so much that I want to keep thinking about them afterward—to take time to reflect on what they said, how they seemed, and what they conveyed without words. But I can't do this if I just rush from one interaction to the next without any time to decompress. I get overloaded. I get overwhelmed. I get cranky. I didn't need a personality test to tell me this.

But maybe I did—because here I was, years later, setting up my workweek in a way that didn't involve any downtime for reflection, processing, solitude, or actual work. Fortunately, though, I had plenty of downtime at night and on the weekends. And I cherished that time. I needed it. Never more so than after that first week of my self-inflicted open-door policy.

So, my big plan (or non-plan) for that weekend was to stay at home, stay quiet, and stay by myself. The one exception was my weekly lunch at the buffet.

I felt reluctant to leave my cocoon for a crowded public place, even for an hour or two. But I reminded myself that, even among the crowds, I usually managed to stick to myself. And people seemed to sense that this is how I liked it, because they generally left me alone.

But just to make sure, from the moment I walked through the buffet's door, I put on my best "give me space" expression, kept my head down as I loaded up my tray with food (stir-fry with extra garlic—all the more reason for people to stay away!), and found an empty table in a secluded corner of the buffet's quietest room. No sooner had I sat down, though, than a man approached me. "Hey there, buddy!" His voice boomed. "This seat taken?"

"Actually, I was hoping to—"

"Well, it is now! Haw! Haw! Haw!" He sat down next to me and extended his hand. "The name's Jim, but you can call me Jimbo." He gestured to his tray of food, which was filled to the point of overflowing. "And if I finish all of this, you might have to call me Jumbo! Haw! Haw! Haw!"

He took a huge bite of his sandwich and turned to me mid-chew. "So, where d'ya hail from? Me? I'm from hither and yon. Been stationed from the east to the west, but I've gotta say, this little burg's been treatin' me right. No complaints, no siree Bob."

"Truth be told, Jim—er, Jimbo—I was feeling a bit—"

"Hey there, fellas!" Jimbo waved to a group of people holding trays and apparently looking for a place to sit. "Plenty of space over here. Care to join us?"

A man in a plaid shirt walked over to the table. "Sure, if you don't mind."

"Course we don't mind!" He turned to me. "Scoot over, son. Make room for my new best friend." He extended his hand to the man in plaid. "The name's Jimbo."

"I'm Stan."

"Stan the man! Haw!" He shook his hand. "Welcome aboard!"

Stan was soon joined by his wife, Betty; his son, Brett; Brett's wife, Molly; and their teenage boys, Cayden and Cooper, who were visiting from out of town. This was their first time all together since last Thanksgiving. And they had a lot of catching up to do—a lot of family news, which they enjoyed sharing with me and Jimbo, who became increasingly gregarious with each new revelation about the family.

I, on the other hand, just smiled and nodded while increasingly regretting my decision to come to the buffet at all this weekend. No offense to the present company (with the possible exception of Jimbo, who could use some work on his listening skills), but after the week of almost non-stop socializing, I was less in the mood for Stan's family updates than for a quiet lunch on my own. But that ship had sailed the minute Jimbo sat down.

Or had it?

Why couldn't I do what I wanted? Why couldn't I go back to my original plan of sitting alone? Why couldn't I just pick up my tray and move to a different table? No reason at all.

"It was really nice meeting you all," I said, standing up.

"Leaving so soon?" Betty said, eyeing my mostly full tray.

"Yeah, I'm sorry. I just remembered I have a…" But I stopped myself. I didn't need to resort to white lies. I wasn't doing anything wrong. "Actually, I was just hoping for a quiet meal alone."

As I walked off, I caught huffy snippets of their conversation: "Well, I never!" "So rude!" "No manners at all!" "Young people these days!" "Not my boys, of course, but…"

I hated disappointing people—especially being criticized and disliked. I really had wanted to be nice. But being nice doesn't mean being a doormat. Under different circumstances, I might have been happy to stay and socialize. But right then, I didn't need to socialize—I needed to decompress, to process, and to eat my lunch in peace.

So that's what I did. I spent the next hour blissfully alone in the crowd, savoring the stir-fry and letting my mind settle. For the first time all week, I felt like I could catch my breath and hear myself think. And what I heard was a revised plan for workplace interactions. No, I wasn't going to follow in my old boss's footsteps—locking everyone out, leaving them to fend for themselves, and feeling disconnected from my team. But I also needed to have time alone each day—time to work, time to think, time to recharge. Maybe I could have set office hours, like my old college professors. Or maybe it didn't have to be anything that formal or rigid. I could just give them a sign: *Open door = come on in. Closed door = not now.*

It might not make everyone happy, but I had to remind myself that it was okay to close the door sometimes. In fact, it was more than okay. It was necessary. And it was another lesson worth writing down, remembering, and living—just like last week's lesson, and the one before that, and…

A chill ran down my neck, and goosebumps popped up on my arms. This was getting uncanny. Week after week, the buffet was teaching me exactly what I needed to learn in that moment. It had started during my very first visit, when, after a week of no decisions and no progress, the buffet showed me that I needed to make choices…or go hungry. It had been such an important and timely lesson that I'd written it in my notebook, just like I'd done with the lessons about looking for what I wanted, asking for help, creating a balanced meal (and team), and everything else I'd learned at the buffet—week after week after week. And after two and a half months, it felt like more than mere coincidence—more like (dare I even think it?)…*magic*.

Another chill ran through me, but I shook it off. No, just a fluke. Laughable. Ha! (Or, to put it in Jimbo's style, *Haw!*) Besides, this week's lesson didn't come from the buffet; it came from Jimbo. The fact that a loud-mouthed buffoon sat down next to me when I wanted to be alone certainly didn't *prove* anything.

In any case, regardless of the explanation, I'd gotten another good meal and another good lesson.

Lesson #11:
Set healthy boundaries.

12. Either/Or

I woke up clear-headed, as if emerging from a fever dream. Then, within moments, my face felt flush once again—not from a fever but from embarrassment as I remembered the dream: I'd been at the buffet and had somehow fallen under the momentary delusion that it was magically answering my questions and providing guidance about work.

Then my embarrassment tripled as I remembered that it hadn't been a dream at all—I'd actually entertained this ludicrous notion. Just for a moment, though. Now, in the clear light of morning, it was plain to see that the buffet was just a big restaurant—an inanimate structure, not some all-knowing business guru. Maybe the spice in that stir-fry had temporarily clouded my reason. Or maybe I just needed to get out more.

In any case, I climbed out of bed, showered, and did my best to wash away all thoughts of this bizarre flight of fancy. I couldn't afford to lose my mind—especially right now. I only had twenty-four hours to pull myself together and get ready for a week of conducting serious business as a serious manager, not some mentally unstable flake. And this was a particularly important week—I'd be making some of the biggest decisions of my professional life.

I already felt like I'd made more decisions in the past month than I'd made in my entire life up to that point. How should I set up the office? Should I get an assistant? What organizational structure should we use? Who should I hire for each position? What should their roles be? How much should I pay them?

After a lifetime of being notoriously indecisive, I'd suddenly turned into a decision-making machine. (If only Maya could see "Mr. Indecisive" now!) It sometimes felt like making decisions was the biggest part of my job. And for the most part, I think I'd made good ones.

But despite all the small and medium decisions I'd made (What kind of chairs should we buy? Should Zoey get her own office or share with Nikhil?), I still hadn't made some of the biggest ones: What kind of office environment did I want to create? Should I foster creativity and fun…or productivity and results? Should our products emphasize style…or substance? And yes, I knew we were a technology company, but what specific type of technology should we focus on?

Although I was proud of my newfound decision-making prowess, I reminded myself that I didn't have to make every decision alone. I now had an entire team I could turn to for advice. So, come Monday, I asked everyone for their input. I thought that would help me gain clarity, but I ended up more confused than ever.

Nora and Yun wanted to make the office fun—a place that people looked forward to coming to, a place that felt less like work and more like play. Sofia and Tamika had the opposite viewpoint: business is about business; let people goof around on their own time.

Keiko and Liam told me that to succeed, we needed style. "People only see the outside of the package," Keiko said. "You sell the shell." But when I shared this perspective with Kareem, he nearly blew a gasket. According to him, the three most important parts of technology are functionality, functionality, and functionality. (And then he went on an anti-superficiality rant that included a few other choice f-words.)

But that still left the question about what type of technology we'd create. In this area, Nikhil was the most vocal. For him, the future was all about one thing: quantum computing—and he didn't mind telling you so…again and again and again. (To put it bluntly, he wouldn't shut up about it—to the point where his officemates started calling him "The Quantum Kid.") When I asked him why, he said it would be faster, safer, and exponentially more powerful. And then he spent the next twenty minutes waxing poetic about qubits, superposition, entanglement, Rydberg atoms, gate-based ion trap processors, and about a dozen other terms that I couldn't even begin to understand. But he sure sounded convincing.

That is, until I talked to Zoey. She had equally strong feelings *against* quantum computing—and, as far as I could follow, equally compelling reasons. People had been talking about this for decades but were still years away, she said. We had to face the reality that we were living, working, and doing business in the *present*—not the future. And that required classical computing: binary bits and bytes. And then she went off on a lengthy harangue about the dangers of decomposition, broken encryption, and a conspiracy theory regarding NASA's fear of extraterrestrial intelligence (which, quite frankly, made me question my choice of VP of technology).

By the time I finished these conversations, all my newfound confidence with decision-making was out the window. (However, I did congratulate myself on deciding not to have Zoey and Nikhil share an office. Given their vehement disagreement on the whole quantum vs. classical computing debate, if they'd been forced into any closer proximity, they might've come to blows.)

All this renewed uncertainty threw me into a serious funk. I thought I'd snap out of it after a day or two, but it lasted all week—even when I was away from work, it seeped into all areas of my life. Suddenly, every decision felt paralyzing. What pants should I wear: jeans or corduroys? What should I do tonight: read a book or watch a movie? What should I buy my cousin for his birthday: tickets to a concert or to a baseball game?

At least I didn't have to decide where to eat lunch on Saturday. But just as I was about to walk out the door, I stopped in my tracks. This would be my first time going back to the buffet since I'd had those ludicrous thoughts about its "magical" guidance, so I wasn't exactly keen to return to the scene of the delusion. On the other hand, it might be good to see it again with clear eyes and a clear head, just to convince myself that it had all been a passing fancy. It would be silly to avoid the place. Besides, if it did give me guidance, great! I could use it! And if not, then that would disprove my bizarre hypothesis. Yes, that was it—I'd take an experimental approach. It was win-win: either I'd get valuable guidance—or confirmation of my sanity. And at the very least, I'd get a break from all those big decisions at work.

Or so I thought.

Once I got to the buffet, though, I was faced with even more overwhelming decisions. Not just the details (pesto or tomato sauce? iced tea or lemonade? soup or salad?), but the big-picture decisions: Should I eat something healthy…or something that tastes good? Do I want something new for me…or something familiar and comforting? Light and invigorating…or heavy and filling?

It was like being back at work. Quantum or classical? Sweet or savory? If I couldn't even decide on a general direction, how would I ever figure out specifics?

Before I could spiral down any further, an alluring aroma pulled me out of my thoughts. I followed my nose and found the source: lasagna.

Unlike the last time I'd seen the buffet's lasagna, this one looked baked to perfection. Suddenly, all my indecision evaporated. Before I had time to think, I scooped out a healthy serving. I wanted to eat while it was still hot, so I quickly grabbed a few other things to round out my meal—a garden salad, an Arnold Palmer (my go-to drink: half lemonade, half iced tea), and a blueberry cobbler for dessert—and found an empty table where I could enjoy my lunch. And enjoy it I did!

As good as the lasagna looked and smelled, it tasted even better. And there was much more to it than initially met the eye: it was packed with breaded eggplant, zucchini, spinach, crushed walnuts, and a spice that gently pushed my heat-tolerance limits but never went too far.

I alternated bites between the lasagna and the salad, letting the cucumbers and raw tomatoes cool my tongue. And then I washed it down with my Arnold Palmer, leaving just enough room to savor the cobbler.

And then, as I basked in the afterglow of a perfect meal, it hit me: I hadn't sacrificed a thing. The lasagna was healthy *and* tasty. It looked good *and* had substance. I'd gotten my sweet *and* my savory foods. And I'd even gotten iced tea *and* lemonade in a single drink.

So why couldn't we do the same at work? We could make the office fun and still be productive. Our products could be stylishly designed and work well. And there was no reason why Kareem and the other techies couldn't keep using classical computing while Nikhil headed up a long-term R&D project centered around quantum computing. (Unless we weren't profitable this year, in which case there wouldn't be a long-term.) And although I'd already bought everyone regular computer desks, there's no reason why we couldn't swap Zoey's for that standing desk she'd requested.

Yes, some decisions were mutually exclusive, but not everything had to be a battle. Sometimes everyone could win.

I shivered. I'd gotten the answer to my work question. But was this also the answer to my experimental question? Was the buffet actually proving its magic? Or was it just a healthy lasagna?

I made a mental note of the result but also remembered to maintain an open mind and a scientific approach. After all, every good scientist knows that you can't *prove* a theory, only disprove it. Plus, I hardly had a statistically significant sample size. I'd have to collect more data before drawing any conclusions.

But whether I'd just experienced true magic or just a random moment of insight, at least I had another good lunch…and another good lesson to add to my notebook.

Lesson #12:
Not every decision is either/or.

13. Unexpected

I had high hopes for everyone I hired. (If I didn't, I wouldn't have hired them!) But I'll admit, I was most excited about Kareem. His résumé was extremely impressive. He blew me away at his interview. And yes, I was awestruck by the fact that he'd sold an app for such a staggering sum (more than I'd earned in all my years with the company). Clearly, he didn't need the money, but he said that after leaving the corporate world to focus on his individual projects, he'd missed working with others and was looking forward to the small-group camaraderie—and he hoped that, along with his teammates, he could make a meaningful impact in the tech world. (As they say on that game show: "Good answer!" Not that there'd been any doubt, but that definitely sealed the deal.)

In any case, he was more than ready to get down to business, so I threw him right into the deep end: tasking him with developing an app that we could market to small businesses. The first part of his assignment was to make a list of ideas, pick the one he thought was most promising, and send me a description of it by Friday. All week long I waited eagerly, wondering what he might come up with. Maybe something to help small businesses manage payroll? Or facilitate employee interaction? Or streamline the onboarding process? (Having just gone through that, I know I would've welcomed anything to make it easier and better—maybe Kareem was thinking along the same lines.)

Late Friday afternoon, his email popped up in my inbox with the subject line "App Proposal." I eagerly clicked on it, opened the attachment, and read his description. And within minutes, one thing became perfectly clear: he had bombed it.

Not bombed as in, *his idea was the bomb*. Bombed as in, *not good*.

Worse than that, he hadn't even done the assignment. I'd given him one very simple guideline: to create an app for small businesses. Instead, he gave me some add-on for VR headsets. I can't say I fully understood his vision, but the gist of it was that it would allow users to superimpose and interact with real-life objects within a virtual landscape. This wasn't a business tool—it was a toy for gamers!

I spent the rest of the afternoon reeling from disappointment, seriously questioning Kareem's judgment…and my own. After all, I had hired the guy! How could I have been so off the mark? How could he have so misinterpreted the assignment? Was this a terrible fit? Was he just a one-app wonder? Would it be best to let him go now, before we invested any more time in each other?

Despite my questions, I knew one thing for sure: we were not on the same page. Not even in the same book.

However, even with my limited managerial experience, I knew better than to make a knee-jerk decision I might come to regret, such as firing him or even just having an awkward conversation about how terribly he'd botched the assignment. Instead, I sent him a vague one-line email (*Thanks for sending—let's discuss Monday*), then I left the office early, went home, and did my best to put the matter out of my mind for the weekend.

I didn't exactly have a busy social calendar (unlike Maya, who, based on her social media posts, seemed to be relishing the single life—girls' night out, happy hour with coworkers, Sunday brunch with friends, and smiles all around—although that was probably just a public façade to mask the deep-seated pain we shared). But at least I had one weekly outing to look forward to: Saturday lunch at the buffet.

So much of my life was up in the air: uncertainty about my new town, my new job, my new staff, and of course my new and very unwanted relationship status—and the resulting uncertainty about whether I'd be able to repair and rekindle things with Maya after she got these wild oats out of her system and I'd become a world-beating business mogul. Anyway, it was nice to have one thing I could count on. That was half of the buffet's appeal.

The other half was the food—row after row, room after room, and seemingly mile after mile of delicious-looking options, many of which were completely new to me. On this day, though, I didn't want something new. Maybe it was a reaction to Kareem's outlandish app proposal, or maybe it was just a random craving, but I was in the mood for a super basic, no-nonsense, delightfully boring lunch. So, when I got to the buffet, I headed straight for the burger and fries.

Not surprisingly, the buffet offered a massive array of options, including crinkle-cut fries, curly fries, waffle fries, shoestring fries, steak fries, cottage fries, sweet potato fries, garlic fries, potato wedges, and a number of varieties that I'd never seen before (including an impressive one that spiraled around a two-foot skewer). But I bypassed all these and went for the standard-cut fries, which I piled onto my plate alongside the most basic-looking veggie burger I could find. Then I dumped no-frills ketchup over everything, poured myself a glass of soda, found an empty table, and sat down to enjoy a plain, simple, and delicious meal.

At least that was the plan. However, the very first bite told me that something was off. What was that bizarre flavor? I put down the burger and ate a fry. Yuck! What was wrong with this meal?

I picked up a fry and examined it closely. It looked pretty normal—just a basic french fry. But there was something odd about the ketchup. It had a weird texture—not quite lumpy but definitely not the smooth consistency it should've been. And the color was off too—a bit too dark.

I put down the fry and lifted the hamburger bun for a closer look. Like the fries, the burger itself looked fine; the problem was the ketchup. I tasted a spoonful of the ketchup by itself. What the...? Then, all at once, it hit me: this wasn't ketchup at all—it was marinara sauce!

Ugh! I had ruined a perfectly good burger and plateful of fries.

Actually, no, the buffet had ruined it. This was all their fault! Why had they put marinara sauce with the condiments? It's not that I dislike marinara sauce, but it had no business being next to the french fries. It should've been in another room, next to the pasta.

Still, I kicked myself. How had I not noticed when I was scooping it out? And what should I do now—throw it all away and start over? It seemed like a waste, especially because there was nothing wrong with any of it—not even the marinara sauce (which, I had to admit, was top notch). But on burger and fries? It was, to say the least, unexpected.

Nonetheless, I took another bite of the burger. No, the sauce clearly wasn't what I'd originally had in mind, but, truth be told, it wasn't terrible.

It actually complemented the burger quite nicely. I swallowed that bite, then ate another french fry—this time, fully aware that the red "condiment" covering it was decidedly not ketchup. Knowing this, I wasn't thrown off by the taste, which, like the burger-and-sauce combo, wasn't half bad. I ate another fry. And then took another bite of the burger. And then another and another and another.

After a minute or two, I decided I might as well finish the meal as is—marinara sauce and all. No, it wasn't a standard condiment for a burger and fries, but that didn't mean it wasn't good. It simply wasn't what I'd expected. At first. But once I came to terms with the fact that it wasn't ketchup, I actually found myself enjoying this new-for-me combination.

And although I'd sworn I was going to forget about work until Monday, I couldn't help but think about Kareem's app proposal. Like the marinara sauce, it wasn't at all what I was expecting. And yes, I'd been taken aback at first. But maybe I should give it a second chance. Maybe once I knew what I was getting, I'd discover that it actually had merit. Who knew? Maybe small businesses would like the fact that it was unconventional—more like a game than a traditional business tool. But instead of brandishing magic wands in an online fantasy game, they'd be able to show a customer a couch or a coffee table as if it were in their living room. Or something along those lines—I'd leave the applications to Kareem and the rest of the development team. But the point was, maybe I shouldn't dismiss the idea out of hand simply because it wasn't what I expected.

Content that I'd received the answer I needed for work, I picked up the half-eaten burger and was about to take another bite. But then I suddenly jolted upright as if I'd received a powerful electric shock. Goosebumps sprang up on my arms, and all my senses shot into a state of heightened awareness. But this wasn't an electric shock; it was déjà vu.

I had lived through this moment before. But when? And how?

Immediately, I knew the answer. No, it wasn't Kareem's app and the marinara sauce. It was the buffet's weekly guidance, which—despite my skepticism and experimental approach—was now way beyond the realm of logical explanation.

Chills spread across my upper back and prickled my arms.

What was this place? Yes, I knew, it was a big all-you-can-eat restaurant with lots and lots of food. But was there something more to it? Week after week, it seemed to read my mind, examine my life, and teach me exactly what I needed to know.

I looked up and scanned the room, watching the other customers serving themselves, eating their food, chatting with one another, seemingly unaware that anything might be out of the ordinary. Then, as I stared, a man at a table across the room looked up, locked eyes with me, and gave me a quick, subtle smile and nod. Was he in on it…or just being friendly?

Immediately, I looked down at my plate, my thoughts whirling. What was going on here? Was I losing my mind? Or had I stepped into some mystical dimension where I could receive exactly the guidance I needed and all my questions would be answered?

No, this was completely irrational. Sure, the buffet helped with work, but this was no way to run a company. If I needed business advice, I could take a course, read a textbook, or hire a consultant—not ask a restaurant!

But, as crazy as it seemed, it was hard to ignore everything it had taught me over the past three months. Then again, maybe I was just finding what I was looking for—like the Baader-Meinhof phenomenon or the RAS (or whatever that brain-filter thing is called). The buffet didn't have supernatural powers. Maybe it was simply a numbers game: with all the buffet's options—room after room of food, drinks, and people—I was bound to find *something* there that answered my questions.

Right?

That was one answer the buffet didn't give me right away. But regardless of the explanation, the buffet was definitely teaching me the lessons I needed—including the valuable one from today.

Lesson #13:
Look for guidance in unexpected places.

14. What's the Catch?

"What's the catch?" Westin asked.

"There isn't one," I said. "At least, I don't think there is."

"There's always a catch."

"I don't know. I guess we'll see."

"Yes, you will."

When I hung up, I felt like a different person than I'd been before the call. Just an hour earlier, I'd been looking forward to going to work the next day. I could hardly wait to hear more about Kareem's idea and see what other brilliant ideas the team would come up with. I wasn't even worried about challenges that might arise, because I had a feeling that the buffet would somehow make everything clear. But after talking with Westin, all the wind was out of my sails.

We'd spent most of the call discussing the various trials and tribulations of his recent life: his annoying landlord, his bout of stomach flu, and the latest ways he'd managed to keep striking out in the world of online dating. And then we got around to how much he was dreading going back to work the next morning.

I felt guilty saying it, but I told him that over the past month, I'd completely forgotten the concept of the Sunday Night Blues—and had started saying "TGIM"…and meaning it! I didn't want to rub it in, but I couldn't contain my enthusiasm, and before long I was gushing about how brilliant Kareem and Zoey were, how helpful Laney had been, how the creative team was overflowing with ideas, and how well the entire staff worked together. "And best of all, I have total creative license with everything: the products, the designs, the marketing, the business strategies…all of it."

Westin scoffed. "And what, the company just hands you blank checks?"

"Yeah, pretty much. The deal is, they cover operating expenses, and as long as we're turning a profit by the end of the year, anything goes."

"A-ha! There's the catch. If they're paying, they're gonna have their hands all over the business—just wait and see."

"No, they really gave me full control. At least, I *think* so." I slumped back on my couch. "I mean, so far it all seems—"

"Hey, I don't wanna burst your bubble, but this sounds like a classic honeymoon phase. And honeymoons don't last—just look at me and Ishani. Or you and Maya."

"Yeah, but isn't it different with a—"

"I'm just saying, whether you think you've found the perfect woman, the perfect team, the perfect job...whatever. Trust me, I've seen enough flies in the ointment, and I just don't want you getting your hopes up and getting hurt again." He sighed. "But hey, if things are going well, more power to ya. Just, you know...keep your eyes open."

So I did. I kept my eyes open throughout the week, looking for any potential flies in the work ointment. And lo and behold, I started noticing things I'd previously overlooked. For instance, I sensed some tension between Yasmin and Diego. (And not the good kind, like what Maya and I felt just before we got together.) And why were Yun and Nikhil meeting so often? As far as I knew, they weren't collaborating. Unless...were they plotting something? And what was Nora telling everyone in those closed-door HR consultations? And why did they have to stay confidential, even from me? After all, as branch manager, wasn't I supposed to know what was going on with my own employees in my own branch?

Westin was right: I had to stay vigilant. Even things that looked positive on the surface could be leading to something disastrous. Maybe Zoey was only interested in Kareem's ideas because she wanted to steal them. Maybe Laney's great work was only the prelude to a coup where she'd take over the branch and vote me out. Or maybe the company would give me the boot midway through the year. Sure, I had a contract, but there was always a loophole, right? There was always a catch.

Until then, I hadn't quite figured out what I should be doing as the branch manager, but suddenly I knew: find the catch and stop it...before it could catch *me*!

I needed help, but I had no one to turn to. I couldn't ask Laney or anyone else at the office—they might be the ones I had to worry about! And Westin was better at spotting problems than solving them. But what if the helper wasn't a person but a *place*?

Of course!

My inner jury was still out regarding whether the buffet had supernatural powers or was just where I happened to be when insights popped into my head. In either case, I'd keep my eyes open during my next visit. One way or another, maybe the buffet could help me find the office's catch—and do something about it before it destroyed all my hopes and dreams.

When I got to the buffet that Saturday, I didn't notice anything different. Just like my previous visits, there was row after row of mouthwatering foods and beverages, all there for the taking. Maybe there were a few more people than usual, but that didn't—

"Hey! Watch it!" I yelled at the man who'd just elbowed his way past me.

"Out of my way!" he said, pushing up to the serving dish of lo mein. "I got here first! It's mine!"

Actually, I had been there first. And technically, the lo mein was not his—it was for any paying customer who wanted it. However, the crazed look in the man's eyes told me this probably wasn't the time to quibble. Still, I couldn't stop myself from speaking up (albeit in a lighthearted tone that I hoped wouldn't provoke him). "Relax, buddy. There's plenty to go around."

He whirled around and glared at me. (So much for not provoking him!) "Don't tell me to relax!" He went back to shoveling lo mein from the serving dish onto his plate, yelling at me the whole time. "You don't know there's plenty to go around! They could run out any minute! And then what?"

"Then they'll bring more," I said. Still doing my best to defuse the situation, I forced a good-natured laugh. "Don't worry, I've been coming here for over three months now, so I can assure you that—"

"Well, I've been coming here for over three *years*!" the man shouted as he kept loading (or, rather, overloading) his plate.

"Then you know they've got a massive selection and massive quantities." Even though I'd initially had my eye on the lo mein, I didn't want to get in his way, so I moved aside to the display of spring rolls, picked up the serving tongs, and put a roll onto my plate. "And even if they did run out, they'd refill the containers."

"You don't know that! Just because they've done it before doesn't mean they'll do it this time!" He turned back toward me and then, with an angry scowl, lunged at me, grabbed the tongs out of my hand, and took the spring roll right off my plate. "Hey! Quit being selfish! You're taking food away from me…and from everyone else!" Waving the tongs, he gestured at the other diners in the buffet (some of whom were glancing our way and giving us a wide berth).

By that point, I should have realized that arguing with this guy was completely futile…and possibly dangerous. (Actually, I should've realized this long before that point.) Instead, I tried taking a more amicable approach. "Don't worry," I said, holding up my hands in what I hoped was a placating gesture. "There's enough for everyone. Here, help yourself." I stepped aside, allowing him to take as many spring rolls as he wanted (which turned out to be a *lot*).

Once he'd filled every square inch of his tray, he darted to the nearest table and immediately started scarfing down his lunch, casting nervous glances left, right, and all around, hunching over his food as if to ward off potential thieves.

In retrospect, I should've just walked away, but for some reason, I couldn't let it go. In my mind, I simply had to convince this man that there was plenty to go around. That he could go back as many times as he wanted. That the buffet's embarrassment of culinary riches wasn't about to run out. That the buffet would keep restocking the food. That by taking our food, we weren't taking it away from anyone else. That he didn't need to stuff his face so quickly—there was plenty of food and plenty of time. That he didn't have to worry about all these good things being taken from him. That the other shoe was not about to drop. That there *was* no other shoe. That he could stop looking over his shoulder at other diners because no one was coming to steal his food. That he could simply relax and enjoy the meal.

So I walked over to his table, cleared my throat, and addressed him in my kindest voice. "Excuse me, sir, I don't mean to keep—"

"Get away from me!" he shouted at the top of his lungs. And this time—as he stared daggers into me (or perhaps forks, knives, and skewers—all of which were disconcertingly within his reach)—I finally got the message and backed away.

Maybe it was the throbbing vein in his forehead, his tensed-up neck muscles, or his bulging biceps, but I finally came to terms with the fact that, try as I might, I just couldn't convince him about how abundant the buffet was. Just like I couldn't convince Westin about how positive my work situation was. But it didn't matter, because by that point, I had convinced myself. Or maybe the buffet had convinced me. But either way you looked at it, I had to admit that, once again, the buffet had provided the lesson I needed.

Lesson #14:
Sometimes there isn't a catch.

15. The Nobel Prize for Potential

It quickly became obvious to me and to everyone else in the office.

Granted, there had been some delays while setting up. And some debate about what organizational structure we should use. And then there was the stress of the hiring process. And the somewhat awkward onboarding phase and the weeks afterward when everyone was still getting used to their roles and responsibilities and where they fit into the company. But now that we'd settled in, one thing had become clear to us all:

We had a fantastic team!

From Brenda's welcoming presence at the reception desk to Sofia's fastidious bookkeeping—and every tech whiz, master marketer, and personnel pro in between—we'd assembled a top-notch group. Before long we started calling ourselves "The Dream Team"—and, I have to say, the appellation was well deserved. We had the vision. We had the technical expertise. And we had the support structure to allow everyone to excel in their roles. I don't think I'd ever seen a team with so much potential.

Other people saw it too. Diego even shared a funny article titled "The Nobel Prize for Potential." He cc'd the whole team, adding the subject line *WE should get this!* I agreed.

As I walked around the office, I felt like a conductor standing on a podium in front of a world-class orchestra, knowing that we could play almost any piece of music—and it would sound incredible. Or like a master painter holding a brush and a full palette of paint, looking down at a hundred blank canvases and knowing I could turn them all into amazing pieces of art. Or like an explorer standing on a mountaintop, looking out over a vast landscape I was about to travel through—a land full of lakes and rivers, abundantly blooming fruit trees, gold mines, and every imaginable natural resource. I just had to decide which path to take, set out on my journey, and enjoy the riches that were sure to come—and know that on the other side of this bountiful land was Maya, waiting to welcome me back and share the fruits of my travels.

This feeling was more than just hope, optimism, and trite analogies—it was a sense of ripening, of strength, of inevitable success. It was boundless potential. And it buoyed me every moment of every day. Everywhere I went, I felt this potential within me. And everywhere I looked, I saw it around me. As I walked through the office throughout the week, I didn't just see employees; I saw the potential for success—technical breakthroughs, innovations, and profit.

I held on to that mindset as I walked through the buffet that Saturday. I didn't just see trays of food; I saw potential meals—healthy meals that could make me stronger, delicious meals that could delight my taste buds, unusual meals that could expand my horizons. Every person at the buffet was more than just a fellow diner; they were a potential teacher. And so was every element of the buffet, every detail, every situation. This was a place that could enlighten me, strengthen me, and nourish me on every level. I just had to open my eyes, open my mind, and let it unfold.

As I stood in the middle of the appetizers room, contemplating all the possibilities—not just at the buffet, but also at work and in all areas of my life—I could hardly fathom the vastness of the potential. Just thinking about it felt amazing. Yes, I should win the Nobel Prize for Potential!

But then a cold wave rushed down my spine, and a sobering thought shot into my mind. There's a reason why "The Nobel Prize for Potential" was a piece of absurdist humor: because there *is* no Nobel Prize for Potential! (Or *any* prizes for potential, as far as I know.) And for good reason: because potential by itself is worthless.

In fact, it could be worse than worthless. As the buffet had already taught me, having so much potential and so many options could be overwhelming. And all the options in the world wouldn't mean a thing unless I made a choice. I didn't have to make the perfect choice or even one of the best choices, but I did have to choose *something*.

So, determined to do just that, I headed to the nearest food display. But as I inspected the options, it became clear that just because I *could* eat something didn't mean I *should* eat it. Yes, I *could* have kimchi, but I already knew I wasn't a big fan of cabbage. Yes, I *could* make an entire lunch out of cupcakes, but I don't think that would be the most nutritious meal. (Also, I might have a serious sugar crash before I even made it home.) And yes, I *could* have the nut loaf, but it was loaded up with Brazil nuts, which didn't agree with me (as I'd learned the hard way at Maya's Christmas party).

Fortunately, there were plenty of appealing options remaining. So, without overthinking it, I grabbed the one that was calling to me in that moment: spinach enchiladas. I rounded it out with a few slices of avocado, grilled corn salad, and a tall glass of fruit punch. Then I took my tray to the nearest table and patted myself on the back for making such excellent selections. Unlike my first visit to the buffet, I wouldn't go home hungry. I'd learned my lesson, and I'd made my choice.

I spread my plates around me and took a minute to admire the well-balanced and delicious-looking meal I'd assembled. I could practically taste the enchilada. I could practically feel my body growing stronger thanks to the spinach and avocado. And I could practically feel my thirst being quenched by the punch.

Then, in a flash, the absurdity hit me—and I burst into hysterical laughter.

I must have looked like a madman because several people at the neighboring tables gave me strange looks. I was sitting alone, and nothing was visibly funny (aside from my uncontrollable giggle fit), so I'm sure they were wondering why I was laughing. But from my position, it was so obvious—and even more absurd than "The Nobel Prize for Potential": No matter how good my meal looked, it wasn't going to fill me up, quench my thirst, make me healthy, or delight my taste buds simply because I'd chosen it, loaded up my plate, and looked at it. I still had to take the crucial next step: *actually eating it!*

And it was just as obvious when I applied this principle to work. Yes, it felt empowering, liberating, and energizing to think that the Dream Team had the talent and potential to achieve greatness. But no matter how dreamy our team was, we weren't going to create any new products, get any new clients, or generate any revenue just by contemplating our potential. We had to take action!

No, I wasn't going to do any work right there at the buffet, but I did take action in the best way for that moment: I pulled my plate toward me and took a big bite of enchilada. I chewed. I swallowed. And I smiled. It was even more delicious than I'd expected.

Not only that, it provided the last piece of evidence I needed to scientifically prove my hypothesis: No matter how hard I'd tried to deny it, I had to admit that the buffet was no ordinary restaurant; it was a business mentor cleverly disguised as a cafeteria. For nearly four months now, it had answered my questions, provided wisdom, and taught me exactly the lessons I needed—including this latest one.

Lesson #15:
It's not what you could *do that matters; it's what you actually* do.

16. Start Small

I walked home in a state of elation. Somehow, my experiment had worked—the buffet really was delivering the guidance I needed, exactly when I needed it. Yes, it defied all logic, but week after week I'd accumulated such overwhelming evidence that it would be unscientific to dismiss it. By the time I got home, I could feel the truth of it, right down to the core of my being: I'd discovered a miracle! Standing in the middle of my living room, I raised my fists and let out a full-throated *whoop!*

Then I spent the rest of the weekend questioning my sanity.

Sure, the buffet had provided some good lessons, but did that mean it was *magic?* Weren't there plenty of other plausible explanations? What was next—praying to tacos?

By the time Monday morning rolled around, I still hadn't resolved my inner debate over the buffet's possible magic vs. scientific explanation vs. possible insanity. But as I pulled into the office parking lot, I realized that *the explanation didn't matter!* Who cared how I got the lessons? As long as they kept coming, I'd keep writing them down—and using them.

More than that, I'd seek them out—asking questions and expecting answers. What a resource! It was like having a secret new member of the Dream Team. (And yes, I decided that I would keep it secret. It was bad enough questioning my own sanity—no need to get the whole team in on it.)

I practically burst through the office doors, barely restraining myself from hugging every employee I saw. I knew that no matter what issues might arise, I had the ultimate ace up my sleeve to solve them.

Not that I needed another ace—the Dream Team was already a winning hand…and then some. And they seemed to grow dreamier by the hour. By the end of Monday's product-development meeting, I was able to lay to rest my earlier concerns about Kareem. Just when I'd made peace with his VR headsets, he'd moved on to bigger and better possibilities. Clearly he wasn't a one-app wonder; he was a visionary, overflowing with ideas for new apps and devices. And he had already planned how we could incorporate them into everyday objects and integrate them into a holistic system. "We could combine nano-technology and ambient computing with XR and IoT," he said. I just smiled and nodded. Later, I looked up half the terms—and the more I understood, the more impressed I was.

But it wasn't just his technical knowledge that impressed me. It was the practical applications he envisioned that filled me with excitement. He explained how these systems could be implemented in retail demos, manufacturing training and educational programs, home design, and even city planning. And if we developed it right, he said, we'd be able to sell not only the final products, but the improved chips and other components that made them effective.

And it wasn't just Kareem who impressed me. Zoey's ideas were equally compelling, and I appreciated her ability to explain them in language that even I could understand. Nikhil was clearly a tech whiz. And Keiko was one of the most talented designers I'd ever met.

But what impressed me most wasn't the individual ideas and contributions but the way that, right from the start, everybody worked together as an integrated team—supporting one another's ideas, building on them, challenging one another, and ending up in places beyond what any of them had envisioned before we'd come together.

Every time Kareem shared an idea, Zoey thought of a dozen ways we could bring it to life with the technology already at our disposal. And every time their visions ran into a technical roadblock, Nikhil came up with a solution or a workaround. And Keiko somehow translated these lofty ideas into hand-drawn sketches of possible designs, which she would whip out while they talked. And then she'd run their favorite ideas through some mind-blowing computer program I'd never seen or even heard of, which would turn scribbled sketches into professional-looking prototypes…within seconds!

Watching these guys work together was a thing of beauty. It was like watching a world-class dance team—one that had been performing together for years—choreographing their next routine and then rehearsing it right before my eyes. It was amazing to think that, just a couple of months earlier, they'd never even met one another.

Their intellect was staggering. Their visions were awe inspiring. And their enthusiasm was contagious. Before long, I was buzzing with the electricity they'd been generating. I felt ready to take the tech world by storm!

But I was also aware of an unsettling thought that had been nagging at the back of my mind: *I don't deserve this.*

It was just a matter of time before they realized that they were light years ahead of me and that I had nothing of value to offer them. Seriously, these geniuses and visionaries could work almost anywhere they wanted. Why would they want to work for me?

The question wouldn't go away, so during our lunch break (which we took together in the conference room), as we chatted about this and that, I casually asked everyone what made them want to work here. (Hopefully it came off as curiosity, not disbelief—like, "Why on *earth* would you want to work *here?*")

It turns out that, although they'd come from different backgrounds, they all had almost the exact same answer: they wanted to make a difference. Before starting here, they'd been working at big companies that moved at a snail's pace. Their ideas would get lost in a maze of bureaucracy. If they were lucky, one tiny thing they contributed to might see the light of day every couple of years. They wanted to work at a small company where their ideas would have a big impact. They wanted to move forward on numerous fronts. And they wanted to move fast.

Well, I was on board 100%. I believed in their visions. I believed in their technical abilities. I believed in *them.* As long as they worked here, they would be sure their voices were heard, their visions were valued, and they all knew that they mattered.

And that's when the light bulb went on over my head. The green light bulb. Suddenly, I knew what I could offer that would be valuable to them: a green light. They already had the ideas and the ability to make them real. They didn't need me for that. They just needed someone to believe in them, to give them the go-ahead.

And the money.

Fortunately, I could provide that as well. The parent office may not have given me any guidance, but they were bankrolling the operation. We still had to end the year in the black, but how I got there was up to me. And if the Dream Team wasn't a safe investment, I don't know who was.

I ended the week on a high note. I was witnessing a miracle: the next wave of the technical revolution, being born right before my eyes. And I had something to contribute! It all boiled down to one word: *yes*. Yes, we could move forward with XR and IoT. Yes, we could develop nano-technology and ambient computing. Yes, we could market the software, the products, and the components we created with them. Yes, we could move into retail *and* wholesale! Yes, we could develop training modules. Yes, we could expand into city planning.

From the micro to the macro, we would cover it all. We would take the tech world by storm. Actually, the *entire* world. And it all started now!

Whatever it took, I would make it happen. If we needed to temporarily go deeper into the red, we would. If we needed to hire more people, we would. If we needed to outsource some of the work, we would. If we needed to rent a bigger office, we would. I was all in. This was going to happen, and it was going to be huge.

Before we left for the weekend, I shared my "go big or go home" philosophy with Laney, so she'd know I was fully committed to our success. I thought she'd be thrilled to know she had my unwavering support, but she didn't seem to share my zeal. "Well, that's certainly *one* approach, but..." She pressed her palms together and stared at them thoughtfully. "You know, you don't have to dive right into the deep end. You can ease in, just dip your toe into the water before—"

"I don't want to just dip my toe into the water. I want to make a big splash! And you don't do that with timid half-measures!"

"Hmm. Well, why don't we take some time to think about it over the weekend." It looked like she was attempting to keep her expression as neutral as possible, but I knew she vehemently disagreed with me. And I knew what she was really saying: *Slow your roll. Play small. Curb your enthusiasm.*

But my enthusiasm wasn't going anywhere. I was buzzing with it when I left the office. I was buzzing all Friday night as my brain raced with the endless possibilities. And I was still buzzing the next day as I walked into the buffet.

I was in such a good mood, I didn't have time for those pesky questions about magic, guidance, or coincidence. Who cared what you called it. I was surrounded by great people during the week and great food on the weekend. And now, unlike before, the endless rows of options no longer felt overwhelming; they felt invigorating. They filled me with a sense of possibility. They called to me with the promise of a mouthwatering meal that would provide an energizing experience from beginning to end. And it was all there for the taking.

Although I'd been coming to the buffet every week for almost four months, it didn't really sink in until that moment: I really could take anything—*everything!* Whatever I wanted. Not as some future hypothetical possibility, but right now. It was all laid out in front of me. And I didn't have to limit myself to just one type of food. I could take whatever looked good.

And SO much of it looked amazing! The veggie fajitas smelled delicious, so I loaded up my plate with them. But why stop there? After all, I was surrounded by all this abundance. Yes, I already had fajitas, but the enchiladas were also calling out to me, so I took a couple. And I'd been meaning to try the paella, so I scooped out a hearty serving of that too. And I'd enjoyed the falafel sandwich when I had it before, so I figured I'd grab another. And dolmas went well with falafel, so I definitely needed a few. There was one problem, though: my plate was completely full—not even room for a single dolma.

But of course there was room—I just needed to get a second tray. After all, the buffet didn't have a one-tray-per-customer limit; it was all you can eat—anything you wanted. And I wanted dolmas! So I took a second tray, and I took the dolmas. And now that I had all this extra room on tray number two, I figured I might as well fill that up. Fortunately, there were still plenty of delectable options all around me.

The quiche looked great, so I took a slice. And I couldn't pass up the stuffed portobello or the tomato and olive focaccia. And there was still room on the tray for a samosa.

Only after I'd filled my second tray did I realize I also felt like some soup. The minestrone looked great, so I grabbed a bowl of that. But where would I put it? My two trays were already full, and I didn't have an extra hand to carry a bowl. I didn't want to leave any of the food there—someone might take it while I went to find a table…or clear away anything I left unattended on the table while I came back for the soup. A real quandary.

But then I had a flash of insight: I could get a third tray and balance it between the first two, like a capital *H*, but loaded up with edible goodies. After I put the soup on the third tray, though, I realized that I had plenty of space left, so I filled that up with dessert—or actually, desserts, plural: baklava and lemon bars and some raspberry sorbet to finish it off. And of course I needed something to drink. But with all these options, why limit myself to just one? I poured a glass of iced tea, a glass of ginger ale, and a glass of cranberry juice, all of which I balanced carefully around my soup and desserts.

There was still more I wanted to try, but I didn't want time to run out on me, so I called it good with my three heavily laden trays. And, using my *H*-inspired balancing technique, I managed to bring everything to a table, intact and ready to be savored.

As I surveyed the trays spread around me, I once again felt like an intrepid explorer on the border of a new frontier. I was exhilarated and eager to embark on this new era—not just in terms of lunch but in all areas of life. Ever since that tech meeting, I felt like a new man—one who embraces opportunities. One who says yes to possibilities, to abundance, to life. I'd broken through not only an inner ceiling but the inner walls as well. Nothing was holding me back. I could already see evidence of this new attitude spilling over into other parts of my life. (In the case of the minestrone, quite literally spilling. But there was still plenty left in the bowl, and lots of other food to savor.) Look out, world. Look out, Maya. Here comes the new me: the boundless, unstoppable go-getter!

"Is this seat taken?"

I looked up from my array of foods and saw a woman gesturing at the chair across the table from me. "No, go ahead."

She set down her tray, took a seat, and smiled. "I wasn't sure if you were waiting for your family or friends or something."

I shook my head. "Just me...and now you."

She looked at my three overflowing trays, then at me, and then back at the food—furrowing her brow as if trying to solve a difficult puzzle. "Not to pry, but are you one of those competitive eaters, like who eats fifty hot dogs in two minutes?"

I laughed. "Nope, just a man with a healthy appetite. And this all looked too good to pass up!"

I caught her glancing at my stomach, which I should mention, is not particularly large. If you were feeling charitable, you might say I had a sleek physique. If you were feeling less charitable, you might say I was scrawny. But, however you put it, I've never been a big guy.

She chuckled. "I used to be like you—eyes bigger than my stomach. But I'd just end up getting stuffed...or wasting food. Usually both." She spread her napkin on her lap, picked up her fork, and stabbed at a cherry tomato in her salad. "Now I start small. That way, if I don't like something, I won't waste much of it. I just go get something else instead. And if I do like it and eat it all, I can always go back for more if I'm still hungry. And if there's something I don't have room for, I can always get it next time."

"Not me! I'm not waiting for next time—I'm hungry *now*! And I plan on giving all this grub a good home." I patted my slightly concave stomach, and the woman gave another good-natured laugh. Then we both got down to the business at hand: eating.

Twenty minutes later, after she'd finished her salad and stir-fry, she said it was nice meeting me, then got up and left. But I was still going strong. Well, maybe not *strong*, but I was still going. Truth be told, I was feeling pretty full. But I didn't want to leave without finishing everything—or at least starting it. I still hadn't even touched the paella or the portobello, though. There were just so many different foods—and SO MUCH of it.

By then, the minestrone had gone cold and the sorbet was melting, so I just kept working my way through the falafel sandwich. I didn't think there was any space in my once-small stomach, but somehow I got through it. But I felt like I'd hit (or passed) my limit. Finishing the falafel didn't just make me feel all full; it made me feel awful. I was stuffed to the bursting point. I still had a tray and a half full of untouched food, but I couldn't take another bite.

Part of me felt like a failure. And another part of me (my stomach) felt just plain stuffed. But a deeper part of me knew that, present discomfort notwithstanding, this had been one of the most important meals of my life. And as much as it pained me to throw out all that food, at least it wasn't wasted. Call it magical guidance or call it big eyes and small stomach, but the experience had driven home the lesson that Laney and the woman at the table had both been trying to tell me—the lesson that I was finally (and somewhat painfully) digesting.

Lesson #16:
Start small.

17. Failure

When I first told my friends I'd accepted the out-of-town job, they couldn't believe it. "Way too risky," Miles said.

"A new branch? Not established in the region? No security after the first year? No way," Ishani said. "Maybe for someone else, but not Mr. Play It Safe."

"Who are you?" Westin asked. "And what have you done with our friend?"

I explained that I was just as surprised as they were, but it was all part of my plan to win back Maya.

They said there were easier ways to do that.

I said this would show her she'd made a mistake—prove that I really was driven, capable, and successful.

They said I'd never last.

"I give him one month," Miles said. "Maybe two."

"Six weeks, tops," Ishani said.

"See ya by opening day," Westin said.

Yet here it was, more than a month into the baseball season (thank you very much, Westin), and I was still going strong. Or, if not exactly *strong*, at least still running the branch—still doing way more than any of them gave me credit for (Maya included).

That's not to say I didn't still feel the lure of safety, especially when Kareem talked about possibilities for new products and services. Yes, he had great ideas that made my heart race as I considered their potential. But no matter how much his enthusiasm pulled me forward, those old tendencies pulled me back again. I felt like a rope in an evenly matched tug of war. As much as I wanted to wholeheartedly buy into Kareem's visions, I couldn't shake that inner voice that kept asking one question— a question I eventually blurted out during a brainstorming session with Kareem: "But what if you fail?"

"Don't worry. No matter what happens, it'll be a learning experience—something to grow from," Kareem said. "There's no such thing as failure."

"Actually, there is," I said.

He told me about his grad school roommate who'd spent five years working on a cure for cancer, only to run into a dead end.

"You're not making me feel better," I said.

"No, no, no." He waved his hands as if frantically erasing a whiteboard. "It was a good thing. It advanced the research and provided invaluable information for the scientific community. That's what we should do—take the same experimental approach: try something, learn from the results, and make adjustments as needed." He raised his eyebrows and held up a finger for emphasis. "*If* needed."

"Hmm," I said. Then I told him I'd think it over. And I did. I thought about it while I reviewed his proposals that afternoon. I thought about it while I ran the numbers the next day. I thought about it during our group meetings throughout the week. I thought about it while I tossed and turned in bed on Friday night. And I thought about it Saturday morning while I walked to the buffet.

Five years of failure might have been good enough for Kareem's scientist buddy, but I had less than eight months left to make our business profitable. I needed a safer bet than a cure for cancer. Then again, nothing ventured, nothing gained. On the other hand, nothing ventured, nothing lost. On yet another hand, Kareem had sold his first app for seven figures all by himself—imagine what he could do with a whole team behind him.

By the time I reached the buffet, I'd run out of hands, but I still hadn't run out of reasons to play it safe...or equally compelling reasons to take a chance on something new. So I decided to use the least-scientific approach imaginable: before opening the buffet door, I whispered, "What should I do?"

Even though no one was close enough to hear me, I felt silly asking a restaurant for business advice. But I needed guidance, and somehow—

whether it was magic, cognitive science, or pure delusion—the buffet always managed to serve it up.

Once I was inside, though, I soon forgot all about Kareem's ideas and became engrossed in a more pressing question: *What should I eat?* Sure, the spaghetti looked good, but I'd had that a million times. Why not try something new? Then again, what if I tried something new and didn't like it? Maybe I should stick with the tried and true. But with all these options, why limit myself to the same old same old?

Before my brain realized what I was doing, my legs carried me into a new area of the buffet (new for me, that is): Russian cuisine, where I scooped myself a big bowl of hearty stew. (Bet you didn't see that one coming, Ishani! So much for Mr. Predictable.)

Congratulating myself on my adventurous spirit, I found an empty spot at a nearby table, slurped down a big spoonful of the stew, and nearly gagged. What *was* that slimy stuff in there? As it slithered over my tongue and down my throat, I answered my own question: *cabbage*. And lots of it. Ugh! How had I not noticed one of my least favorite foods on the planet?

I couldn't give up that easily, though, could I? After just one taste? Reluctantly, I took another spoonful…but I just couldn't bring myself to eat any more. So much for the spirit of adventure. So much for taking a risk and trying new things. My friends had been right—and so had my inner voice: I would've been better off playing it safe and sticking to the known.

As much as I disliked the stew, it pained me to dump out my leftovers (basically, the entire bowl). What a waste! But it would've been an even bigger waste to ruin my whole lunch because I'd made one mistake. So I poured it into the garbage, grabbed a new tray, and started over.

Despite the stew fiasco, I decided to extend my new-food experiment for at least one more bite. So I wandered into a different part of the buffet—Australian cuisine—where I noticed something that looked familiar but that I'd never tried: vegemite. I'd seen it on TV and had always been curious. And wasn't there a song about it? If people were literally singing its praises, how bad could it be?

I soon found out—very bad. No, I won't be judgmental and call it *bad*. I'm sure many people think it's delicious. But I'm not one of them.

Undeterred, I tried a third meal—something I'd heard people calling a "ploughman's parcel." It seemed promising…until I hit a pickled onion lurking in the middle. Yuck! What were those ploughmen thinking?

As I rinsed out the taste with a glass of water and a few spoonfuls of sorbet, I realized that the buffet had spoken: Kareem was wrong. There *is* such a thing as failure, and I'd just experienced it—three times in a row! I'd wasted three perfectly good meals. (Perfectly good in the sense of *not rotten*, that is—but far from good in terms of taste.) And I'd ruined what could've been a perfectly good lunch experience.

Stewing in defeat (which, in my case, involved literal stew), I scurried back to familiar ground: pasta. And I didn't waste time with anything fancy; I headed straight for the spaghetti and marinara—a far cry from the culinary adventure I'd set out to experience, but still a perfectly enjoyable meal.

But just as my serving spoon was poised over the spaghetti, I heard someone nearby say, "Ooh! Look! That's different!" I froze. Then I turned around, trying to figure out who'd said those words and, more importantly, what food they'd been talking about.

Amid all the people bustling about—and all the food surrounding me—I couldn't tell who'd spoken or what they'd been referring to. But maybe those words weren't meant for someone else. Maybe they were the buffet's way of speaking to me: *Look…different.*

I set down the serving spoon, reconsidered those words, and reconsidered my meal. Maybe I just needed to look at the situation from a different angle. What if the new foods hadn't been failures? What if they were simply the "errors" of a trial-and-error process that would eventually lead to a brilliant discovery? Maybe lunch wasn't ruined after all. I still had more than an hour left—plenty of time to try a few more novelties. I just had to embrace Kareem's experimental attitude. I knew there was no guarantee of success, but there was at least the possibility of finding something great. And that was worth a shot.

I stepped away from the spaghetti and set off in search of something out of my culinary comfort zone.

I'd love to say that I instantly struck gold, but that was definitely not the case. Instead, I learned that Persian rice with dill and fava beans was not my new favorite food, and neither was the Hungarian goulash (which, unfortunately, in this variation, included brussels sprouts). More tossed food—and almost tossed cookies! But everything suddenly turned around the moment I took my first bite of peanut stew.

OMG! Where have you been all my life?!

This unassuming bowl of culinary heaven was packed with goodness: sweet potatoes, kidney beans, and mixed veggies (including bell peppers, carrots, and kale) swimming in the most delicious peanut broth I'd ever had in my life. Every bite was absolutely divine—and *so* worth all the missteps, mistakes, and mis-tastes I'd gone through to find it.

The stew (which I later learned was Senegalese maafe) provided more than just a satisfying and delectable lunch; it convinced me of just how valuable Kareem's experimental mindset could be. After all, if it had led to this culinary gold, it could lead us to gold in business too. I just had to accept that we wouldn't necessarily strike that gold right away—or every time we tried—or perhaps ever. But we definitely wouldn't strike it if we never tried. And we wouldn't set ourselves apart from our competition simply by peddling the same old products everyone else had.

Thank you, Kareem. Thank you, maafe. Thank you, buffet. And thank you to that part of me that was willing to look at things differently—to not give up after a few setbacks. To keep going until I found something that worked for me.

So maybe Westin had been right—I *wasn't* the friend they'd known for so long: the predictable, risk-averse "Mr. Play It Safe" who never took a chance. Of course, I fully realized that trying Kareem's new products would be chancy. There would probably be some trial and error, some disappointments, and some waste. But we could minimize the waste by conducting market research, performing split tests, and gauging consumer interest before we rolled out a new line of products. Still, there were no guarantees. Regardless of the outcome, though, we could be proud of ourselves for trying something different. We would learn something valuable, even if we didn't get the results we wanted. And, at the very least, we'd be one step closer to success.

Lesson #17:
Everything you try is either a success or a learning experience.

18. More or Less

It had been over a week since I'd been converted to the "start small" philosophy—that's why we were focusing on one small product rather than trying to take over the tech industry. But starting small didn't mean we had to be minimalists, right? With so many great features and possibilities in mind, why couldn't the team include them all? Let the users decide which ones to enable or disable. Maximum freedom! Maximum power! What was there to discuss?

Let me back up a moment. I was at the Friday afternoon product-development meeting where Kareem, Zoey, Nikhil, Yasmin, Diego, Tamika, and Laney were discussing possibilities for a technological breakthrough. Despite my job, I never became particularly tech-savvy. Unlike the others (especially Kareem, Zoey, and Nikhil), I couldn't tell you half of what their gadgets did, much less how to make them. But I still liked to sit in on some of their meetings for two reasons: 1. I could play the role of a "normal" customer (namely, not an IT expert), and 2. as branch manager, I wanted to know what was going on in my own office.

But I was a little late to this particular party (or at least their idea of a party—namely, discussing tech gadgets). I'd missed their meeting earlier that week when they'd brainstormed ideas for possible products. After they'd come up with a few dozen, they'd chosen one to focus on: augmented reality navigation glasses. Next, they brainstormed possible features and again came up with dozens. Now we were at the next stage: narrowing down the features.

At least, that was their plan.

I, on the other hand, argued that we shouldn't be narrowing anything. Why not be the company that delivers *more*? More products! More features! More options! Wouldn't that lead to more business, more sales, more revenue, more growth, and more success? (Maybe this is why they put me in charge: I could step back and see the big picture rather than getting lost in the tech-weeds with these admittedly brilliant but often narrow-minded nerds.)

These aforementioned nerds had come up with a ton of what I thought were fantastic features: a mini speaker built into the glasses' stem, a mic in the bridge, navigation instructions, points-of-interest identification, customizable maps, traffic information, safety alerts, virtual tour guides, real-time language translation, and much more. If this wasn't a gotta-have-it gadget, I didn't know what was!

Admittedly, not every proposed feature sounded essential. But why not add them anyway? Maybe some customers would appreciate extras like real-time social media sharing, weather updates, a retractable selfie stick, celebrity-sighting alerts, games and challenges (scavenger hunts, obstacle courses, team competitions, and more), and virtual date avatars and/or holographic pets (which might not sound essential, but once they saw Keiko's adorable puppy sketches, who could resist?). And sure, most people could probably do without the ads (although they could be personalized to appeal to each individual user—and just think of the extra revenue they could generate!). With all these great features, I could already imagine the marketing campaigns that Yasmin and Diego could come up with—and the sales that Liam could bring in!

I was the odd man out, though. Everyone else seemed to share the same vision: a lightweight, sleek design that looked just like a normal pair of prescription lenses but contained features to help pedestrians find their way around an area they're not familiar with—without using any handheld devices. No selfie sticks (too heavy). No virtual pets (cute but irrelevant to the glasses' purpose). No driving features (too many risks—not to mention legal liabilities, as Tamika emphatically and repeatedly reminded us).

At the heart of it, though, our debate wasn't about any of the individual features; it was about our underlying philosophy: less is more vs. more is more.

By the end of the day, we were still at an impasse, so we decided to pick it up the following week. (That is, if they didn't have a secret meeting over the weekend where they finalized the design without me—which, based on Diego's frequent eye rolls and exasperated sighs after my comments, didn't seem entirely out of the question.)

I was committed to keeping my weekends free, so I wouldn't be attending any work meetings (secret or otherwise)—unless you count my weekly "secret meeting" with the buffet. Maybe *it* would help me navigate the situation with the glasses—and help me see things more clearly, as it had done so many times before. Or maybe it would just provide another tasty lunch.

In either case, by the time Saturday arrived, I had set aside all thoughts of work, navigation glasses, and debates over their possibly superfluous features, and was simply enjoying the day. The gorgeous spring weather certainly helped. The gentle sunshine seemed to put an extra pep in my step as I walked to the buffet. And once I got there, things got even better as I savored a delicious mushroom risotto with green onions, leeks, and fresh herbs. As good as the meal was, though, I limited myself to a small portion, intentionally saving room for dessert. For weeks, I'd had my eye on some fresh-baked pies, but I was always too full by the time I finished my entrée. However, today was the day. No, it wasn't March 14, but it was my own personal pie day!

There was a wide variety to choose from (peach, cherry, strawberry-rhubarb, pecan, pumpkin, key lime, and dozens of less common types), but I went with the tried and true: apple pie. I served myself the biggest slice that would fit on my plate and practically ran back to my table to devour it.

Just when I got there, however, a man glanced at my plate and gave me a weird look. "I see you got the, um, 'apple pie.'" I'm not sure why, but he made air quotes around *apple pie*. Then he smirked. "Enjoy," he said, walking off before I could ask him what exactly he meant.

Oh well. Air quotes or not, I *was* going to enjoy this pie! So I sat down, picked up my fork, and dug in.

Just as I'd hoped, the crust was soft yet crispy. The apples were baked to perfection: expertly balanced on the border between gooey and firm. And the sugary cinnamon sprinkled on top added just the right touch of sweetness and flavor. As I chewed my first bite, however, I realized that these weren't the pie's only ingredients. There was something more in there. Something unexpected.

It was gooier than the apples and even sweeter than the sugar. Finally it came to me: caramel sauce—yum! Mixed with a bit of maple syrup—double yum! What a great idea. So far, this pie was surpassing my expectations. This baker really is a genius.

The pleasant surprises didn't end there. I bit into something crunchy—some sort of toasted nuts, as far as I could tell—and then something chewy that I think was a mix of raisins and cranberries. Again, unexpected. Again, delicious.

In the next bite, though, things started to get a bit weird. I was struck by the unmistakable flavors of ginger, lemon zest, and balsamic vinegar—all of which I usually love, but none of which went particularly well with the maple-caramel sauce.

But the third bite is when things really went south. It was all I could do not to spit out the atrocious blend of flavors (and I use the word loosely) that assaulted my taste buds. Maybe the chef had accidentally mixed up two recipes, but regardless of how it happened, I couldn't take another bite. Just out of curiosity, I dug my way through the rest of the pie, searching for the bizarre ingredients that had ruined such a promising start. What I uncovered left me absolutely stunned and horrified: a mashup of pineapples, artichoke hearts, olives, capers, and full cloves of garlic.

Again, these are all ingredients I love…in other contexts and in moderation. Together, though, they ruined the dessert, turned my stomach, and made me swear off pie for the foreseeable future.

But not until I'd eaten a big serving of humble pie—realizing that, on Monday morning, I'd be forced to admit to the tech team that they'd been right all along.

Lesson #18:
Sometimes less is more.

19. Half-Baked

The plan was that Zoey and Nikhil would work on the navigation glasses while Kareem focused on his new project: an app to help businesses follow up with their customers. It seemed straightforward enough, but something was fishy about Kareem. All week long he'd been talking out of both sides of his mouth. I didn't know whether he was flat-out lying or just obscuring the truth in order to placate me…or save his job. In any case, I didn't like it.

It all started on Tuesday afternoon when I asked him how the app was going. He smiled and gave me two thumbs up. "Fantastic!"

I've never liked to meddle or micromanage, but as head of the branch, it's my job to know what's going on. So I asked him if he could put it on my phone so I could check it out.

That's when his smile faded. "It's not quite ready for that."

"No worries. I know it'll just be a beta version."

"Actually, it's not even at that stage. It can't go on a phone yet."

I tried to disguise my anger as concern. "What do you mean? How can you have an app that can't go on a phone?"

"I'm still working on backend coding, but it's getting there. Gimme till next week."

As a guy who's done my share of putting people off to buy myself time, I saw right through his ploy. But I decided to cut him some slack. Maybe he was going through personal issues and couldn't properly focus on work right now. It happened. (Hey, I was in the same boat, with Maya still occupying at least half my thoughts.) But I had a business to run. And we needed results.

As a compromise, I agreed to give him until the end of the week. And when I checked in again on Friday, he seemed excited to talk about the app. "Right on schedule. Going great!"

"Fantastic! So now can I get a copy? I wanna show some potential clients next week."

Clearly, I'd called his bluff. He sighed heavily and shook his head. "You could…but I'd worry about your phone. I'm still working out the bugs and—"

"Bugs!?" I slapped my forehead harder than I'd meant to. "This doesn't sound 'great' to me—it sounds awful! What are we talking here? Functionality problems? Mistakes? Viruses?"

"No, no—nothing like that. It's just…part of the process. Testing. Refinement. Quality assurance."

My first thought was to fire him on the spot, but I didn't want to make any rash decisions. So I took a deep breath and told him we'd revisit this on Monday. What I didn't tell him is that I'd be revisiting it on Saturday— with my secret mentor.

As I walked to the buffet Saturday morning, I couldn't even enjoy the beautiful spring weather because I was so distracted with all the questions swimming in my head: Was I being too demanding? Unreasonable? Unrealistic? Was it really too much to ask that things go smoothly—just once? No surprises. No delays. No bugs. What should I do?

By the time I reached the buffet, I had such a splitting headache that I didn't even care about solving my work problems anymore. I just wanted to forget it all and enjoy a nice quiet lunch at my favorite table, and I knew I could count on the buffet for that—or so I thought. But when I got to my usual spot, the tables had been removed. Instead, a crowd was gathered around some sort of spectacle in the middle of the room.

Curious, but also worried that something had gone wrong (was someone hurt?), I nudged my way toward the center until I could see what everyone was looking at. Fortunately, it wasn't an injury, accident, or emergency. In fact, it was the most innocuous thing imaginable: a bread-making demonstration.

The buffet had set up counters and portable ovens in the middle of the room, where a baker was teaching a lesson. "For sourdough, you'll need a starter," she said, holding up a jar of bubbly goo. "This'll make the bread rise."

"Why don't you just use yeast?" asked a man standing near me.

"You could," she said. "But then it wouldn't be real sourdough. Different flavor." She poured some of the goo into a bowl. "This mixture of flour and water has been sitting for three weeks, and—"

"Three *weeks*?!" the man yelled. "Are you telling me it takes three weeks to make a loaf of bread?"

The baker smiled as she put the lid back on the jar. "Could go faster—maybe just a week or two. But some people keep their starters going for years—sometimes even passed down from one generation to the next, like this baby here." The baker reached behind the counter and pulled out a second jar of bubbly goo.

"Yuck!" said the man. "That looks gross. I would never eat that."

"Me neither," said the baker. "Not raw, at least. But if it's baked just right…*mwah!*" She made a chef's-kiss motion. "Lemme show you." She added water and flour to the bowl of starter and kneaded it all into a doughy ball.

"Still doesn't look edible," the man muttered.

"Still isn't," the baker replied. "First it's gotta autolyze. That's just a fancy way of saying it sits there for a long time." She covered the bowl with a damp cloth and set it aside. "Fortunately, I've got one I made early this morning." She uncovered a second bowl, stretched out a clump of dough, and folded it over on itself.

"This is taking forever! Why don't you just stick it in the oven already?" said the man.

"You like eating bricks?" She winked. "Trust me, this makes it better." The baker mixed in a bit of oil and salt, then repeated the stretch-and-fold procedure four or five more times as she spoke.

I wasn't sure how she kept her cool while having her every move questioned by this guy who was quickly seeming less like a curious student and more like a belligerent heckler. I would've been tempted to invite *him* to lead the demo, seeing as he seemed to think he was smarter than the expert baker. But she kept right along doing her thing with apparent good humor.

"Next, it goes in the proofing basket for a second rise."

"*Second* rise?! Isn't one enough?" the man asked.

"Not for sourdough," said the baker. "Here's a loaf I started last night that's just about ready, but first..." With a theatrical flair, she pulled out a long knife and made a series of cuts across the top of the loaf. "A few decorative touches to—"

"If you're just gonna eat it, who cares about decorations?" asked the man, who by now had pushed his way to the front of the demonstration.

"Well, the cuts also let off some steam, which I'm sure we could all use." The crowd gave a sympathetic chuckle as she transferred the loaf into a small pot, which she covered and stuck into the oven. "After it's been baking twenty minutes, like this one"—she pulled a second loaf out of the oven—"you'll pull it out and—"

"And then eat it?" the man interrupted.

"Not yet." She inspected the loaf. "Although it does look perfect."

"Clearly, it *isn't* perfect, or we'd be able to eat it!"

The baker smiled. "Perfect for this stage. Exactly where it's supposed to be. But first we have to uncover it and put it in for another forty minutes, and *then* we—"

"Finally eat it, right?"

"Sure...if you want gummy bread. Otherwise, don't cut it for an hour."

"So you spent all that time making gross, gummy bread?"

At that point, I had to leave. As much as I wanted to hear the baker's comeback—and, even more than that, stick around for the free samples I assumed were forthcoming—I couldn't take any more of the bread heckler. What was it with this guy? I mean, I was hardly a master baker, but even I could grasp the basic concept that bread takes time—and that just because it's not ready yet doesn't mean there's anything wrong with it. Of course a half-baked (or unbaked) loaf of bread isn't ready to be eaten, just like...

Of course.

It was suddenly so clear: Whether you're making sourdough bread or developing an app, it's a process. It takes time. You can't rush it.

Kareem wasn't being cagey or evasive. He was being honest. Presumably, everything was moving forward right on schedule and coming along perfectly—but still not ready to release.

As I walked away from the demonstration, I knew what I would do first thing Monday morning: apologize to Kareem, ask him when the app would be ready, and then let him get back to baking.

Lesson #19:
Trust the process. What looks imperfect is often
just unfinished.

20. Chili Man

It had been a long week at work—full of struggles, setbacks, and stress. There were more delays with Kareem's app and problems with the navigation glasses. Then our server crashed right in the middle of Liam and Laney's Zoom presentation to a potential client (who, needless to say, did not become a client). Plus, everyone was in a foul mood because our air conditioner broke—right in the middle of a heat wave.

But the worst part of the week had nothing to do with work. It had to do with Maya.

The news was bad enough, but to make it even worse, she didn't even have the decency to tell me herself. I had to find out on social media, during one of my daily checks. (Okay, twice daily—sometimes three or four times, or more, depending on the level of urgency and how much free time I had on my hands.) It's not like I was cyber-stalking her or anything, but since she wouldn't tell me what was going on in her life, how else was I supposed to know?

Anyway, everything looked normal during the Monday morning check and again at lunchtime—no new updates. But then at 3:45, when I'd almost gotten through the workday, there it was:

Status: In a Relationship

I blinked, refreshed the page, double checked that it was actually her profile, and blinked again. It must be a typo, I thought. Or she just clicked on the wrong button. Happens all the time. Someone will point it out and she'll fix it. Maybe I should tell her. Or does she still consider *us* a couple? Maybe *I'm* the one she's referring to! Maybe she had a change of heart, and there's still hope for…

But then the pictures started popping up: Maya and Bradford at dinner. Maya and Bradford at the park. Maya and Bradford laughing, holding hands, looking as happy as could be. It was enough to make you puke.

After I'd taken a few deep breaths and waited for my head to stop spinning and my heart to resume beating (which it eventually did, albeit unenthusiastically), I had no choice but to investigate this Bradford character. First of all, I wasn't convinced that was actually his real name. (Bradford? Sounds more like a snobby, overpriced college than a real person.) He could be some internet scam artist—people fall for that stuff every day and the next thing you know, you're wiring someone money across the world and you never see them again. Or someone's harvesting your organs. Maya could be in serious trouble. Maybe I should warn her!

But then, as I studied his profile, it hit me: this wasn't a stranger; this was Brad the HR guy. The one who'd been "so sensitive and sympathetic" when Maya was having problems with her boss. "Such a caring guy." Yeah, now I see what he really cared about.

It was bad enough that Maya was with this creep in the first place, but how did it happen so soon? I hadn't even been gone for six months! And why did they feel the need to litter the internet with their PDA? Nobody wants to see that! Who did they think they were, some sort of reality-show couple who felt the need to broadcast every detail of their supposedly private life? Their insecurity was mind boggling. If it weren't so disturbing, it would've been downright sad. And now I had to put up with a constant barrage of this—all day, every day. (Or at least every moment I could spare between work drama, which, as I mentioned, was already causing more than enough agita for one week.)

Anyway, by the time Saturday rolled around, my nerves were shot. All I wanted was to put work and Maya and Bradford and everything else out of my mind and just stuff my face. I could hardly wait until noon, when I could go to the buffet and enjoy a nice peaceful lunch…without my phone's incessant stream of nauseating posts and pictures.

I didn't even care about getting guidance this week, and I didn't have any pressing questions for the buffet to answer. I just needed food and forgetting. So, as soon as I arrived, I headed straight for the Thai green curry (one of my go-to comfort foods—on a day when I desperately needed comfort). I ladled out a big bowlful, found a secluded table in the corner, and had just taken my first bite when, all of a sudden, a man a few tables away from me started screaming. "Ow! Ow! Ow! My mouth is burning!" He ran to the nearest beverage station, pushed ahead of several people waiting in line there, and poured himself a glass of water. He immediately drank the whole glass, refilled it, and then drank that glass too.

I shook my head with disgust and went back to eating my own lunch (which, despite the disturbance, I enjoyed tremendously).

I would've felt bad for the guy. After all, I've been in similar situations—eating something that's way too hot for me, urgently draining the nearest drink, and nursing a burnt tongue for hours or even days to come. It's no fun at all. But I had no sympathy for this guy because this was the third week in a row this had happened.

I know because I'd been next to him two weeks earlier when he filled his bowl with five-alarm chili. I'd warned him about it (just as I'd been warned the first time I contemplated trying the aromatic chili in the small red serving bowl, rather than the less spicy varieties in the nearby brown bowls). But he just waved me away. "Not a problem, my boy," he said as he took a final scoop and walked away with nothing but his chili—no side dish, no bread, and no beverage.

I thought he must have a tongue of steel to withstand that heat, especially without a drink. But apparently his tongue wasn't so heat resistant after all: two minutes later, he was screaming and running around and making a scene until he'd gotten a glass of water. Not that I didn't see it coming, but I still felt sorry for him.

But then the same thing happened the following week. Again, he'd taken the five-alarm chili. Again, he hadn't poured himself a glass of water (or any drink) ahead of time. Again, he'd screamed in pain. Didn't this guy learn?

Now I didn't even have to look to know what had happened, but just to confirm what I already knew, I stood up and glanced toward his table. Sure enough, there was the big bowl, loaded up with the distinctively red five-alarm chili (minus one spoonful) and not a drink in sight.

What an odd fellow, I thought. (Actually, I'm censoring myself here. My real, honest thought was, *What a <bleep>ing idiot!*) Seriously, why did he keep doing the same thing? Why didn't he eat something different? Or if he likes chili that much, why didn't he take one of the milder options that are right next to the five-alarm bowl? And why didn't he at least pour himself something to drink *before* he sat down to eat?

The first time, it could happen to anyone. The second time, maybe he forgot—or meant to take a milder chili and got mixed up. But the third time, well, he had no one but himself to blame.

I returned to my meal, which, mercifully, was peaceful from that point on. And I didn't think of Chili Man again for the rest of the day. Or the next, or the next.

Sometime around the middle of the week, though, he popped into my head again. It had been a week just like the previous one—full of work, full of stress, and full of rehashing last week's failures (especially that ill-timed server crash). And when I did get a bit of time to myself, I had to check up on Maya and Bradford and their latest nauseating shenanigans.

They'd set up an infuriating rabbit hole: They'd post what looked like a single new picture, but when you clicked on it, it led to a whole slideshow—one sickening image after another, sometimes even including short videos of them frolicking about like a couple of self-centered exhibitionists. And just when you thought you'd reached the end, they would tag each other, and clicking on their names would lead you to the other one's page, which had a whole other batch of enraging pictures, posts, and videos—and the cycle would start all over again.

After being led through this a few dozen times, though, I suddenly thought of that idiot from the buffet who kept eating the five-alarm chili, even though he knew it would burn him. I was just about to click on yet another picture of Maya and Bradford, but then I thought, *Don't be like Chili Man!* And so I didn't click. I put down my phone and went to get a glass of water. And after I'd calmed down a bit, I pulled my *Lessons* notebook out of my desk drawer, opened it to the first blank page, and wrote down these words:

Lesson #20:
Don't keep doing what you know will hurt you and help no one.

21. The Pasta Guru

Even though I was no longer checking Maya's social media pages (for the most part), I knew the clock was ticking. I didn't have another minute to waste on all this negativity. If I wanted to win her back, I'd have to prove that I was the better man, which, for starters, meant turning this business into a roaring success.

Of course, that depended on the team—and the team depended on me to guide them, support them, and perhaps most of all, *inspire* them. Yes, we'd gotten off to a reasonably good start (despite a few hiccups), but it was time for me to make a bigger splash as a manager—to be the kind of leader who would inspire each individual to reach their potential, the kind of leader who would inspire the team to work together to achieve greatness, the kind of leader who would inspire Maya to marry me.

In my mind's eye, I played this role perfectly. I saw myself onstage, wearing one of those hands-free headset microphones, standing in front of a theater-sized screen that displayed key phrases from my rousing speech—taglines that would become mantras that would inspire a generation.

I wasn't sure why I'd need a stage, a microphone, or a large screen to address a team that was small enough to fit comfortably in our little conference room. More to the point, though, I didn't know what exactly I'd say in this hypothetically rousing speech. What could I possibly come up with that would motivate our humble office to rise as one and create something that transcended our individual lives and touched others in profound, meaningful ways? Anytime I tried to get specific, all I could think of were old advertising slogans ("Think Different," "Just Do It!") or song titles ("You Can Fly," "Don't Dream It, Be It"). Who was I kidding? I didn't have anything original to say—much less an uplifting message that would elevate our spirits and our business to the next level of success. I was no skilled orator, and I certainly was no guru.

But I knew someone who was: the Pasta Guru.

Of course! Why hadn't I thought of him sooner? Actually, I know why—because every time I saw him at the buffet, I scoffed at the reaction he elicited: adulation, adoration, exaltation. It was ridiculous the way people spoke of him in hushed tones of veneration: "He's so wise." "His advice is perfect." "I feel like he knows me better than I know myself." How repulsive.

But wasn't this exactly the kind of reaction I was hoping to achieve at the office?

True to his title, the Pasta Guru spoke about pasta, but if he was really as wise as everyone made him out to be, maybe his message would be universal—something I could apply to our business.

Over the past four months, I'd only seen him a few times, always from afar—a bearded face in the middle of a crowd in the middle of the buffet's pasta room. I'd never been close enough to hear his actual words, but from the glowing secondhand reports I overheard, maybe there actually was something to all the hype. Maybe I just needed to open my mind to the possibility that his wisdom might transcend the pasta bar. Maybe he would turn out to be the source of wisdom I longed to apply to our business. If not, the worst that might happen is I'd get some bad rigatoni.

The one potential fly in the ointment (or the marinara) was that the Pasta Guru didn't operate on any fixed schedule, so I didn't know how long I'd have to wait for the meeting that I hoped would inspire my rousing managerial speech. I might get to see him immediately, or I might have to wait months. The next time I entered the buffet, I crossed my fingers and headed for the pasta room. And as fate would have it, there he was.

As usual, he was surrounded by an adoring crowd, including a long line of devotees waiting to stand before him, ask their questions, and receive his wisdom. And as much as it pained me and offended my sense of independent thinking, I joined the crowd and got in line.

Even from the back of the line, I could hear the Pasta Guru's voice clearly above the crowd of acolytes. I'm not sure what I'd been expecting, but it wasn't this: a thick New York accent that oozed impatience. "Let's go, people. Who's next?" He snapped his fingers. "Come on, move it. We got places to go and pasta to eat."

An older woman shuffled diffidently toward him. "Oh, Pasta Guru. I humbly beseech you to guide me toward a dish that is both light and filling—healthy and delicious."

"Go for the pasta primavera. Third steam tray on the left. *Buon appetito, signora.*" He looked over her shoulder and snapped. "Okay, who's up? Come on, people—while the sauce is still hot."

A middle-aged man stepped up and bowed his head reverently. "Oh, wise Pasta Guru. I come before you seeking the best sauce for my vermicelli."

"You don't want nothin' too heavy for those skinny noodles—your alfredo, your bolognese, your carbonara?…nah, forget about it. Go for something light—like marinara, pomodoro, or arrabbiata if you wanna spice it up."

"Thank you, oh wise one. You have shown me the way to a land of culinary delights, the likes of which I have never—"

"Yeah, yeah. Enough yappin'. Go eat. *Mangia! Mangia!*" Again, he snapped his fingers. "Who's next? Let's go!"

A young man with thick glasses hesitantly approached the guru. Staring at his own shoes, he began to mutter something unintelligible.

"Spit it out, kid. We got hungry people waiting."

The young man cleared his throat. "Well, I know I'm not worthy of your wisdom, great Pasta Guru, but my question is: can you take a big piece of pasta and put something inside it, like vegetables or—"

"Are you joking me? How long you been on this planet and you don't know about stuffed pasta?" The guru pinched the bridge of his nose and shook his head in disgust. "You got your ravioli, your tortellini, your mezzelune, your cappelletti, your…geez, kid. Next time do your homework. You're wasting the Pasta Guru's time. Okay, who's next?"

And so it went: one person after another sought answers to their pasta-related questions, and one person after another was treated to the most mundane drivel imaginable. This guy couldn't even manage to keep his story straight. He'd give one piece of advice ("use a lighter sauce") and then two minutes later, he'd say the exact opposite ("use a heavier sauce"). So which was it? "Pasta Guru"? Ha! More like "The Contradiction Kid"!

None of this was going to help me be a better manager. What I needed was a clear, consistent message—a piece of guidance that could unify the whole team, something broad enough to apply to everyone, but specific enough to inspire.

And that's when it hit me.

My reverie was suddenly broken by the Pasta Guru snapping his fingers mere inches in front of my face. "Wake up, buddy. I don't have all day. What do you wanna know?"

I smiled as I stepped away from him. "It's okay. You already told me."

Lesson #21:
There's not usually one "right" answer to every question. The best guidance may be different for each person and each situation.

22. The Sweet Spot

Even though I decided against delivering a rousing, one-size-fits-all message to the entire team, I still wanted to connect with them. But how? All week long I mulled over this question. Then, on Friday morning, I read an article about the importance of making one-on-one contact with employees—not only to discuss business strategies but also to make personal connections and show that you see them not just as workers but, first and foremost, as people.

I couldn't agree more. Since I'd revised my open-door policy, I'd mostly been meeting with my coworkers to discuss business in group meetings and private work sessions. But I needed to let everyone see that, in my eyes, they weren't just cogs in our company wheel. So, as soon as I finished the article, I walked up to the front desk to check in with Brenda—not just about the emails she was sending but also about how she was doing on a personal level. How was the family? Had she been to any more of her granddaughter's soccer games lately? Any plans for the weekend?

She seemed pleased that I took an interest and, unless I was imagining it, a little relieved that there was no ulterior motive (such as giving her another huge stack of folders to process in addition to everything she already had on her plate). After our pleasant little chat, I moved on and had similar check-ins with Keiko, Yun, and Tamika—all of which seemed to be similarly well received. Liam seemed to enjoy teaching me the proper technique for folding a pocket square. And I even got Laney to open up a bit about her home life—something that had never come up in our previously all-business interactions. (Who knew she had three ferrets and an Olympic-medalist brother?)

I was rather proud of myself for following the article's advice so well. I remembered, though, that the article stressed touching base *regularly*— not just making a nice connection and then disappearing indefinitely. So, a few hours later, I made the rounds again.

The second time didn't seem to go quite as well. It may have been my imagination, but some of the people I reconnected with didn't seem as happy to see me this time around. When I again asked Brenda about her weekend plans, there was definitely a note of sarcasm in her smiling response: "Well, as I mentioned during our conversation *two hours ago*, I'm going to watch my granddaughter's soccer game and then go out to lunch with my friends."

Oh yes, I remembered. I was just trying to keep it light, keep it personal—an intention that I maintained as I continued making the rounds. But despite my easy-breezy demeanor, several people I talked to seemed suspicious the second time. Yun point-blank asked me if he was in trouble, if there had been complaints about customer service.

"No, no," I reassured him. "Just checking in. Touching base. Saying hi."

He looked equal parts relieved and confused. "Oh, okay. Hi."

And my visit with Tamika consisted of little more than eye rolling and exasperated sighs.

At first I chalked up the irritability to the fact that it was just before lunch, but my post-lunch visits were received similarly. Still, I wasn't going to let this deter me. It would just take a bit of time for people to realize that this was the new me: a steady presence, unwavering support, constant contact.

So, determined to persevere with my new best-practice personable approach, I made a third round of contacts just after four. I'd hoped my persistence would pay off. It did not.

Whereas the previous check-ins had mostly just annoyed people, this time I was met with open hostility—most notably in my last check-in of the day. The moment I set my foot into Laney's office, she snapped at me. "No! I have work to finish up before the weekend."

"It's okay, Laney, I just wanted to chat and—"

"Leave!"

"But I thought maybe we could—"

"Get out NOW or I will literally choke you."

I know that a lot of people use *literally* to mean *figuratively* (one of my pet peeves), but I don't think this was the case with Laney. Either way, I didn't stick around to find out.

By that point, I'd had it with all the attitude. If they didn't want to see me, they wouldn't. I slunk out of the office at 4:40, feeling more rejected and dejected than I'd been since Maya had dumped me. I was also confused. What had happened? I thought my employees liked me. I thought they enjoyed touching base—especially after all those nice chats we'd had earlier in the day. I was just trying to be a good manager and a good friend. Is this the thanks I got?

Some people like to drown their sorrow in alcohol or lose themselves in a guilty-pleasure TV binge, but my drug of choice has always been chocolate cake. And the best chocolate cake in town was definitely at…you guessed it: the buffet!

So, when I arrived for Saturday's midday meal, I quickly strode past the salad bar, the soups, the appetizers, and the entrées, and headed straight for the dessert section. And once there, I made a beeline for the most decadent-looking chocolate cake I'd ever seen. I served myself the biggest slice that would fit on my plate, grabbed a nearby seat, and proceeded to gorge myself on my favorite form of "vitamin C"!

The cake tasted even better than it looked. It was perfectly baked. It was moist. It was creamy, fudgy, and rich. And it was absolutely delectable. In fact, it was so good that after finishing the slice, I'd almost forgotten my troubles from the previous day.

Almost.

But just to finish the job, I thought I should probably go back for seconds. I certainly deserved it after how much I'd suffered during those afternoon chats that had gone so horribly awry. I still couldn't get to the bottom of it. But I could get to the bottom of another slice of cake.

The second piece tasted just as good as the first, but about midway through, my stomach told me to stop. I didn't care, though. I wasn't about to give up midway just because I was getting full.

In fact, I wasn't even going to stop after two slices. Hey, I was my own boss, and if I felt like having a third slice of cake, then I would darn well have a third slice of cake. So that's just what I did. Was it the best decision? Probably not. Did my stomach protest louder and louder with each bite? Absolutely. Would I regret it? Most certainly.

But I'd been so good. I'd stuck to a reasonably healthy diet for so long. And I deserved a little treat after all I'd been through—first with Maya and Bradford, and then with all the attitude I'd gotten at work. I'd tried so hard, and somehow it had backfired...almost as badly as that third piece of cake.

I'll spare you the details of my dash to the bathroom or the rest of the afternoon—also spent largely in the bathroom or groaning on the couch. Suffice to say, it was not a pleasant weekend, but at least I got the answer to my question about how to connect with people. No, the lesson didn't come from the article I'd read. It came from a chocolate cake.

Lesson #22:
Find the sweet spot between not enough
and too much.

23. Eat Here Now

It was the best of weeks, it was the worst of weeks.

On the plus side: Kareem finished the customer-contact app—and two days later, we made our first sale! Back in the old days, a company would have celebrated this landmark moment by taping their first dollar bill to the wall. But since the transaction was digital, we simply gave ourselves a round of high-fives and let out a big *woo-hoo!*

Then, ten minutes later, I got called into Zoey's office for an emergency update on the navigation glasses. It turned out, the parts they'd ordered for the prototype weren't compatible with one another. So, after a hasty and heated debate, we decided that they'd modify the design and order some new parts that would fit. Which meant additional expenses and delays to what was supposed to be our signature product. Hopefully, it would all be worth it in the long run, but for now it was eating away at me…and my bottom line.

Meanwhile, the Maya-and-Bradford situation was also eating away at me. For the most part, I refrained from checking their social media updates, with occasional exceptions. (Hey, I'm human. Of my few slip-ups, the most grating were the photos of their weekend getaway at the beach house. Oh, and also their dinner with Maya's family—including Bradford eating MY aloo saag! The audacity!) But even when I did step away from their posts and pictures, they lingered in my mind and gnawed at my heart.

As with the navigation glasses, I knew that everything would work out eventually. We'd all look back and laugh at the bumpy, twisting path that led us where we were supposed to go—to success, joy, and love. But for now, the path felt far too twisted for my tastes. And all week long, it didn't leave me a moment of peace. Which is why, more than ever, I looked forward to the buffet—my personal haven where (for the most part) everyone just left me alone so I could relax, enjoy my food, and let my mind drift.

Not that my mind did much drifting on this day (or most days, for that matter). No sooner had I grabbed my meal and settled into a secluded corner, than my thoughts started swinging back and forth like a pendulum. First they went back to the good old days when I was with Maya. Back when we were still a happy couple, surrounded by happy friends, and building a good life together. Or so I thought.

But inevitably, these thoughts led to regrets about what had gone wrong. What *had* gone wrong? Was it really that I wasn't driven enough, ambitious enough, successful enough? Or was it that I wasn't really "there" for her, as she often complained? Didn't she remember all the good times? I sure did, but now those happy memories just made me pine for everything I'd lost.

And that's when the pendulum would swing in the other direction: looking ahead. Ahead to when we'd get back together. Ahead to when I'd tell her all about the successful branch I'd created. Ahead to when the navigation glasses were fixed, Kareem's apps were household names, and our products had revolutionized the industry…at least enough to impress the heck out of my skeptical ex-girlfriend.

But that meant that first these products actually had to get finished. Which meant I had to spend a lot more time overseeing their development. Which meant, as much as I wished I could just skip forward to the end of the year, I was stuck where I was for another six months. Which made me wish I could just go back to when things already were good—or at least good enough.

And so the pendulum kept on swinging—back and forth, back and forth—as I sat at that corner table, picking absent-mindedly at my food, wishing I could go back in time. Or forward. Or—

"Excuse me, young man. Is this seat taken?"

I looked up to see whose voice had jolted me out of my thoughts. It was an older woman. Three of them, actually.

Before I had the time (or the presence of mind) to respond, the second woman sat down across from me. "Aah," she sighed. "I've been looking forward to this all day."

"All week!" the third woman said. "I've been dreaming about this tiramisu every night."

"Now don't go spoiling your appetite, Ellie," the first woman said. "Dessert comes last."

"I know, I know! But can't a gal dream?"

By that point, all three women had settled into their seats—one across from me and one on either side. (As I said, people at the buffet left me alone...*for the most part*. There were exceptions, though. And, despite my recent commitment to healthy boundaries, I didn't want to be rude. Besides, these three seemed like they'd be interesting enough to provide a welcome distraction, pulling me away from my anxiety-regret pendulum.)

As they settled into their seats, I tried to determine their ages, which could've been anywhere from low sixties to high eighties. I guessed it was on the higher end of that range, based on their matching dresses, which were the same floral-print style my grandma and her friends used to wear. They also had the same matching hairdos: poofed-out gray curls that looked like they'd just been done at the salon. Between their clothes, hair, and carefully applied makeup, they were fully decked-out for the occasion, which I sensed was their big outing for the week. (Not that there was anything wrong with that. After all, it was also my big weekly outing, even if I didn't go to the salon first.)

They introduced themselves as Edith, Edna, and Eleanor ("but call me Ellie"), told me that two out of them were sisters (but didn't say which one wasn't), and continued their rapid-fire conversation with utter disregard for the general convention of not speaking with your mouth full.

"You think *this* is a big meal?" Edna said. "This is nothing compared to the shepherd's pie I had last week. Hoo-wee!" Her eyes glazed over with joyous contentment. "I could barely waddle back to the car...but it was worth every bite, I tell ya. Every last bite."

Edith scoffed. "I'll take my quiche over your so-called pie any day of the week." I looked at her plate and was somewhat confused—she was eating what appeared to be mushroom stroganoff...with not a quiche in sight. When I looked up, she was peering into my eyes and chewing with frightening intensity. "You know, young man, I've had quiches in the finest restaurants in Paris, and they don't hold a candle to the ones they make here. Mmm-mmm-mmm!" She closed her eyes and took another bite of her stroganoff.

"Well, you two can keep your tarts and pies," Ellie said. "And I'll keep my tiramisu. That's what I—"

"Not yet!" Edith said. "First you've got to—"

"I know! I know! *After* I finish my vittles. Keep your bloomers on, old girl."

Edna made a sour face. "No more dessert for me. I'm sworn off the stuff ever since that atrocious strudel."

"That was over two months ago, Edna!" Ellie shouted. "You've gotta get back in the saddle. That's what I say." She twirled some stir-fry noodles around her fork. "Tiramisu, here I come!" she shouted as she shoved the noodles into her mouth.

Edna looked at me with fervent appeal in her eyes. "That strudel was absolutely raw inside. *Raw!*" She quivered with disgust. "After that fiasco, I had half a mind to swear off food altogether."

"Not me," said Edith. "I've got the rest of month all planned out." She put down her fork and counted on her fingers as she enumerated each upcoming meal. "Next week it'll be stuffed peppers. After that, potato latkes with applesauce. And then I'll finish off the month with the best of all: paella." She smiled as she took another bite of stroganoff. "Quite a month we've got ahead of us. Quite a month."

As the meal continued, the trio continued to rhapsodize over the fondly recalled highlights of meals past—and the upcoming treats they eagerly anticipated—while intermittently bemoaning their culinary disappointments. But never once did they mention their current meals. In fact, they didn't even seem to notice them.

To test my theory, I asked, "How's your food today?"

Sure enough, they all appeared utterly perplexed, looking down at their plates as if they were only just noticing them. "I couldn't rightly tell you," Edith said. She took another bite and ruminated. The others did the same with their respective meals.

"I suppose it's good enough," Edna said.

"Mine too," Edith agreed.

Ellie groaned slightly. "Well, mine *was* good, but quite filling. I'm afraid I haven't got any room left for my beloved tiramisu." She scooted her dessert plate in my direction. "It's all yours if you want it, lad."

Taking their cue from Ellie, they all promptly stood up, bid me adieu, and headed for the exit—leaving behind only the untouched tiramisu.

It would've been easy to make fun of them, but I was essentially in the same boat. After all, even before they arrived, I'd been so wrapped up in my regrets about Maya—and my big plans to win her back with my stunning business success—that I'd barely noticed the fajitas I was eating. After the sisters (and one non-sister) left, though, I took another bite…and was pleased at just how tasty it was. I savored the rest of my meal, as well as Ellie's tiramisu (which more than lived up to her hype).

Then I walked home and enjoyed the rest of the weekend—more than I'd done since I'd moved. And on Monday, I arrived at work feeling eager but also calm. And when I made my morning rounds, instead of asking my two usual questions—*What are your goals?* and *What are your plans?*—I asked two different questions: *What are you working on now?* and *How are you doing?*

As the employees answered—each one brilliant, thoughtful, and full of life—I didn't think about Maya. Or the past. Or the future. I just listened.

Lesson #23:
Be present.

24. To Finish or Not to Finish?

For the most part, I stuck with my newfound commitment to being present while I was at work. When it came to Maya, however, I was slightly less successful. But my biggest fail in the stay-present department was related to food. Instead of focusing on my current meals, I kept thinking about pasta.

Not just any old pasta—one particular dish that had caught my eye during my previous visit to the buffet. By the time I saw it, I'd already filled my plate with fajitas, so I decided to get it next time. Based on how good it had looked and smelled, I had a feeling it would be well worth the wait.

Try as I might to avoid the future-thinking trap, all week long I kept fantasizing about that pasta dish. Just thinking about it whet my appetite. The sauce looked like a perfect combination of creamy and chunky—packed with vegetables, spices, and little touches (capers? peppercorns?) that called to me from across the room. It's like the head chef had hacked into my private gastronomical files and constructed a work of edible genius specifically tailored to my tastes. Even before I'd tried a single bite, I was smitten—even worse than Ellie with her tiramisu!

I could hardly wait for the weekend, when I'd actually get to taste my new culinary obsession. On Saturday morning, however, I awoke in a panic. What if the meal wasn't there? What if it was a one-off that was only available the time I saw it? Or what if it was there but other people got to it first and they were all out by the time I arrived? I couldn't risk it—I had to make sure I reached the buffet by twelve o'clock sharp!

In my haste, I arrived twenty minutes early and ended up pacing back and forth in front of the entrance until they opened—at which point I barged inside to make sure I was first in line, not caring about being pushy. That pasta was too important for such trivial concerns.

Once I'd paid, I raced past the salad bar, the soups, the appetizers, and everything else that stood between me and my dream pasta…assuming it was still there. I got to the right room, made my way to the right spot, and…YES! Hallelujah! There it was, in all its steaming-hot, creamy-chunky, aromatic glory—just waiting for me to load up my plate, find the nearest table, and chow down.

As I took my first bite, I could hardly believe I was actually eating this meal. It was a dream come true. It was the fulfillment of a weeklong fantasy. It was perfect…for about half a second. And then I realized that something was wrong. Very wrong. There's probably a culinary term for it (acrid? astringent? ashy?), but since I'm not a chef, I'll just say what I thought: *This is freaking gross!*

What I'd expected to be a delicious creamy sauce turned out to be some sort of greasy, viscous slime. Those glorious toppers tasted like my least-favorite spice: anise (or, actually, more like a similar word). And let's just say the veggies had seen better days.

But I'd served myself a full plate of this stuff. I couldn't just throw it out—that would be a waste. After all, I'd been dreaming about this meal all week. And I'd only taken one bite. Maybe I should take another bite or two just to see if the taste grew on me. Maybe this meal and I would be like a rom-com couple who can't stand each other at first but end up falling in love.

In the spirit of optimism, I took another bite.

Nope. Not the rom-com fantasy-twist ending. Still gross. If anything, the second bite tasted even worse than the first.

Still, I couldn't just give up. I'd already wasted too much food lately. Besides, I'd been taught to persevere. To finish what I start. To be part of the Clean-Plate Club. I steeled myself and took a third bite and then a fourth and a fifth. It still tasted just as bad, but soon that was the least of my concerns. I was starting to feel queasy.

But that wasn't enough to stop me. I was no quitter. I wasn't some commitment-phobic, cold-footed waffler who jumped ship at the first sign of trouble. I would tough it out and find a way to finish.

I came up with a strategy: Instead of focusing on the food, I would think about something else. And since I didn't have much else going on in my life at the time, I had two options. I knew that thinking about Maya and Bradford would just make me queasier, so instead I thought about work. But that wasn't much better—because it meant thinking about the navigation glasses nightmare.

Six weeks earlier, when we'd started working on this project, it had seemed so promising—something we hoped would be a real breakthrough, a landmark, a product that would help thousands and make millions. It all looked good on paper. It sounded great when we discussed it. And the whole team was on board, enthusiastic, and dedicated to its success.

But it just wasn't working. And the more we tried to fix it, the worse it got.

Over the past week, Zoey and Nikhil had told me that the more they worked on it, the more they realized that it simply wasn't a viable product. Sofia ran the updated numbers and assured me that it wouldn't be cost effective. Yun said it wouldn't help our customers. And Yasmin said that, even if we could get it to work, a bigger company was sure to put out something better and cheaper. They all agreed: it was time to pull the plug.

But I disagreed. Vehemently. We couldn't just walk away—we'd already invested so much time, effort, and money trying to develop it. And we'd all had the same lessons drilled into us: *Where there's a will there's a way. Don't quit three feet from gold. Winners never quit, and quitters never win.*

So, playing the role of the good motivational manager, I told the team we weren't quitters. We weren't some wishy-washy, flip-flopping company that started one product then abandoned it midway and started something different, only to ditch that too in favor of something else (and then something else and something else and something else) without ever bringing a product to market. We stuck to our guns. Put our noses to the grindstones. Forged ahead where lesser mortals would have given up. One way or another, we would make this project work.

And as I sat there in the buffet suffering through the worst meal I'd ever eaten, thinking about the worst product I'd ever worked on, all these voices rang through my head—from my childhood, from college, from my years on the job, and from countless motivational books, videos, and posters. *Don't quit! Don't give up! Persevere!*

But from amid the cacophony, a different voice emerged—possibly my better judgment, possibly the buffet itself—a voice filled with compassion and quiet confidence. It told me that when you find yourself in a hole, the first thing to do is to stop digging. It told me that when you realize you're heading the wrong way, stop driving. It told me that nearly every great company had to abandon its Plan A (and, in many cases, Plans B, C, D, and well beyond) before they found their path to profitability. It told me that it's okay to make mistakes—that they're part of the path of learning, improving, and evolving—but that the key was to not keep making the same mistakes over and over…and certainly not to double down on the ones you're in the middle of!

Then I thought of a friend who'd stayed in a toxic relationship long past the point of hope. Of leaders who'd dragged out wars they knew they couldn't win. Of a cartoon character optimistically trying to hammer a square peg into a round hole.

And I thought of myself: spurring on a doomed project, eating a disgusting lunch, and refusing to try a new course—simply because I'd told myself I wasn't a quitter. But in that moment, I knew what I had to do: put down my fork, throw out this plate of half-eaten food, and get a different meal.

So that's just what I did.

And as I ate my new meal (polenta with roasted veggies—simple enough to settle my stomach, tasty enough to savor), I decided that first thing Monday morning, I would pull the plug on the glasses. I'd tell the team I was proud of them for trying but that now it was time to try something new. And we'd brainstorm until we came up with an idea that seemed worthy of our time, talents, and efforts. Then we'd get started on that—knowing that it also wouldn't be guaranteed to succeed. But, unlike the glasses, it wouldn't be guaranteed to fail. And that was a step in the right direction.

Lesson #24:
Winners know when to keep going, when to try
something different, and when to quit.

25. The Waiter

One of the regulars at the buffet was a guy everyone calls "The Waiter."

When I first overheard people talking about him, I was confused because the buffet doesn't have waiters—it's self-serve. Yes, the buffet has a staff: chefs who prepare the food, people who refill the serving containers, and washers who clean the plates and utensils after they've been used. But "The Waiter" wasn't one of them—he didn't work for the buffet at all.

So why did people call him "The Waiter"?

I decided to surreptitiously watch him to see if I could find out. And it didn't take long.

The next time I went to the buffet, I spotted him sitting alone. So I took my lunch to the table behind him, where I could watch without him noticing me. I wanted to see what exactly he did. While I sat there, savoring every bite of my avocado sushi roll, The Waiter did nothing at all. He just sat there—not eating, not drinking, not talking to anyone, not even moving. He was just...*waiting*.

After about half an hour, he suddenly got up, grabbed his coat, and stormed out of the buffet, casting sidelong glances at the other diners and muttering angrily the whole time: "What a lousy place! People here are so inconsiderate, so selfish!"

My first instinct was to never go near this wacko again, but curiosity got the better of me, and I found myself watching him every chance I got.

The next time I saw him, I once again sat at a nearby table where I could unobtrusively observe. Again, he did the same thing: *nothing*. Or, to put it another way: he waited. And this time, his waiting paid off: eventually, a man approached him and asked if he'd like anything to eat. The Waiter immediately perked up and, for the first time since I'd been watching him, actually smiled. "Why, yes. That would be very nice, thank you."

A few minutes later, the man returned to The Waiter's table with a tray of food and drinks. Again, The Waiter thanked him and then turned his attention to the meal, which he ate with evident pleasure. Once he'd finished, he got up, put on his coat, and strolled out of the buffet, smiling at the other diners while musing aloud: "What a great place! People here are so kind, so thoughtful! And the food is absolutely delicious!"

Aha, I thought—that's his deal: He waits for someone to bring him food. If they do, he's happy; if they don't, he gets mad.

But the next time I saw The Waiter, I realized it was more complex than that. As usual, he sat alone and waited in silence. Eventually, like the previous time, someone approached him and asked if he'd like some food. As before, The Waiter graciously accepted. This time, however, after he'd taken the first bite, he grimaced and shoved away his plate. "Ugh!" he groaned. "This is horrible!" He glared in the direction of the man who'd brought the food. "How could you insult me with this slop?! Is this all you think I'm worth?!" Then he got up, grabbed his coat, and stomped toward the door, continuing to yell at everyone and no one in particular: "What a dump! Crummy food, crummy service, crummy people!" And with that, he stormed out and slammed the door behind him.

What was this guy's problem? The other man had gone out of his way to help him, and this was the thanks he got? I'd been watching The Waiter closely, so I know he hadn't asked the man for any particular food or given any clue regarding his preferences, so it wasn't the man's fault that he didn't like it. And it's not like he'd brought him rotten food.

Or had he? Maybe that would explain it.

I walked over to the table where The Waiter had been sitting and took a peek at the offending plate of food. It was a steaming hot vegetable casserole that, as far as I could tell, looked perfectly fine. Taking a look around to make sure no one was watching, I surreptitiously snuck a bite of it. (Yes, I know this is gross, but I used my own fork and took a bite from the side that The Waiter hadn't touched.) In any case, the casserole tasted great! In fact, I liked it so much that I made a mental note to get it for myself at some point. It clearly wasn't to The Waiter's taste, but there's no way someone else could have known that.

More baffled than ever, I left the buffet and did my best to put The Waiter out of my mind. However, just the opposite happened: Throughout the week, I found myself thinking of him almost incessantly. And I started seeing him everywhere.

No, I didn't see The Waiter from the buffet again, but I noticed other people who acted similarly: passively waiting for someone to give them what they wanted, even though they didn't ask for help or give any indication that they were looking for it. And just like The Waiter, these people would either be happy or upset depending on whether they received help and, if they did, how it worked out.

It seemed like everywhere I looked, I saw "Waiters": My friend Westin was upset because the woman he liked never asked him out on a date— even though he'd never asked *her* out or even shared his feelings with her. My aunt was mad that the free accounting service that reached out to her wasn't able to save her more on her tax return. And there were even some people at work who just sat around doing nothing until someone gave them an assignment. (Although they both seemed like nice people, I couldn't help notice that Nora and Diego fell into this category: she waited in her office until someone came in to discuss HR concerns, and he wouldn't initiate his own copywriting projects unless point-blank told to.)

Not everyone acted like this, though. Plenty of people took initiative and went after what they wanted. They took the "self-serve" approach. It wasn't in a selfish way, as The Waiter had accused; if anything, these people were also the most likely to help others, while Waiters selfishly expected people to serve *them*! I thought of my old neighbor who'd started his own lawncare company while his brother complained about not being able to find any work. Now the neighbor was doing booming business and had hired three other people to help—including his brother! Our office certainly had its share of Self-Servers (most notably, Laney, Zoey, and Kareem, who frequently initiated new projects and, without being asked, followed through on the most promising ones).

I was feeling very pleased with myself for coming up with this "Waiters and Self-Servers" theory, and I frequently found myself musing about it—which is just what I was doing on Friday afternoon when Yun barged into my office and announced that he was quitting. "I'm fed up with working here!" he said. "I've got tons of great ideas, but no one ever asks for my input! I'm going someplace that actually values me!" And then he turned around and marched right out of the office, leaving me in flabbergasted silence.

What was he talking about? Of course his ideas were valued here. He was our customer service manager—serving customers was literally the most important thing we did. And I for one would have welcomed any input he cared to offer. But as far as I knew, he'd never suggested anything. So what was his problem?

Then it hit me. I knew exactly what his problem was: he was a Waiter. He had all these ideas, but rather than share them with anyone, he just waited around for someone to ask him—and when they didn't, he got upset. Well, good riddance. This office needs Self-Servers—not Waiters!

After I'd cooled down and mulled it over, though, something else hit me: *I* was a Waiter. I was the one who'd been waiting for Yun (and who knows how many others) to bring ideas to me. I had no right to get mad if people didn't volunteer their ideas when I'd never even asked them to! As branch manager, it was up to me to seek them out, solicit their input, and encourage them to share their ideas.

By the time I realized this, the office was already closed for the weekend, but I resolved that from that point on, I would approach people—individually and in groups—and ask them if they had any ideas that might help the company, make their jobs (or their lives) any better, or create a better work environment for all of us.

And starting Monday morning, that's just what I did.

Lesson #25:
If you want something, don't wait for someone to
give it to you. Speak up, take action, and invite
others to do the same.

26. Reality Check

When I got back to the office the following week, the first thing I did was to get in touch with Yun. I assured him I'd seek out his input from then on and asked him to consider coming back, but he'd already accepted another job. I was disappointed, but my downcast mood didn't last long—for three main reasons.

First of all, I quickly thought of a possible replacement for Yun: Rohan, the man who'd applied earlier in the year and had taken the rejection so well. I gave him a call and found out that since our last talk, he'd followed my suggestions: taking courses to fill the gaps in his training while volunteering at a local nonprofit to get experience in the field. Laney agreed that although Rohan was still learning, he was ready to come on board as customer service manager. I offered him the position, and he accepted on the spot.

My mood was also improved by our booming business. Kareem's app continued to sell, and he'd already created a couple of add-ons for it. Also, since pulling the plug on the navigation glasses, Zoey and Nikhil had created an app of their own: a social media time-management tool that tracked screen time, set limits on platform usage, and provided insights into usage patterns to promote healthier digital habits. Within days they were running beta tests and getting glowing feedback from businesses and individuals alike.

All this new business meant that the office was suddenly hopping. After a few slow months, Yasmin (our director of marketing) and Liam (director of sales) now had products to market and sell. Tamika finally had contracts to write. Brenda spent her days fielding a steady stream of calls, texts, and emails. And Rohan was able to hit the ground running as customer service manager—because we actually had customers to serve!

Most of all, Sofia finally had some positive numbers to enter in her bookkeeping files. Which brings me to the biggest reason I was excited: anticipating her second-quarter report, which she said she'd deliver by the end of the week.

When Friday arrived, I could hardly sit still. Initially, I'd been hoping to make the branch profitable by the end of the year, but I had a feeling we were already well past that goal. The only question was, by how much?

I was doubly ready for a comeback after the Q1 report, which had been dismal. But I'd expected that. At that point I had just set up the office and hired everyone, so of course we weren't raking it in. But now business was booming. I could see it with my own eyes. I could feel it in the office's energy. And Sofia had even hinted that the numbers were looking up.

I checked my watch: 10:43. Sofia had said she'd drop off the report mid-morning, so it should be any minute now. Or so I thought. But by noon, she still hadn't brought it.

I was too excited to go out for lunch, so I went to the break room for a candy bar and a third cup of coffee. (Probably not the best antidote for a case of the jitters, but I needed to do something other than pace around my office or hover over Sofia's desk.) When I got back to my office, I looked down at my desk, and there it was.

I saw why it had taken Sofia a little extra time. She'd created a stunning, professional-looking report—complete with a beautifully designed full-color cover (featuring high-quality photography and graphics that suggested Keiko's involvement), a protective plastic front, and spiral binding that gave it an air of dignity and durability. This wasn't the report of some fly-by-night operation that printed out a few black-and-white pages and stapled them together. This was a company that was built to last, and here was the report to prove it.

I picked it up, reread the simple yet stately title (*Second Quarter Report*), took a few moments to admire the cover (and a few more moments to wonder whether *Second Quarter* should be hyphenated), and then opened it to page one.

The multi-level table of contents hinted at the depths within: income statements, balance sheets, cash flow statements, gross revenue, and other financial data and analysis. I would soon read all of this thoroughly, cover to cover, several times. First, though, I just wanted to see the bottom line—that big number I'd been anticipating for months.

I hastily flipped through page after page of charts, tables, and text until I found what I'd been looking for. Contrary to its nickname, the number was not the literal bottom line, but Sofia (or Keiko) had increased the font and put a box around it so that it couldn't be missed. And there, in the middle of the report's penultimate page, was the YTD net profit.

The number was even larger than I'd expected—significantly larger, in fact. Unfortunately, though, it was red and preceded by a minus sign.

I've seen countless movies where a character has a mind-altering experience or receives some shocking news—often dramatized by some sort of trick photography or special effect that makes it look like the character is getting bigger while everything around them is getting smaller. No matter how many times I saw this effect, it always made me laugh, but I never really felt what those characters were supposed to be feeling. Until that moment.

As soon as I saw that big red negative number, I felt like the floor was dropping out from under me—like the walls were receding and the room was growing dark…aside from a spotlight shining down on that one horrible number. There it was: the sum total of all my labors. The number on which I'd been basing all my hopes and dreams. The brutally honest assessment of my worth as a manager, a provider, a person. Not even a big fat zero. Less than zero. *Much* less.

I felt like passing out, but I didn't. That would have been preferable. Instead, I had to stare at that irrefutable number. Even when I closed my eyes, I saw it—burned into my brain like an afterimage of the pitiless midday sun. And, as clear as day, it said one thing:

I was a failure.

After six months of steady effort, I'd managed to get us deeper in debt than ever. And now, with just under six months left until my profitability deadline, I couldn't see how I could possibly climb out of this hole by the end of the year. It was time to face the facts: I was toast. And thanks to my crazy wager, so was the whole office.

Most of the team was out on lunch break, so it was easy for me to slink out of the office undetected. But instead of going out to lunch, I went straight home. And I stayed there. I was done for the day. Done for the week. Done period.

I just couldn't bring myself to go back and face the team. But after a few hours of sulking around the house, I realized that it wasn't the team I dreaded facing, it was the one person I couldn't avoid: myself.

There was no one else to blame. As manager, this was my responsibility. The buck had to stop with me. But thanks to me, the branch didn't have a whole lot of bucks. (Negative bucks, in fact.) This was all my fault. I had messed up.

But actually, no, I hadn't messed up—that was the worst part. It would've been easier if I'd made an obvious mistake. Then I could've just fixed it. But as far as I could tell, I'd done everything right: I'd hired a great assistant, put together a top-notch team, brainstormed ideas, developed high-quality products, offered valuable services, tested the market, put together great advertising campaigns, and made sales. Not to mention the invaluable guidance I'd been receiving—and applying—from the buffet. Of course there'd been a few missteps along the way, but I'd learned from them and made the necessary adjustments.

So what had happened?

That was the question that plagued me all night. The question that my entire fate rested on. The question that, for the life of me, I couldn't even begin to answer. So I did the next best thing: tried to put it out of my mind. I binge-watched two seasons of an old cop show, ate three bags of microwave popcorn, and fell asleep on the couch.

Mercifully, the next day was Saturday, which meant the office was closed and the buffet was open. And never before had I needed the buffet as much as I needed it then. I needed guidance, I needed answers, and I needed a decent meal. (With all due respect to microwave popcorn, my body was crying out for something a little more nutritious.)

I set out that morning with high hopes but low expectations. Yes, the buffet had helped me before—every week for half a year, in fact—but this time was different. I didn't just need to set boundaries or find balance, I needed to save my business and my future. So, as much as I wanted to have faith, I needed to be realistic. Even if the buffet seemed to have some mysterious guidance-giving power, at the end of the day (or, in my case, the middle of the day), it was still just a big cafeteria.

So, it wasn't shocking that I didn't get any business-saving, life-fixing guidance the moment I stepped inside the door. However, I did get insight about what to eat: Thai green curry.

This wasn't what I'd had in mind. For the past few weeks I'd been eyeing some new-for-me meals that I wanted to try. But after my Q2 failure, I needed a guaranteed win. And the buffet's Thai curry was a sure thing. I'd already had it twice before, and both times it had been better than anything I'd had before, even at top-tier Thai restaurants (including Royal Dragon, where Maya and I went for our second anniversary). I'm not sure what the buffet's secret was, but they'd clearly found the magic formula for curry, and on this day, that's exactly what I needed.

As I made my way through the rooms, I did my best to push aside the worried voices in my head. (What if they moved the curry and I can't find it? What if they discontinued it altogether?) Turns out, my fears were unfounded—the curry was exactly where it had been before, and it looked and smelled as good as ever. Before anything could go wrong, I scooped out two ladlefuls and a side of sticky rice, found an empty table, and prepared to savor the flavor.

From the very first bite, however, it was painfully obvious that this was not a flavor I would savor. It wasn't awful (nothing rotten, rancid, or whatever you'd call the taste equivalent of the Q2 report), but it certainly wasn't good. Was this even the same curry I'd enjoyed so much just over a month ago? It looked and smelled the same, but something was different—and not in a good way.

I dug through the bowl, trying to figure out what had changed. As far as I could tell, the ingredients were the same: potatoes, eggplant, carrots, and cauliflower in a coconut-curry broth. But somehow the flavor was off. I don't have a refined enough palate to know why (not enough basil? too much lemongrass? missing cumin or coriander?); I just knew that my taste buds were not happy.

I thought this would be my consolation meal. (If I couldn't make a profit, at least I could enjoy a decent lunch.) But instead of providing solace, it just heaped more misery onto my already sizable pile. Was this my punishment for being such a lousy manager? Was the buffet trying to teach me a lesson? Or was it just being mean to me?

Maybe it was telling me I needed to stick with it—to plow through the rough patch to get to the good stuff. Maybe the curry would start tasting better after a few more bites, once I got used to the different flavor—like when I got used to marinara sauce on french fries. I tested this theory for three more spoonfuls, but the curry still tasted bad, and I was no closer to solving my problems.

Then it dawned on me: maybe the business was too scattered—marketing low-cost apps to retail and wholesale customers while simultaneously developing high-impact products (not to mention Nikhil's long-range nanotechnology and quantum-computing projects)—just like the curry with all those different vegetables. What if I focused on just one thing? It was worth a try. (At this point, the meal and the business couldn't get any worse, so why not experiment?) I dug through the bowl and fished out nothing but eggplant. But every bite tasted just as slimy and disgusting as the last.

I was at my wit's end. What the heck was I supposed to do? Why was everything going so horribly wrong? I felt like I was being punished, but for what? I'd tried my best—I really had. I'd done everything I thought I was supposed to. I'd been the best boyfriend I could be to Maya—trying to become the person she wanted me to be and provide the life she deserved. I'd been the best manager I could, and I'd tried to learn enough to overcome my shortcomings. I'd been kind and encouraging to my employees, followed the best practices for business, and strived to create win-wins for our customers and our branch. And even at lunch, I'd tried to pick out a surefire-winner meal—something I'd already had and enjoyed. My life should have been perfect—or at least decent—at the buffet, with Maya, and at work. We had all the ingredients of a successful branch, just like this curry had all the ingredients of a delicious lunch. In theory, I should have been running a profitable business and eating a great meal. But the reality was…

I dropped my spoon with a clatter that jarred me back to my senses (and turned a few heads at neighboring tables). Of course! In *theory*, everything seemed great. But I wasn't living in theory, I was living in reality. And, for whatever reason, the reality simply was not good. Even if I was doing everything "right" at work, even if the chef was doing everything "right" in the kitchen, even if it all seemed perfect on paper, the business and the curry just weren't working. The Q2 report was my reality check at work, just like this bad curry was a reality check at the buffet. And they both told me the same thing: *something needed to change.*

Fortunately, there was still time. I still had almost six months left to turn the office around—and almost an hour left to get a better lunch. So, without wasting another moment trying to figure out what was wrong with the curry, I simply threw it out and went looking for a new meal. I didn't yet know what I'd choose for a replacement; I just knew it would be something different.

Lesson #26:
No matter how good things seem in theory, if the reality falls short, it might be time to change.

27. Look and Learn

I thought I was done with the world of cliques when I left high school. However, the adult world seemed to be full of them—in virtual and in-person communities, at work, and even at the buffet. Somehow I didn't notice it during my first six months of weekly buffet lunches. But once I did, I couldn't believe I'd ever missed it.

It was like high school all over again. There were jocks, who sat together humblebragging about their workout regimens while pounding protein shakes and inventing reasons to flex their bulging biceps. There were class clowns (or "buffet buffoons"), who kept everyone at their table laughing so much that it was hard to eat. There was the theater crowd, who always managed to make a scene—treating the buffet as their personal stage and the eaters as their adoring crowd (most of whom, I sensed, met their theatrical antics with less adoration than irritation). There were computer geeks. (I spent all week with them, so I'd learned to identify them outside the office too, sometimes by just a snippet of conversation—especially when it involved algorithms, APIs, firewalls, qubits, or anything "borked.") There was the popular crowd, who lots of people tried to follow and/or imitate. There were rebels, who seemed on a mission to be the polar opposite of the populars. And then there were loners, like me.

Not that I minded. In fact, after my busy weeks of constant interaction, I relished my weekends alone—time to unwind, process, and refuel for the week ahead. I liked spending time at home or even being alone in a crowd, like I usually was at the buffet.

But today I wasn't enjoying it at all.

I felt uncomfortable on a deep level. I couldn't quite pinpoint the reason, but I think it had something to do with being around all these different cliques. Not that they were bothering me (even the theater crowd seemed to be on their best behavior that day), but I didn't like the fact that I was so focused on them. It went against everything I believed in. It went against who I was. It went against one of the most important lessons I'd been taught—something that had been drummed into my head throughout high school.

As early as ninth grade, I'd shown some promise as a runner, but I had this bad habit of constantly checking on the other runners. "Keep your eyes on your own lane!" Coach Hopkins would shout. "Don't worry about what everybody else is doing. Just run your own race." He yelled the most during sprints, when even a quick glance to one side or the other could cost me a split second, which often cost me the race. But he also got on my case during the medium- and long-distance races. Even when I trained alone, I'd want to compare my time with everybody else's, which drove Hopkins nuts. "You're competing against *yourself*, period. You do you. Just be a little better than you were last time, and the results will take care of themselves."

I never became the star athlete some people had predicted, but I did take Hopkins' advice to heart in other areas of my life. I tried to focus on self-improvement rather than competing with others (even Bradford—I just had to become the best man I could be and trust that Maya would see that the best man should be her groom). In terms of wealth, I never cared about "keeping up with the Joneses"—I just wanted to live in a way that felt good to me. I didn't worry about what kind of impression I made on others. (In addition to Hopkins' teachings, another one of my life mottos was "What you think of me is none of my business.") Basically, I did what Hopkins had taught me: I stayed in my own lane and kept my eyes focused ahead.

Yet I was surrounded by a world that tried to convince me to do otherwise. Books, movies, magazines, websites, and even well-meaning friends and family reinforced the same message I was getting from the buffet: you have to act a certain way to be accepted by others and be part of a group. (Or you have to make a point of acting *differently* from others in order to be accepted by those who also make a point of acting differently.) I'd even been getting this message all week at work.

It started at Tuesday's all-staff meeting. After that dismal Q2 report, I knew I had to do something to turn things around—*fast!* So I invited Yasmin to give a presentation on marketing. I thought she'd inspire us all to look at things from fresh, creative angles and get the word out about our unique, innovative products; instead, she spent over an hour harping on about my least favorite subjects: market share, niches, and, worst of all, competition. She used dozens of examples, perspectives, and statistics, but they all boiled down to the same message: *We've got to keep an eye on what everyone else is doing.*

Afterward, during our private meetings throughout the week, she followed up with variations on this theme. And every time she did, I felt a little more unsettled. Not just because this approach went completely against the way I'd tried to live my whole life (at least ever since I met Coach Hopkins) but because I started to get the sense that Yasmin might actually have a valid point.

A month earlier, I would've immediately rejected this approach. But that Q2 report had woken me up, shaken me to the core, and made me realize I couldn't live in a bubble. I didn't want to turn into a copycat—a pale imitation of our competitors. But I also didn't want to go too far the other way: completely ignoring the competition—or trying to be radically different (or adversarial) just to prove that we *weren't* copycats. There had to be a happy medium. But by the end of the week, I still hadn't found it.

With a sigh, I turned my attention back to my lunch—twirling another forkful of sesame noodles and taking a sip of my new favorite drink: bubble tea. I thought of how I'd discovered this delicious drink: because I noticed a bunch of people with what I initially thought were blueberries in iced coffee. To be honest, it looked gross, but so many people seemed to be enjoying it that I decided to give it a try. And I'm so glad I did! I'm also glad that I experimented with several variations until I found my personal favorite: mixing popping boba and tapioca pearls with a cup of coconut milk and adding a dash of brown sugar and cinnamon—a perfect combination of ingredients. And, now that I thought of it, a perfect combination of other people's tastes and my own.

This wasn't the only time I'd benefited from watching other people at the buffet. Just a few weeks earlier, I'd seen a bunch of people eating the stuffed peppers, which looked great. But before I could get one of my own, I noticed the looks of disgust that emerged as soon as each person tried it—and saw that none of them had eaten more than a bite or two. Sure enough, a week later I overheard people saying that the peppers had been off and made several people sick—which could have been my fate if I'd dogmatically "kept my eyes on my own lane."

I shuddered. Had I been conducting "market research" without even realizing it? As much as I'd resisted Yasmin's way of doing business, I had to admit that I'd learned a lot from the lunchtime equivalent of "checking out the competition" or "surveying customer reactions." Seen in this light, even the cliques all seemed to have something to teach me: The "cool kids" might be on to something good with their popular food choices, as they were with the boba tea. The rebels might also have a valuable lesson or two for me. No, I wasn't about to pour tabasco sauce on a vanilla cake (as I'd seen one of them do), but you had to hand it to them: they sure knew how to differentiate themselves and stand out in a crowd. And speaking of standing out, whatever you thought of the theater crowd, they always managed to get attention. Even the health-obsessed jocks reminded me that my food (and my products) should be good for you. And the "buffet buffoons" reminded us all not to take things so seriously—to lighten up and have fun, no matter what we were doing or eating, or what clique someone was part of.

And then there were my sesame noodles, which didn't fit squarely into any of these categories. The meal wasn't cool or rebellious or flashy or some kind of ultra-healthy superfood, but it was exactly what I felt like eating just then—cold noodles on a hot day. And it hit the spot.

As I polished off the noodles and slurped down the last of the bubble tea, I realized that the buffet had shown me a happy medium between Yasmin's market research and Coach Hopkins' eyes-forward philosophy: an approach that applied equally to lunch and business and would let me learn from others without losing the race…or losing myself.

Lesson #27:
You can learn from others, but ultimately you have to do what feels right to you.

28. A Fitting Trend

The more I looked at the world around me, the more amazing developments I learned about—especially in the world of technology. And the more I learned, the more excited I grew about the prospects for our business. Yes, we would always strive to incorporate new developments in our own unique ways—not simply copying what other companies did. But we were running a business. And, as the Q2 report had made abundantly clear, we wouldn't be in business for long if we didn't turn things around fast.

There was no time to waste on wishful thinking and timid half measures. We needed to find a big wave and ride it! Fortunately, the tech industry was full of big waves—I just had to pick the best one for us. So, learning from my "market research" at work and at the buffet, I spent some time studying what cutting-edge companies were working on, what consumers were interested in, and how we might be able to provide something similar or, ideally, even better. And after identifying the most potentially lucrative options, I gathered the team into the conference room to let them know about our new direction.

"From now on, we're going to focus all our energy on the metaverse," I told them, only to be met by a roomful of blank stares. It's not like I expected instant, unequivocal enthusiasm, but I was disappointed not to get even a hint of support. Still, I was prepared to win them over. "It's definitely the next step in the tech world—and the world in general," I explained. "It goes beyond VR and AR and has a ton of applications in business and personal life—everything from online games to virtual workplaces, meeting rooms, and even entire worlds." Summoning my inner tech-guru, I paced around the room and gesticulated passionately. "Some experts predict that in the not-too-distant future, people might spend most of their lives in the metaverse. Besides, it's possibly the coolest thing ever. But we have to get on board *now* or we'll get left in the dust! So, are you all in?"

I leaned forward and froze in an attitude of positive expectation. But as I scanned the room, the blank stares gave way to downcast expressions and shaking heads. Admittedly, this was a pretty sophisticated concept. Maybe they just needed me to explain a bit more. I shifted from tech-guru mode to tech-professor mode. "You see, it's a way to connect and collaborate while—"

"We know what the metaverse is," Zoey said. "And we also know who we'll be up against if we try to compete in that arena."

I'd prepared for some resistance—bold new ideas are rarely accepted immediately—but I wasn't about to back down without a fight. "Yeah, but we're a small, sleek, hungry company."

"And we're going to stay *very* hungry if we try to compete with—"

"Let me put it this way," Sofia cut in. "We'd be going up against industry giants with almost unlimited resources. We just don't have the money."

"But if we get in on the ground floor, we can revolutionize the industry! We can—"

"Let me repeat," Sofia said. "Industry giants. Resources. Money."

Unlike everyone else, I still didn't think that focusing on the metaverse would be a losing battle, but trying to convince them definitely was, so I pivoted to Plan B. "Then how about another hot trend: *cloud computing*?"

This suggestion was met with more shaking heads and several groans. "That was a trend like, ten years ago," Kareem said. "We'd be way behind the competition."

"Yeah, besides, edge computing is cutting into cloud's market share," Nikhil said. "And with all the nonlocal devices involved, there'd be way too many variables for us to—"

"Okay, okay—I get it," I said. "You hate the cloud, and you hate the metaverse. However..." I paused for dramatic effect—and to pull myself together before my sulking made me look more like a petulant toddler than a visionary leader. "Here's something I know you won't hate. A trend that can help us make money *and* make a difference." I pushed my luck with one more dramatic pause before finally laying my ace on the table:

"MedTech."

At least this time I wasn't met with blank stares or vehement resistance, but the team did look skeptical, so I launched into my pitch: "Think about it—the applications are virtually endless. And I do mean *virtually*!" (No laughs, so I continued.) "Everything from virtual-reality training for surgeons to AI for early detection of diseases. We could also branch out into 3D printing for medical equipment or even vaccines for—"

"Whoa! Let me stop you right there," Tamika cut in. "First of all, we're not doctors. Nobody here knows how to train surgeons. Second of all, do you have any idea of the legal liabilities? The medical insurance alone would be staggering. And that's if everything went well, which it most likely wouldn't since, as I mentioned, *we're not doctors!*"

I may not be the world's greatest manager, but I do know how to read the energy in a room, and I could sense we were at an impasse—one that we weren't going to resolve anytime soon. So I adjourned the meeting, but not before I told them we'd pick up this conversation next week. I wasn't about to give up on my dream of being part of the Next Big Thing. Not after all that time I'd spent studying tech trends (not to mention learning surfing terminology so I could describe my vision in terms of waves: basically, we wanted to get on top of a wave at its peak, stay in the pocket as long as possible, and avoid getting caught in the impact zone).

The thing about studying a topic is that after a while, you start to see it everywhere. Even when you're not reading about it, watching videos about it, or even consciously thinking about it, it has a way of showing up in your life. That's what happened with me and trends: even when I tried to turn off that part of my brain, I saw trends wherever I looked: at the grocery store, on TV, and even at the buffet.

During my weekly visit to the buffet, I normally just grabbed my tray, loaded it up with whatever looked good, and ate my lunch at the first available table. But this Saturday was different. As I browsed the food displays, I couldn't help but notice that a lot of people were heading toward the door just beyond the condiments and going into the next room. At first it was subtle—just a few people more than usual. But it definitely picked up over time. And the more I watched, the more I realized that this wasn't just a coincidence. This was a trend.

As I studied the people coming and going from that side room, I couldn't figure it out. What was the mysterious draw? Was this something new, or had it always been this way and I'd just never noticed until now? And what was everybody getting in that room?

I tried to spot a pattern with their food, but it seemed like the same old meals as always: soups, salads, sandwiches, noodles, casseroles, and a wide variety of cuisines. So what was different?

Then it hit me: it wasn't their food that was different; it was their drinks. Regardless of what they were eating, everybody had the same kind of juice—something purple, but not grape juice or prune or borscht. It looked familiar, but I couldn't quite place it, so I stopped the next person I saw with the juice—a young woman with a friendly smile—and asked her what it was.

"Acai," the woman said.

Of course—now I recognized it. I'd tried it a long time ago and wasn't a huge fan. But something was clearly drawing these people to it—dozens or even hundreds of them. "And why is everyone drinking it today?" I asked.

"Monica," she said.

"Who?"

"On *Monica's Meals*."

"What's that?"

Her friendly smile dissolved into a look of eye-rolling contempt mixed with a hint of pity. "No offense, but have you been living under a rock?"

I tried to ignore her condescending tone and get to the bottom of the mystery trend. "So what does Monica have to do with acai juice?"

"She did a whole episode about it yesterday. Raving about how good it is—all the antioxidants and anti-inflammatories. It has so many health benefits, and it's super delicious." As if to prove her point, she took a big sip, which seemed to restore her beaming smile.

As she walked off, I wondered: was I being filmed for some sort of hidden-camera commercial for acai? (That woman seemed suspiciously perky, and her hair and makeup looked a bit *too* perfect. Hmm.) Well, commercial or not, her pitch worked, because I also wondered if I should give acai another try. Maybe I'd been too quick to dismiss it that first time. Maybe it was an acquired taste. And, on another level, this was my chance to practice what I'd been preaching at work: the importance of spotting trends and getting in early. If I truly believed that, I should put my mouth where my mouth was.

So I followed the crowd flowing into the next room, waited impatiently at the juice bar, and filled up a nice tall glass of the trendy purple potion.

In order to focus fully on the drink, I took it to a table before I got anything to eat. With high hopes, I took the first sip. Maybe this would be the moment when I finally realized what all the craze was about.

Nope, just as gross as I'd remembered.

But I wasn't going to give up so easily. I took a second sip and a third. No better.

All of a sudden, I remembered another reason why I hadn't tried it a second time—it hadn't agreed with my stomach. But maybe my body chemistry had changed since then. I should at least finish the glass. I took another sip and told myself to forget the taste and just think of all those health benefits: the fiber for improved digestion, the vitamins for a stronger immune system, the antioxidants that would…

No, I just couldn't do it. Trendy or not, I couldn't keep going. I hadn't even made it halfway through the glass, but I was done. I was glad for Monica and the smiling woman and all the other people around me who were enjoying their acai. Maybe it was right for them, but it wasn't for me. Just like…

Of course. The buffet's message of the day hit me right over the head (or, more accurately, right in the taste buds): There was nothing wrong with acai—just like there was nothing wrong with the metaverse, cloud computing, or MedTech. They just didn't align with our team's skills, strengths, and resources.

That didn't mean I was giving up on trends. I'm sure there were trendy foods out there that I'd love. Just like there were tech trends that the team would love. I just had to find the one that fit.

Lesson #28:
A great trend won't help
unless it's the right fit for you.

29. You Can't Please Everyone

Ever since that nice woman in the buffet pointed me toward the Belgian waffles, I'd never forgotten that it's okay to ask for help. Over the last few months, this had made my life so much easier at work. Instead of trying to figure everything out by myself, I'd turn to one of our experts. Yasmin helped me develop a marketing strategy. Nikhil helped me when I had tech problems. And Laney helped me with just about everything.

Getting all this help was so comforting. It was so reassuring. It was so…well, helpful.

Recently, though, this approach had been more difficult to follow— mainly because people's advice had been more difficult to follow. It started when I asked Laney about two conflicting strategies I'd been considering: should we diversify and create multiple streams of income, or should we focus on just one product or service?

For once, Laney didn't have a strong opinion (otherwise, I probably would've just gone with her suggestion); she said that either approach could work, but it was up to me to choose. So I polled the rest of the office.

Unlike Laney, Yasmin had a very strong opinion: she thought we needed to pick a lane, focus on that, and niche down as much as possible. "How can I create a consistent marketing campaign if I don't even know what our company is or what exactly we do?" she asked. "If we're all over the road, customers are going to be confused…and look elsewhere."

Liam completely disagreed. He said that, as director of sales, he wanted to give his customers as many options as possible. "I don't want to be stuck with just one product that I'm trying to ram down everyone's throat, even if it's not right for them. Give 'em choices! That's what I'd want."

Kareem said that the tech team was way too creative to focus on just one single product. "These guys are brilliant; I don't wanna rein them in." He shrugged. "Then again, developing even one product takes time, so it's not like we can give you a ton of options right out of the gate. Maybe we could focus on one thing for a while and then diversify over time." It made sense. Then again, so did the opposite approach: trying lots of things and then, after we saw which one was most successful, focusing on that.

To make matters even more confusing, Nora said that her HR feedback was pretty evenly split. Some employees said they already felt scattered with too many projects. Others said they liked the variety—it kept things from getting boring. After she summarized the opinions, she took off her purple-rimmed reading glasses, looked straight into my eyes, and said, "Personally, I think it's important to establish a clear brand. You only have one chance to make a good first impression, right?" Although she was younger than me, she flashed a comforting-grandma smile and softened her gaze. "But remember, it's okay to change your mind. At some point, most successful companies pivot."

I walked out of her office more confused than ever. Which approach was she advocating? Which one made sense to me? And which one made the most sense for our business? So much for clarity—I was still stuck at square one: torn between Option A (focus) and Option B (diversify).

So I chose Option C: put off a decision for as long as possible.

Under the guise of "mulling it over," I went home each night and did everything I could to put the question out of my mind. Instead, I focused on completely unrelated activities. I watched action movies. I read old novels. And I spent a lot of time talking with friends and family—making it clear that I did not want to discuss work. This meant that we usually ended up discussing the only other topic I was obsessed with: Maya.

As painful as this was, at least it managed to get my mind off the business dilemma and all the conflicting opinions about it. But it seemed like the same thing happened when I talked about Maya: everyone had strong opinions about what I should do, and everyone's advice was different.

Westin said I should forget her and move on with my life. Ishani said I just needed to give her some space, focus on my job, and prove to her that I really was a go-getter who valued my career. And Miles urged me to go back to her immediately and show her that *she* is the most important part of my life—not work, not money, not anything or anyone else. Give up everything else in order to gain what matters most: love.

Augghhh!

Saturday couldn't come soon enough. Never had I been more ready to spend a few hours away from the office, away from my phone, and away from my dilemmas—a few hours when my biggest decision would be whether to start with a soup, a salad, or an appetizer.

It was a beautiful morning, with just enough cloud cover to keep the July heat at bay, and the walk to the buffet boosted my spirits. Despite my confusion with work and Maya, I felt confident that the buffet would once again come through for me. So, with hope in my heart, I offered up a silent prayer as I strode along: *Please, buffet, provide the guidance I need and help me gain clarity.* I didn't know whether this request was brilliant, blasphemous, or just plain foolish. But I did know that, whether it was because of the buffet's magic or just my dumb luck, the buffet hadn't let me down yet. I quickened my pace and arrived just as they were opening the front door.

I was glad enough just to get to the buffet, and I felt even better when I saw a friendly, familiar face: the Belgian Waffle Woman. (I never did get her name.) Clearly, I hadn't made as big an impression on her as she had on me, so I had to remind her about how much she'd helped me when I so desperately wanted to find some comfort food. She looked a little puzzled but smiled and said she was glad she could help. Then her eyes lit up. "Hey, if you're looking for more comfort food, you might like what I got today." She glanced down at her tray. "It's not as sweet as waffles, but it is delicious: shepherd's pie."

I'd had shepherd's pie plenty of times and had always liked it, but for some reason it always felt like more of a fall food to me—not exactly what I had in mind for this warm summer day. Nonetheless, I didn't want to be rude, so I followed her into the next room, where she walked to a table in the corner and started scooping out a big serving of the pie. Before she could get it onto my plate, though, a stranger stepped between us.

"Hey, sorry to butt in, but I've gotta warn you—that's not the greatest shepherd's pie. They put some weird ingredient in there that—"

"I know just what you mean!" another woman cut in. "It's the bell pepper. Tastes funny…and it makes my arthritis act up. Stay away from those nightshades, young man!"

"Bell peppers are perfectly delicious," the Waffle Woman said. "Besides, he doesn't have arthritis, do you?"

"Well, I've never been officially—"

"Excuse me," another man said. "I couldn't help but overhear that you're looking for a good lunch, and I've got to recommend the pad Thai—it's absolutely delicious."

"If you want to *die*!" said a woman holding a young boy's hand. "My son's got peanut allergies, and if he takes even one bite of that stuff, he'll end up in the hospital."

Two young men walked up holding funnel cakes and big sticks of teal cotton candy. "Hey, if you're looking for a treat," one of them said, "they set up a carnival-food section in the next room." He pointed with his cotton candy.

"Are you kidding me?" said the woman with arthritis. "That stuff'll rot your teeth and clog your arteries."

"Aw, come on," said the man, glancing between the woman and me. "He looks healthy. One churro isn't gonna kill him!"

"You say that now, but that's how bad habits start. He gets a taste for fried food, and it's a slippery slope."

A man in a tight t-shirt walked over and clapped me on the shoulder. "You wanna stay healthy, my man? Stick with the Mediterranean Diet. I started it two years ago, and now that's all I eat. And check out these guns." He rolled up his sleeves and flexed his sizable biceps.

"That's not from your diet," one of the Cotton Candy Men said. "That's from—"

"You should've seen me two years ago," said the Mediterranean Man. "Trust me, there's no reason to eat anything else."

The Waffle Woman jumped back into the discussion. "Are you telling him he should only eat one thing for the rest of his life?"

"Hey, once you've found perfection, why mess with it?" He gestured at his torso.

"That's ridiculous! What about variety? What about fun? What about…"

As the argument grew increasingly heated, I was able to slip away unnoticed. At that point, I didn't even care where I was going or what I'd have for lunch—I just wanted to be on my own, clear my head, and get as far away as possible from everyone else's opinions. Without looking back, I scurried through room after room until I was confident I'd escaped the arguers.

When I finally felt safe enough to look up, I found myself right in front of one of my old favorites: spaghetti with pesto sauce. This would do the trick. The spaghetti provided the comfort I so desperately wanted, and the sauce would bring the flavor. One sniff of the aroma told me they'd used fresh basil and garlic. And it was topped not only with almond slivers but also pine nuts—a decadent treat that I usually avoided due to the price, but hey, as long as the buffet felt like being generous, who was I to pass it up?

Without thinking twice, I served myself a plateful and found a spot in a secluded corner—facing toward the wall so I wouldn't be spotted by the arguers. I could just imagine their critiques: "You need more variety!" "Where are the veggies?" "You took too much." "No, he didn't take enough." "He can always go back for more." "You should've gone for the enchiladas—they're so much better than what you've got."

I shook my head to clear out the imaginary debaters. I know they'd just been trying to help, but enough was enough. I'd listened to their suggestions, and now it was my decision, my lunch. And I was thoroughly enjoying my pesto and spaghetti.

And maybe that's what reminded me of that old saying—"throw spaghetti at the wall and see what sticks"—which made me appreciate everyone's input. After all, you never know when someone will suggest something that really sticks. And then, as much as I'd tried to forget about work, I decided that, starting next week, I'd use the spaghetti approach with our business: try a bunch of different products and services, see what sticks, and then focus on that.

I knew that some people would disagree (particularly Yasmin) and some would find it impractical (such as Kareem), but that's what I'd decided. And, just like the pasta, it felt right to me.

Lesson #29:
Advice can be helpful, but you can't please everyone. Ultimately, you have to do what feels right to you.

30. Beyond the Front Row

The following Saturday, I went to the buffet just like I'd done every other Saturday that year. I walked past rows and rows of food—an endless array of appetizers, entrées, side dishes, and desserts. Everything I saw looked wonderfully prepared, fresh, and delicious. And I didn't want any of it.

I didn't want pizza or tacos or chili or spaghetti or lasagna or even my beloved aloo saag. I didn't want french fries or mashed potatoes or macaroni salad or corn on the cob. I didn't want apples or oranges or bananas or strawberries. I didn't want peanuts or popcorn or potato chips or pretzels. I didn't even want apple pie or brownies or oatmeal-raisin cookies or chocolate cake.

It's not that there was anything wrong with any of these foods. In fact, they were all among my favorites—my go-to staples. So why didn't they appeal to me that day? I was hungry, and I was ready to eat. So what was wrong with me? I'd heard that no longer enjoying what used to give you pleasure can be a sign of depression. Was I depressed?

I did a quick check of my emotions. Admittedly, I wasn't in the greatest mood—a bit irritated, perhaps, a bit nervous about my looming work deadline, and more than a bit bummed about Maya—but I didn't feel depressed. It was something else, something different. In fact, *that's* what it was: *something different.* I was looking for something different. And all the foods I saw as I first walked through the buffet were things I'd eaten a million times before. They were obvious, predictable.

Normally, that would be fine with me. I don't need anything fancy or unusual. I enjoy apples, oranges, and peanut butter and jelly sandwiches as much as the next guy. Most days. But on this day, I was already maxed out on obvious. I'd spent the whole week immersed in obvious.

I'd been trying out my "throw spaghetti at the wall" approach—brainstorming possibilities for our company. But during the product-development meeting, each "new" idea someone suggested wasn't new at all; it was the same old thing everyone else was doing. And when I met with people one-on-one to ask for their input, they all repeated the same things we'd discussed at the meeting. Even Keiko's updated website design looked basically like the old site—minus any sign of pizazz. For some companies, this would be fine, but we were supposed to be known for our innovation, for thinking outside the box, for being the kind of company that doesn't rely on clichés (such as "thinking outside the box").

I don't know if it was a "summer slump" or just a creative rut, but all week long, I'd felt surrounded by banality. Even at the buffet—my usual haven of insight and inspiration—I couldn't shake my lingering annoyance with boring, predictable, and obvious options. So, no, I was not in the mood for an obvious meal. But every room I walked through seemed filled with cuisine I'd had more times than I could count: Chinese stir-fry, Italian pastas, Indian curries, Japanese sushi, and American comfort food, which, on this day, offered me no comfort at all. Even when I got to the room of Lebanese food, where I'd never eaten before, I saw tray after tray of familiar foods: hummus, pita, falafel, tabbouleh, stuffed grape leaves, and olives. (Granted, about a hundred varieties of olives, but still…olives.)

I was just about to move on to the next room when I happened to look just past the tray of falafel, where I saw what looked like more falafel…but wasn't. Upon closer inspection, it seemed to be fried potato balls—not exactly what I was looking for. But then I looked at the tray behind that and saw some sort of stew that looked good and smelled even better. It seemed to be packed with eggplant, peppers, and a smattering of herbs that I couldn't identify but couldn't resist. Before I realized what I was doing, I ladled myself a bowlful. But I didn't stop there.

As I pressed deeper into this section, I found something that looked like a pizza but with sauce and toppings I'd never seen on any pizza. After I took a slice of that, I helped myself to a few triangular pastries, which I'd initially thought were spanakopita but seemed to be filled with mushrooms instead of spinach. In lieu of my typical salad, I took a scoop of what looked like a combination of grains, parsley, onions, and what may have been pomegranate seeds (but don't take my word for it;

contrary to public opinion, I'm no expert on pomegranates). Regardless of what they were, though, they looked fantastic. Lastly, not to go without dessert, I took a crispy treat filled with pistachios and drizzled with honey.

Not only did this turn out to be the best lunch I'd eaten in ages, it was exactly what I needed that day: the antidote to obvious. It took me in a new direction with food and with business. And it taught me what I needed to do at the next meeting: press people to dig deeper, to look beyond the first choice, and to try something new.

Lesson #30:
Obvious ideas can work. But for true innovation, you have to dig deeper, pass up the low-hanging fruit, and reach beyond the front row.

31. A Slice of Truth

It had been the most contentious week of work we'd ever had. Maybe tempers were shorter because of the August heat wave, but all week long, it seemed like everyone was at everybody else's throat. And it all came to a boil in the Friday afternoon staff meeting, where everyone had their own idea of how we should move forward:

- Kareem, Zoey, and Nikhil thought we needed to focus on bringing new software to market.
- Liam, Yasmin, and Diego thought we needed to promote the products we already had.
- Nora thought we needed to come together through team-building exercises—and maybe even a weeklong retreat to build esprit de corps.
- Sofia thought we needed to address our cash-flow problem by tightening our belts, bringing in more money *now*, and not wasting our resources on long-term projects, marketing, or frivolous retreats. ("Perhaps it's time to downsize," Sofia concluded, looking ominously around the room.)
- And everyone thought that everyone else's ideas were stupid, bad for the company, and just plain wrong.
- Meanwhile, I thought my head was going to explode from all the competing ideas.

Everyone's ideas seemed to have at least some validity, but they seemed mutually exclusive. So who was right and who was wrong?

By the end of the week, I desperately wanted to get away from all the contentiousness and just clear my head for an hour or two. So on Saturday, I knew just what to do: head straight to the buffet, load up my plate (preferably with something spicy that would clear my sinuses—and maybe clear out some of those voices still echoing from the meeting), and find a secluded table where I could eat in solitude.

By this point, I'd learned that the buffet could be a bit of a wildcard; you never knew exactly what you'd get—in terms of food, atmosphere, or your fellow diners, who could range from quiet and polite all the way to wildly disruptive and downright bizarre. But today the buffet seemed to grant my every wish. The food all looked fresh and delicious, and the room I chose had just enough people so that I wouldn't stand out, but few enough so that I had no problem finding an empty table. And everyone seemed to be keeping to themselves—nobody making a racket, nobody causing a scene. It looked like I would actually get what I hadn't gotten all week at work: an hour of peace and happiness.

As planned, I took the spiciest food I could find—a Nigerian soup (recommended by a fellow diner, who told me it was called "egusi") and a side of hot-pepper pilau—and brought it to an out-of-the-way table in the least well-lit part of the room.

The food was every bit as delicious as I'd hoped and even spicier than I'd expected. So it wasn't long before I had to return to the beverage station to refill my drink. Just as I was pouring a glass of water, though, somebody bumped into me, spilling my (much-needed) drink all over the table. Before I could even turn around to see who'd caused the spill, I heard their voice: "Hey, watch it!"

Are you kidding me? *They* were the one who'd bumped into *me*! I should be telling *them* to watch it! I whirled around, ready to launch into them for their rudeness, but felt too flabbergasted to speak. Not to mention that my mouth was still burning from the spicy food—and, thanks to this clumsy fool, I hadn't gotten a sip of water yet.

But as soon as I saw who it was, it made a bit more sense: the offending bumper was a short old man with the thickest glasses I'd ever seen. Even though I was standing right in front of him, I'm not sure he saw me. So, hoping to avoid a repeat of our recent collision, I got out of his way and let him take my spot at the beverage station.

He leaned over, putting his nose right in front of the pitchers of water. Then he shuffled to his left and did the same thing with the pitchers of iced tea, lemonade, and fruit punch. With a huff, he walked to the soda fountain just beyond that, repeating his routine of close-up examination followed by a huff of disgust. Finally, he started hollering: "What a rip-off! There's nothing but drinks in this place! I can't make a meal out of this! I'm hungry! I need solid food!"

Was he talking to me? To the entire room? To an imaginary friend?

A yelled response from behind me told me that his friend wasn't imaginary after all. "What are you talking about, you fool?!" came the maximum-volume response. (Whoever these guys were, the concept of an "indoor voice" clearly had never reached them.)

Turning around, I saw another man of approximately the same age and size who wore equally thick glasses. Like the first man (maybe his brother?), this one was bent over a table—in this case, though, it was the dessert table. "There's plenty of food, but it's all too sweet—I want something healthy!"

"It looks healthy to me!" shouted a third voice. I looked across the room and spotted the new speaker: the spitting image of the first two, right down to the thick glasses. "But too spicy. No thank you!" I didn't have to move any closer to see the table he was examining—the one I'd just come from with the spicy soup, rice, and plates of hot peppers.

"Ha! You're a lightweight!" I turned to my right and identified the latest speaker (or, rather, shouter). Once again, it was a man who looked almost exactly like the others (who, given the striking resemblance, I now suspected were quadruplets), except that his glasses were the thickest of the bunch. "This is the blandest-looking food I've ever seen in my life!" Taking a few steps in his direction, I saw that he was examining (at extremely close quarters) a selection of white bread. "I wanted something fancy! Full of flavor! I could get this boring stuff at home!" Like the others, he huffed in disgust and turned away from the food.

"Come on!" shouted the first man. "Let's get out of this place!" And with that, the men convened in the center of the room, linked arms, and made their way toward the exit—nearly bowling over anyone who happened to be in their way—continuing to shout with every step:

"What a rip-off!"

"Totally overrated!"

"Nothing good to eat!"

"No variety at all!"

By this point, I'd seen some pretty odd characters at the buffet, but these guys might just take the cake. Aside from their unusual appearance and penchant for talking at bone-rattling volume, they were flat-out wrong. The buffet had a ton of variety—something for every taste imaginable: hot and cold, spicy and mild, soups, salads, entrées, desserts—you name it.

As glad as I was to see them go, part of me wanted to chase after the brothers (as I'm assuming they were) and explain the situation: Each of them had only looked at a tiny slice of the buffet's offering—and then assumed that the entire place was like that. Yes, each one of them was right in their own limited way (there was indeed an assortment of beverages, sweets, spicy food, and bland food), but they were also partly wrong—because they only saw one piece of the puzzle. If only I could help them see the entire picture.

But it was too late. They were gone.

However, it wasn't too late to do something similar at work. Right then I decided that in the coming week, I'd get everybody back together and explain my perspective: Everybody was right. Partly. Yes, we did need to promote the products and services we already had, but we also needed to create new ones. And yes, we did need to be mindful of the bottom line—for everyone's sake. But we also needed to invest in ourselves in order to grow. And, despite our differences, we had to pull together as a team. And that started with seeing the validity of everyone's point of view while also acknowledging our limitations—and understanding that the only way to grow was to respect others' perspectives and stay open to new ones.

In short, each of us (myself included) needed to take off our blinders, move beyond myopic tunnel vision, and embrace a "yes and" approach. If we each contributed our own special piece of the puzzle, together we could make it through this rough patch and create something beautiful.

Lesson #31:
Your perspective is valid,
but it's just one piece of the puzzle.

32. Matcha Man

When I returned to work, I was committed to boosting morale and avoiding the tunnel vision that had led to last week's contentious meeting—as well as the nearsighted brothers' complaints at the buffet. So, throughout the week—in meetings, memos, and private messages—Laney and I conveyed to each team member why their individual role was important and how it fit in with the bigger picture of the company's mission. Before long, team spirit started to improve—helped, no doubt, by the fact that sales had been picking up.

Our customer follow-up app had developed a small but loyal following, and the social media time-management tool was steadily gaining traction. We were also seeing decent returns from Nikhil's personal-finance app and its business-oriented counterpart. But the best results of all came from Zoey's latest endeavor: RateWise, an app that helped companies optimize international business by assisting with currency conversions and fluctuations—including AI-driven forecast models to help companies determine the best time to convert their holdings (e.g., from euros to dollars) based on current and expected rates.

The response was overwhelmingly positive. Customers loved RateWise. Dozens of four- and five-star reviews praised how much easier it made international business—and how much money they'd saved. Several reviews even mentioned that, by following RateWise's suggestions, they made more from the conversion process than they did from their actual sales. And every day, the glowing reports came pouring in—and so did the sales.

But then the inevitable happened: we got our first negative review.

Not just negative—scathing. Scalding. Vendetta-level.

The reviewer spent paragraph after lengthy paragraph describing why this product was a swindle, a scam, a scourge on humanity—evil incarnate. Why it didn't even deserve their one-star rating (the lowest allowed by that platform) or even zero stars, but "negative infinity" stars.

Zoey wrote a polite, professional reply, explaining that the app was not appropriate for all users, such as those who conducted only in-person local business, especially if they dealt mainly in cash (which was the case for the reviewer, as they mentioned somewhere around paragraph seven of their rant). But that didn't seem to satisfy them. As we'd soon learn, they were just getting going.

Not content to merely post a one-star diatribe and leave it at that, they went up and down the thread and replied to every other reviewer, telling them why their positive assessments were wrong, why this was the world's worst app, and why they should demand a refund and boycott our company.

Rohan went through the proper customer-service protocol, including refunding the reviewer's money in full, but that still didn't stem the tide of vitriol. Clearly, this person was on a mission. They went to every other platform where anyone had reviewed this app and, like they'd done in the initial thread, offered ruthless rebuttals to every positive review. And once they'd exhausted the available review platforms, they took to other channels: writing critical reviews and blog posts and even making a video denouncing not only the app but also anyone who used it—and, above all, the company that produced it. Us.

Sure, it was just one person's opinion, but it was enough to take the wind out of our sails—and our sales. Almost immediately, we saw a drastic reduction in downloads. And by the end of the week, our spirits were lower than they'd been in months.

By the time I got home Friday night, all the optimism I'd been feeling just a few days earlier had drained out of me, replaced by a crisis of confidence. Maybe the reviewer had been right after all. Maybe this app was morally depraved, part of everything that was wrong with modern society—eliminating face-to-face connections, destroying communities, and undermining our country's economic foundation. It's like the reviewer had infiltrated my mind, making me question everything our company did.

On top of that, I also had a splitting headache, an upset stomach, and a nagging case of déjà vu. That reviewer reminded me of someone. No, it wasn't the countless other irate reviewers who seemed to think the internet was invented for the sole purpose of public griping. Someone else. Someone I'd seen in person. But who?

The mystery bothered me all night long, all Saturday morning, and throughout my walk to the buffet. By the time I reached the buffet, though, I'd finally put it out of my mind. And that's when it hit me. Not because I remembered but because the person was literally standing right in front of me:

Matcha Man.

As I've mentioned, many of the buffet's regulars are highly irregular—people who I will charitably describe as "colorful characters" who sometimes made the dining experience what I will (again, charitably) describe as "suboptimal." One such character was Matcha Man.

The Matcha Man hates being called Matcha Man—because he hates matcha (a tea that, depending on who you ask, tastes like a cup of heaven or like a cup of grass). Truth be told, I fall into the latter camp. The one and only time I had it, I almost spit it out. So I never drank it again. And I never thought much about it…until I encountered Matcha Man.

Matcha Man seems to have made it his life mission to prevent people from drinking matcha tea. Almost every time I've been to the buffet, he's standing in front of the tea station, proclaiming to anyone who comes within earshot: "Stay away from the matcha!" And most people do—either because they don't want to invoke Matcha Man's wrath or, like me, they simply aren't fans.

But every now and then, despite MM's warnings, someone will pour themselves a cup of matcha tea. And that's when he really lets them have it: "How can you drink that swill? It's disgusting! *You're* disgusting!" Some of the accosted people seem to find MM amusing—they shake their heads and laugh. Others react with hostility—yelling right back at him, telling him to mind his own business (usually with language that's more colorful than I care to repeat). And some don't react at all—they just take their tea, go back to their table, and drink it.

I've heard that Matcha Man's efforts didn't stop with the customers. He actually took his case to the buffet's management, urging them to stop serving matcha. Supposedly (and keep in mind, this is third hand, so take it with a grain of salt—or, since we're talking about tea, a cube of sugar), he told them that black tea was the only "real" tea, and they shouldn't serve any other kinds. But he was willing to compromise as long as they stopped offering matcha, "the most evil of all beverages, consumed only by filthy degenerates" (according to MM...according to my third-hand reports).

But management stuck by their principles. "We pride ourselves on offering our customers a wide variety—something to suit every taste," they said. And so, week after week, alongside black tea, green tea, yellow tea, chamomile, chai, rooibos, earl grey, oolong, and dozens of other varieties, there was the usual pot of matcha. And week after week, right next to it, there was Matcha Man—ranting, raving, and railing against the evils of this heinous tea and the morally despicable people who drink it. Just like he was doing on the Saturday after I'd been dealing with the negative reviewer.

But unlike our previous encounters, this time I was actually glad to see him. First of all, it cleared up that déjà vu mystery. More than that, though, he cleared away my nagging doubts about Zoey's app and our business in general.

We weren't doing anything wrong. We were creating products that made life better for many people. Of course, no single product was a good fit for everyone, but that's true for all business.

Above all, Matcha Man taught me how to handle that bad reviewer— or any others who would (most likely) arise from time to time. I would handle them just like most of the buffet's customers handle Matcha Man: I would let them say their piece, and then I'd go about my business, doing whatever I would have done anyway. Maybe I would even find an amusing element in the whole experience. (After all, Matcha Man was eminently laughable.) And although I wouldn't respond with hostility, as some customers did with MM (which never seemed to end well), I would stick by my principles, like the buffet's management did. And if I had to tell the reviewers anything, I'd tell them exactly what I would tell Matcha

Man—which is exactly what I wrote in my *Lessons* notebook the moment I got home:

Lesson #32:
If you don't like something, that doesn't necessarily mean it's bad—or that the people who make it, offer it, or like it are bad. It's just not your cup of tea.

33. The Next Big Thing

I was sick of losing. And lately, that's all we seemed to do. Ever since that negative review, we were losing business. We were losing the technology race. And I was quickly losing hope.

Even with all our talent, how could we compete? There were simply too many other companies vying for the same market share. Companies with better reputations, better experience, and (if I'm being completely honest) better managers. Some of them were bigger companies with more resources. Some were small, sleek, hungry startups. And some weren't companies at all but individuals with the brains, the vision, or just the dumb luck they needed to make a big splash—and a big profit.

In the meantime, we kept sinking further and further into debt. And although it was only August, the ticking clock of the year-end deadline was growing louder every day.

To make matters worse, everyone around me seemed chipper, sanguine, and full of go-get-'em platitudes. "Cheer up, buddy," they said. "Success is just around the corner." Yeah, and so is New Year's Eve, when I'll officially lose my branch, my livelihood, and Maya.

"You're so lucky," they said. "You've got such an amazing team." Which just made me feel like the weak link who was holding everyone else back.

And every time I walked into the HR office, I had to stare at Nora's *Don't Quit Three Feet from Gold!* poster and listen to her pep talks. "We really do have a gold mine here," she said. "It's just a matter of time until the team comes up with the Next Big Thing." That was the worst of all. Not because I was opposed to gold or the Next Big Thing, but because I knew that countless other people were having this same conversation in countless other boardrooms and basements all around the country and all around the world. Everyone was trying to strike gold, but most of us were just striking out.

Maybe the rest of the team knew something I didn't that made them believe they were on the cusp of something big. But I knew something they didn't: we had a hard deadline. So if that Next Big Thing didn't show up by the end of the year, it would be the end of the line for all of us.

On the positive side, I knew something else they didn't: I had a secret advisor. And that advisor had been steering me right all year long. It had been guiding me through ups and downs, through personal and professional matters, through big decisions and small details. Maybe it could guide me toward the Next Big Thing.

The moment I remembered my mealtime mentor, adrenaline surged through my body. Of course! I didn't have to rely on the team to come up with the Next Big Thing. I could do it myself! The power was within me. Or, actually, within the buffet, but that was close enough for me.

I could hardly wait for Saturday to come so I could go on my secret mission. On the outside, it would look like just another lunch. But I knew the truth: I'd be walking into an ordinary-looking cafeteria and walking out with the Next Big Thing.

In my eagerness to get to the buffet sooner—and hence get my guidance sooner—I must have walked faster than usual, so I arrived well before noon. The front door was still locked, but a steady stream of people flowed inside through a side door. Unlike the small group waiting by the front, none of the side-door people were empty handed. They carried boxes and bags. They pushed dollies loaded with coolers and cases. They wheeled shopping carts filled with fruits and veggies.

What was going on?

I walked around the side to investigate, looked through the open door, and saw…I didn't know what. People setting up for a party? A farmer's market? A cooking demo? Or was this exactly what I'd been looking for: the Next Big Thing?

"Excuse me! Comin' through!"

I spun around and got out of the way of two women carrying a large display case. After trying several angles, they tilted the case just enough to get it through the doorway and into the room, where they soon disappeared among the bustling throng. I followed them inside and looked around, still unable to crack the code on this mystery event.

Rather than simply guess, I decided to ask someone, but everyone seemed too busy to talk. They were either setting up tables, filling up displays, or conferring with one another in urgent tones. All except for one woman who sat quietly by herself in a corner. She was so unobtrusive that I didn't notice her at first. Unlike the others, who clamored in large groups around massive displays, her only "equipment" was a folding chair and a TV tray.

"Hi," I said, approaching the woman. "Can I ask you a quick question?"

"Produce is over there." She pointed to a crowded section of the room where dozens of people were bustling around tables, laying out fruits and veggies.

"Actually," I said, "I wanted to know what's going on here?"

She smiled. "Oh, it's the vendor fair. First time?" As I nodded, she continued. "They do this every year—a way for the buffet's management to meet potential food-service providers. Mostly local farmers, but there's also delivery truckers, equipment manufacturers, kitchenware suppliers, and anyone who wants to work here: cashiers, dishwashers, chefs, bookkeepers, and even managerial positions. It's a great gig if you can get it, hence all the competition." She gestured toward the jam-packed room.

"What about you?" I glanced down at her TV tray, which contained only a few pamphlets and a small stack of business cards. "No offense, but you don't seem to be competing very hard."

She laughed. "You know a lot of people around here who repair industrial-sized ovens?" As I shook my head, she said, "That's because there's only one, and you're talking to her." She handed me a business card that read:

Annie's Oven Repair
Industrial Kitchen Specialist

I returned the card to the TV tray and tried to back away, but it was too crowded to move. Since Annie and I were stuck together for the moment, I tried to think of a way to keep the conversation going. But what could I say about industrial oven repair? Unfortunately, what I came up with was probably one of the rudest things I could've asked a stranger (or anyone, for that matter): "You really make a living doing just this?"

"Nothing else. Twenty-two years now." She shrugged. "I admit, it isn't exactly a gold mine, but at least I don't have to fight off those guys." She pointed at the produce vendors jockeying for position across the room.

As she said the words *gold mine*, the back of my neck shivered and my brain kicked into another gear. "What did you say?"

"Yeah, it's just me. So all I've gotta do is show up once a year, give my standard pitch, and sign the renewal contract. Basically a formality at this point, but they still make me—"

"No, no, no. About the gold mine."

She laughed again. "Yeah, well, let's just say it's more of a *copper* mine. But hey, you can make a decent living from copper—even if it isn't the Next Big Thing."

The crowded room suddenly seemed to grow quiet, and enough space opened up for me to squeeze out. I muttered a few parting words and made my way back to the buffet's front door just as it officially opened.

I was so preoccupied by Annie's words that I barely noticed my lunch. But that wasn't why I'd come. I'd come to find the Next Big Thing, but I left with something even better: the next small step.

Lesson #33:
Instead of running the same race as everyone else,
carve out your own lane…and win.

34. Stick with It

The buffet had lied to me. And just like that, the whole façade came crashing down.

It was bound to happen sooner or later. After months of magical thinking, my whole buffet-as-business-guru delusion was shattered in a single week.

The worst part is, I'd never been more confident in the buffet's abilities. I'd trusted it. I'd put my fate in its hands. When I wanted to find the Next Big Thing, I looked for it at the buffet. And when it told me to forget about the Next Big Thing—to focus instead on a slow-and-steady, niched-down offering—that's the approach I took.

Looking to come up with our own "copper mine" equivalent of Annie's Oven Repair, I pitched ideas to Laney first thing Monday morning. For once, she was completely on board. So was the rest of the team. And together we came up with a new direction and a new tagline: "Customized Technology Solutions."

We decided to market our services to big companies with big budgets and big goals—but without the technology know-how to bring them to life. We would provide the tech, and they would provide the money. With our proposed arrangement, we wouldn't get credit (kind of like tech ghostwriters), but we would get paid.

No, it wasn't as flashy as developing a universally used software suite. And because of the ghostwriting (or "ghost-teching") arrangement, it wouldn't even put us on the map. But although it wasn't a million-dollar app or a billion-dollar business model, it was a path to profitability. And right then, that's what we needed.

Monday afternoon, Keiko created a functional webpage, Yasmin devised a marketing plan, and Diego wrote an irresistible sales script. And Tuesday morning, Liam organized a sales force—which, for this project, meant almost all of us—and we hit the ground running. We hit the phones. We hit the pavement. And no matter how many prospects we talked to, we always hit a brick wall.

By the end of the day, we had absolutely nothing to show for our efforts.

But we all knew that Silicon Valley wasn't built in a day. So we picked up where we left off on Wednesday. And although we got the same results (or lack thereof), we tried again on Thursday and again on Friday—methodically working our way through our list of leads.

Over the course of the week, we contacted dozens of prospects in person, hundreds more on the phone, and thousands via email. And it all amounted to a big fat zero. No clients. No contracts. No follow-up meetings. Not even a nibble.

I'd love to tell you that we kept our spirits up and our can-do attitudes intact. But I won't lie; it was discouraging. The team was demoralized. And I was furious.

Not furious at the team or even furious at myself. Furious at the buffet. I had put my faith in its guidance, and it had betrayed me. I'd done everything it had told me to: Niche down. Differentiate. Forget about the Next Big Thing. Stop trying to strike gold and just go for "copper"—something boring but safe and reliable. In other words, get rich slow. Instead, we were getting nowhere fast.

That Saturday I had half a mind to blow off my weekly "lunch date" and go somewhere else—or just stay home and heat up another frozen meal. Or maybe I'd order takeout. I had plenty of options, even without the buffet. And if it was expecting me, too bad. It would see how it feels to be let down.

On the other hand, I had a few choice words for this betrayer, and I wanted to deliver them in person (even if the words were only in my mind). And I wanted to see what it had to say for itself, what excuse it might come up with for steering me so wrong. Also, if I'm being honest, I was still holding out hope that this had all been a big misunderstanding, that my delusion wasn't a delusion after all. Maybe the buffet wasn't just a big heap of bricks, mortar, linoleum, and lunch. Maybe it really was a wise mentor that cared about me and had my best interests in mind. And maybe it would provide some new guidance that would make everything better…or at least make sense. Not likely, but worth a shot.

So, with a mixture of vengeful fury, swallowed pride, and skeptical curiosity, I set out on my weekly pilgrimage. And this week, I didn't just want guidance for my business, I wanted to reveal the mystery of the buffet itself—to find out once and for all whether it was the real deal or just a delusion.

It didn't take me long to get my answer: the buffet was a fraud.

There was nothing magic about it. Nothing supernatural, wise, kind, or nurturing. All that supposed guidance had just been in my head. Wishful thinking. Coincidences that I'd assigned meaning to.

Actually, this was a generous interpretation. Because if it did have special powers or awareness, then it wasn't a wise, benevolent guru after all; it was just plain cruel. All year I'd done exactly what it had suggested, especially this past week, when I'd revamped my entire business in order to avoid an overcrowded field. Yet at the end of the week, what did it give me?

A crowd!

Ah, the cruel irony of it all. As if it weren't bad enough that the buffet's guidance had gotten me nowhere, now it had to rub salt in my wounds by plunking me right in the midst of the biggest crowd I'd ever seen. And not just any old crowd—a crowd of hot, sweaty, stinky, rowdy, and obnoxiously loud teenagers and young adults (and I use the word loosely—based solely on estimated age, not behavior).

Chronologically, I wasn't *that* much older than them (I still felt too young to consider myself middle aged, regardless of what these whippersnappers might think of me and my suddenly stodgy attitude), but they somehow seemed to be from a different generation, a different era—like they'd been transported here for the sole purpose of tormenting me. And right off the bat, they were doing a good job of it.

Before I even got to the buffet, I was being jostled by this crowd of…what exactly were they? A flash mob? No, they weren't dancing. Maybe some sort of large-scale scavenger hunt or geocaching event? Couldn't be—no one was looking for anything. Maybe a sporting event? There seemed to be a pickup football game in the parking lot, but there were way too many people for that—and too many other games going on simultaneously: frisbees, hacky-sacks, beach balls, and several bizarre-looking objects being thrown, kicked, and occasionally caught by various members of the sweaty swarm. The whole scene felt way too chaotic to be any sort of organized event, but also way too big not to be. Well, whatever this was, I'd be glad to get inside the buffet and enjoy a quiet lunch far from the madding (and maddening) crowd.

I tried to push my way toward the buffet, but the closer I got, the denser the crowd grew. Maybe it was from seeing all those footballs flying around me, but I suddenly felt like a running back trying to push my way through a wall of linebackers. And before I could get to the door, the heftiest linebacker of all nearly tackled me to the sidewalk.

"Hey! No cutting!" he yelled.

"It's okay," I said, swallowing hard and pointing to the door, "I'm just going to the buffet."

"Yeah, so are all these people." He gestured at the chaotic throng around us. "Back of the line!" To provide a head start toward this destination, he gave me a forceful shove. I staggered back a few steps, stopping only when I bumped into someone behind me.

"Watch it, man!"

I tried to mutter a half-hearted apology to the guy I'd collided with, but I couldn't get the words out. My mind was too busy processing the full horror of the situation: all these people weren't just milling about or passing through on their way somewhere else; they were going to the buffet.

Now the question became: *was I?* Or, more realistically: *could I?* Would there be time to even make it in the door—much less eat a decent meal—before closing time?

Keeping my options open, I made my way to the back of the "line" (which, by the way, didn't remotely resemble an actual line—more like an elongated blob—but this was no time for geometrical hair-splitting). As I walked through the crowd, the shock gradually wore off and the anger kicked in. I was angry at the jerk who'd pushed me. I was angry at the guy who'd yelled at me (as if it was my fault I'd bumped into him). I was angry at the entire crowd. But most of all, I was angry at the buffet.

It had misled me. It had told me to avoid crowds but then thrown me into the biggest crowd I'd ever seen. If it was intentionally tormenting me, it was just being needlessly cruel. And even if it didn't know what it was doing, it had still led me on and let me down. In either case, it had led me astray and, if I'm being honest, broken my heart.

So why would I give it another chance?

I wouldn't. That was it. I was done. I was going home. Or going somewhere else. In any case, *leaving*.

By the time I emerged from the crowd, my mind was made up. Yet for some reason, my feet had other plans. They stopped walking, turned me around, and planted me at the back of the so-called line. It made absolutely no sense to stay there. And to make matters worse, I was directly behind (and, unfortunately, well within smelling range of) a sweaty college-age kid wearing nothing but cutoffs and flip-flops.

Had I really not gotten the message? Or was I just a glutton for punishment? Why would I stay here after all the buffet had put me through? And if I really was going to stick it out for one last meal (that is, if I even made it to the front door before closing time), why did it have to be today—when I'd be forced to wait behind this shirtless sweatmonger?

Again, it made no sense. And yet, I stayed.

As I parked myself behind the sweaty young man, he gave me a micro-nod laced with the merest hint of a smile. Oh, no—did he expect me to talk to him? Just because we were stuck together in this so-called line didn't mean we needed to buddy up, did it? With everything swirling around my brain, the last thing I wanted was to get into a conversation, especially with someone who smelled like a high school locker room. But I knew I'd be stuck next to this guy for at least half an hour, and I didn't want to get off on the wrong foot (as I'd done with the linebacker), so I returned the nod and introduced myself. He said his name was Steve (which instantly led me to dub him "Stinky Steve"), and then, thank goodness, he kept to himself. So he did have a saving grace after all. After ten or fifteen slow-moving minutes, however, curiosity got the better of me, and I was the one who initiated a conversation. "So, what exactly is going on here?"

He looked confused. "What do you mean? Like—"

"All these people. What's with the crowd?"

A girl in front of Steve whirled around, looking like I'd just mortally offended her. "Are you kidding me, gramps? Like, what planet are you on?"

"I just…I didn't know if—"

"It's Triple M-Fest, dingbat." She turned back around as if she'd thoroughly answered my question, but I was more in the dark than ever.

Fortunately, Stinky Steve explained: "The Mongo Megillah Music Festival. It's at the Fairgrounds."

"So why is everyone here?" I asked.

"The buffet's giving a free lunch with every ticket."

Ugh! This day just kept getting worse! First this ravenous swarm was going to make me get to the buffet late, if at all. Then they were going to eat everything in sight for free, leaving me with scraps, if anything. But worst of all, I found out I'd been taking business advice from an establishment that gives away its food to a hungry mob. What kind of "best practice" is that? They'd be out of business by the end of the week…and so would I! No wonder nothing was working out for me. *This* was my mentor?! This was my model?! Suddenly, it all made sense—not that this made things any better.

And yet, for some reason, I stayed.

Steve pulled a small book from his back pocket and quickly became absorbed in reading. And I was left to my thoughts. Which was not a good thing. After replaying my mental tirade against the buffet, I turned my wrath inward, berating myself for staying here. From an emotional, psychological, and business standpoint, I had plenty of reasons to leave, but my biggest reason was a practical concern: I'd been waiting for almost twenty minutes, the line had barely moved, and I was still a long way from the entrance. Eventually, my need to vent overcame my aversion to conversation.

"We're never gonna make it," I said. "They close in just over an hour."

Steve lowered his book, glanced toward the buffet's entrance, then looked at me. "Let's stick with it."

I shook my head. "It's pointless. The line's moving too slow. We won't make it in time."

He shrugged and, as he turned his attention back to his book, said softly, "We'll see."

He didn't know what a fine line he was walking with those two words. With just the slightest change of tone, they might have sounded patronizing and made me want to smack him. (Not that I'd actually smack anyone—I'm a peaceful guy—but it might've taken a little extra effort to hold myself back.) However, his words came across without any judgment—more like a little experiment he was curious to observe and see how it played out. So, I did my best to stuff down my exasperation and adopt Steve's experimental attitude. Would we make it to the buffet in time? The odds were not in our favor, but…we would see.

After another ten minutes I *could* see: we were not going to make it. It was no longer a question of odds; it was basic math: at the line's current rate of progress, it would take us over an hour to reach the front door. The buffet would be closed, and I would have wasted two hours of my life inhaling Steve's B.O. But at least I'd be able to tell him I told ya so. So, if for no other reason than the bitter satisfaction of being miserable but right, I took Steve's advice and stuck with it.

And eventually, the line began to move faster—almost imperceptibly at first, but after ten or fifteen minutes, we were making decent progress. Looking around, it wasn't hard to see why—people were doing exactly what I'd been on the brink of doing: giving up and leaving. And with every drop-out, the line moved a bit faster. It was still far from certain that we'd make it to the buffet in time, but it was no longer mathematically impossible.

And sure enough, by 1:15, the front door was in sight. As we approached the entrance, Steve put his book away in one back pocket and, from the other one, pulled out a crumpled tank top (which, along with his flip-flops, met the bare minimum for the buffet's shirt-and-shoes requirement). When we reached the door, he held it open for me.

"Well, you were right," I said as we stepped inside. "We made it."

Again, he offered just the merest hint of a nod and a smile. I intended to return the subtle acknowledgement, but before I could, I saw something that filled me with too much horror to even think about smiling: we had just gone out of the frying pan and into the fire. (Forgive the cliché, but it seemed appropriate for a restaurant on the hottest day of the year.) By making it into the buffet, we hadn't beaten the crowd; we'd joined them. The place was so packed, we could hardly move.

I groaned. "Look at this place! I don't even know if we should keep going."

Steve shrugged. "Let's stick with it."

"But we can barely move. And with all these people in front of us, there won't be any food left."

"We'll see," he said. And with that, he dug out a ticket from his front pocket and stepped up to the cashier, who stamped his ticket and ushered him inside.

Because I didn't have a festival ticket, I had to pay the usual fee. Would it be worth it? After all, there'd probably be nothing left to eat. Nonetheless, I figured I'd once again take Steve's advice and stick with it, even if just to prove him wrong. So I forked over the fee and took a step toward the food. Or rather, I attempted to take a step toward where the food used to be. Given the crowd, I could only manage a shuffle or two, but that was enough to see that my fears had been justified: all the serving dishes had been picked clean.

Steve and I shuffled our way through room after room, doing our best to avoid elbows, feet, and head-on collisions but nonetheless got continuously jostled by the crowd. As we passed row after row of steam trays that contained nothing but scraps, I was reminded of a book I'd read as a kid where a swarm of Australian locusts eats every leaf from a forest of eucalyptus trees, leaving nothing for the koalas who live there. As I watched the crowds devouring the little bits of remaining food, however, I realized that a more apt comparison might be a feeding frenzy of piranhas. Every time I saw a morsel of available food, someone pushed in front of me and snatched it up.

After this scene had played itself out a dozen times or more (culminating when I missed getting the last falafel by mere seconds), I let out an exasperated sigh and turned to Steve. "This is ridiculous! We're never gonna get anything to eat."

Once again, Steve offered his standard bit of advice: "Let's stick with it."

I glanced at my watch: 1:27. "But we've only got half an hour. Even if there is something left, we don't have enough time to find it and eat it."

Once again, he shrugged. "We'll see."

Maybe he was right. We *will* see! In fact, I already could see the situation quite clearly. I turned around to survey the room, and everywhere I looked confirmed what I already knew: there was nothing to eat!

I turned back to Steve to point out this obvious fact, but he was gone. Well, good riddance. His two-line shtick was getting on my nerves. And it hadn't gotten me any closer to getting a decent meal.

But I'd already come this far, so I figured I might as well see this thing through to the bitter end—no matter how bitter it ended up being. So I kept on pushing, shuffling, and groaning my way from one room to the next, always finding variations of the same scene: a boisterous crowd snatching up the few remaining bits of food.

Every cell in my body (especially those in my stomach) was telling me to leave—to turn around, walk out the door, and find another place to eat—someplace where I wouldn't have to fight crowds and make do with scraps (if I was lucky), someplace where I could simply order whatever meal I wanted and eat it in peace. But, although this sounded like a sensible plan, an inner voice told me not to give up, to keep going and keep looking. So I did.

I kept walking from one room to the next, looking for food, and running into the same situation: full rooms with empty serving dishes. However, as I walked on, I noticed that the rooms were getting slightly less full. I even saw a few empty spots at some of the tables. With every room I passed, it seemed like more and more people had either gotten their meals already or given up and left. And although I still didn't find anything that would constitute a meal, I did feel a glimmer of hope. (And another childhood memory sprang to mind: a cartoon flea singing, "There's food around the corner, food around the corner, food around the corner for me.")

But there wasn't food around the corner...or the next or the next or the next. And by 1:38, I began to despair of getting even a morsel before closing time. Eventually, though, I found my way to a nearly empty room. And although I didn't see any remaining food, I did see something else that caught my eye: a small wooden door partially obscured behind a curtain. I investigated and found that it was slightly ajar. I pushed it open and walked through, into a dimly lit room I'd never been to before. It took a moment for my eyes to adjust to what I will generously call "mood lighting," but once they did, I beheld...no, it wasn't exactly the miracle I'd been searching for (the buffet's usual cornucopia of endless gourmet options), but it was something that, in that moment, felt even better: a serving table full of ready-made meals.

There were only a few other people in the room, so I didn't seem in danger of having the food snatched away once again. Still, after my many near-misses, I knew better than to hesitate. And hey, the food was there for the taking, so I took.

In another minor miracle, I had no problem finding an empty table. So, with not a minute to lose, I sat down and started scarfing down the food. It wasn't the most gourmet meal I'd ever had—a veggie wrap with a side salad, a pear, a brownie, and a tall glass of room-temperature water—but it was the most satisfying meal I could remember eating in a very long time.

I didn't even look up from my food until I'd almost finished. But as I polished off the last few bites of brownie, I scanned the room and noticed a familiar face at a table in the opposite corner. And just as I saw him, Stinky Steve looked up from his own meal. As we locked eyes, he offered me one last micro-nod and the hint of a smile, which I acknowledged and returned.

And in that moment, I also acknowledged that he'd been right to encourage me to stick with it. And I acknowledged that maybe the buffet hadn't misled me after all. Maybe it had taught me my most important lesson of the whole year—one that I definitely needed to apply outside of the buffet as well. In fact, I was so eager to get back to work so I could pass along Steve's message to the whole team—to tell them not to give up on our new "copper mine" plan—that I could hardly wait for Tuesday morning. (Because we were off Monday for Labor Day, I'd have to wait an extra day—something that brought joy to most people but impatience for me. Plus, my arrival at the office was further delayed by a prescheduled appointment [a standard physical check-up—no issues, fortunately]).

When I finally got into the office—just after eleven on Tuesday morning—I practically burst through the door and ran to see Laney. I didn't want to waste another second before I told her that we needed to stick with it, persevere, and above all, be patient. But she was preoccupied—deeply engaged in conversation with a man I'd never seen before. I didn't want to wait to talk to her, but I also didn't want to interrupt or pry into her personal business (although I didn't know if the situation was personal or business). Nonetheless, I let curiosity get the better of me. I walked over to the front desk and asked Brenda, "Who's that man with Laney?"

Looking up from her computer, she glanced across the office at the two of them and then turned back to me. "That's Dave from Pinnacle," she said.

"What's Pinnacle?" I asked.

She flashed a Stinky Steve-esque half-smile as she casually replied. "Oh, they're our new client."

Lesson #34:
Perseverance doesn't guarantee success, but it does make it possible.

35. How to Eat a Watermelon

Overwhelm. That was the word of the week. Everyone was pushing hard to keep up with their various projects: Kareem's new mobile app, Nikhil's security upgrade, and Zoey's mission of converting Kareem's old headset idea from VR to AR, which (as she explained) would create an augmented reality that allowed users to overlay digital products (such as home-furnishing prototypes) into their real world (such as their living room). Now, on top of all this, we also had the Pinnacle project.

Don't get me wrong—we were all thrilled to have the account, but it was requiring way more time and effort than we'd initially expected. Somehow, we were supposed to design and test new proprietary software for them and have it ready in time for their seasonal training program, six weeks from now.

It seemed doable enough at first, but each step forward seemed to reveal two more hidden steps we'd have to take. I had a hard time imagining we could finish it before next *year*, much less by next month.

All week long, the project consumed my mind and took up almost every waking hour. So by Saturday, I really just needed some downtime— even an hour or two to clear my head. I needed some peace and quiet. I needed the buffet.

Just my luck, though—the buffet was far from peaceful and quiet. Jam-packed with a raucous crowd, it felt less like a quiet lunch spot than a…oh no, was that Mongo Megillah thing still going on? I'd thought it was just last weekend, but maybe some of the people had stayed longer. The crowd wasn't nearly as big as last week's, but it was still bigger than anything else I'd seen all year.

I couldn't figure it out—until I saw the three-word banner that made everything clear:

WATERMELON-EATING CONTEST

At least it wasn't a music festival, but it was still a far cry from my visions of a relaxing lunch. Nonetheless, curiosity got the best of me, and I followed the flow into the central dining room. After a few minutes, I managed to make my way to the front of the crowd where I could watch the action: a long table where about a dozen men and several women shoveled bite after bite of watermelon into their mouths.

A poster to their right explained the rules:

- Each contestant had two hours to eat an entire watermelon (everything but the rind—no red remaining).
- Each watermelon had to be at least twenty pounds.
- Anyone who succeeded would be given vouchers for ten free meals at the buffet.

The contest was just getting underway, so the watermelons were still mostly intact, which meant I could see just how huge they looked compared to the people who were eating them. How on earth could anyone eat twenty pounds of *anything*—much less in two hours?

Once again, I cursed my terrible luck. I'd just wanted to forget my work problems for a while, but here I was, confronted with exactly what I'd been trying to escape: a seemingly insurmountable task with a seemingly impossible time frame.

Already, some of the contestants' faces seemed to be turning green. Or maybe it was just the rinds' reflection. Or maybe I was projecting how *I* felt. Just the sight of all those people gorging themselves sickened me. It was nauseating. It was unnatural, unnecessary, and, in my opinion, undoable. How could anyone possibly succeed? Especially that older woman near the end. She couldn't have been more than ninety pounds, so the watermelon was roughly a quarter of her weight! As I watched her, two thoughts flashed through my mind: 1. This can't possibly end well for her, and 2. I hope the buffet has good insurance and at least one EMT on hand.

I knew exactly what I should do: just walk away. After all, the buffet still had plenty of rooms that weren't occupied by watermelon eaters. I didn't have to watch. I could just treat it like any other Saturday: find a good meal, find a quiet table, and enjoy my lunch.

But something about the whole spectacle mesmerized me. As disgusting as it was, some internal force compelled me to watch. With a sigh, I resigned myself to an afternoon of gluttony-gazing.

Not wanting to miss out on my own meal, I grabbed a few slices of pizza (not the buffet's specialty—but good enough…and easily portable) and brought them back to the site of the main attraction: the watermelons.

At second glance, I realized that the watermelons weren't abnormally big, but they were still pretty sizable: the kind you'd expect to be shared among a few dozen people at an all-day picnic—not scarfed down by a single person in a single sitting. Underneath the rules, the poster explained that a twenty-pound watermelon yielded about sixty-six normal-sized wedges—enough for about thirty-three people to eat a normal serving size of two wedges apiece. But this contest was anything but normal.

The poster also noted that a twenty-pound watermelon had approximately 2700 calories. That was a lot…but not impossible—about a third more than a typical day's caloric intake. Still, the contestants didn't have all day—they just had two hours (or, by this point, just under ninety minutes). To get through it all, they'd have to really rush. And they were doing exactly that.

All of them except the small woman, that is. She was taking her sweet old time. Not exactly dawdling, but not going even close to fast enough to finish the watermelon in two hours. At this rate she wasn't likely to win the contest, but at least she probably wouldn't end up in the hospital.

I wondered if she was even *trying* to eat the whole thing or if she just liked watermelon and felt like having that for lunch. In any case, she clearly had her own methodical approach: One spoonful, one bite, then another. Take a scoop, spit out the seeds, chew, swallow, repeat.

Although she didn't stand a chance in the competition, I found my eyes drawn to her. Watching her make her way through the watermelon was meditative—almost hypnotic. And in spite of myself, I found myself getting sucked in by the process. And then I found myself doing the last thing I wanted to do: thinking about work. Except now, that huge, impossible project suddenly didn't seem so huge or impossible. I realized that we didn't have to do it all, just one small part of it: Clarify Pinnacle's target user. Period. Pinpoint their objectives. Period. Write a training manual. No, not even that—write the *outline* for a training manual, and then write the first section.

Yes, it was a big project. But no single step was too big to handle. The small woman didn't have to "eat a watermelon"—she just had to eat one bite (and then another and then another). Likewise, we didn't have to "finish the project"—we just had to take one small step. And once that was done, we'd take the next. And then the next and the next and the next, until—

A megaphone's screech snapped me out of my work ruminations. "Attention watermelon eaters! You have ten minutes remaining!"

Along with the rest of the crowd, I pushed as close as I could to the contestants, cheering them on as they came down the home stretch. By this point, only two of the original contestants remained. One was a big man who'd been speeding through the early portion of the contest but now had slowed to a near halt and didn't look close enough to finish in time. He seemed to realize this at the same moment that I did, and he set down his spoon with an expression that mixed nausea, exhaustion, and relief.

And that left only one remaining contestant: the small woman.

As the final minutes ticked down, she finished off the watermelon in exactly the same way as she'd eaten throughout the competition: Calmly. Methodically. Steadily. One bite at a time. There was no rush, no worry, no overwhelm. She knew what she had to do.

And so did I.

Lesson #35:
***Even the biggest task is manageable if you break it
into bite-sized pieces.***

36. Mr. Macaroni

The old couple was so engrossed in their conversation that I don't think they noticed me, even as they sat down directly across the table. While I silently worked my way through a plate of tamales, the couple kept right on talking as if no one else was around. "I told you," the woman said as she set down her tray.

"But you didn't know," the man replied. "You were just guessing."

"It's the same every week."

"But you didn't *know!*" He emphasized his final word with a theatrical shake of his napkin, which he then spread in his lap. "It could've been different this time."

The woman shook her head and spoke to me, as if continuing a conversation with an old friend. (So I guess they had noticed me and just had far fewer social inhibitions than I did.) "Can you believe this clown I'm married to?" She jerked her thumb at her husband, who had closed his eyes and was chewing a huge bite of macaroni salad in rapturous silence. "It's always here, always good. But every Saturday morning we go through the same thing: 'What if they're out of macaroni salad? I gotta have my macaroni salad! We need to hurry before it's gone!'"

The man swallowed his bite, opened his eyes, and dabbed his lips with his napkin. "Forgive me if I enjoy my weekly indulgence." Just as his wife had done, he spoke directly to me without any preamble or introduction. "You have to admit they make a fine macaroni salad here. And I, for one, do not wanna miss out."

As her husband stated his case, the woman kept speaking to me, vying for my attention. "And every week I tell him the same thing: 'They're not gonna run out!'"

"But you don't *know!*" He turned toward her and flipped his palms up, gesticulating as he spoke. "Just because they've had it before doesn't mean they'll have it again."

As if her husband hadn't said anything, the woman kept right on speaking to me. "The whole morning, he worries. The whole ride over, he worries. Even when we get here, he still worries…until he finally gets his beloved macaroni salad." She shook her head and laughed. "But even then, do you think he's satisfied? Ha! As soon as we get home, he starts worrying about *next* time!"

A wave of concern washed over the man's face. "But you never know—what if that's the week they run out…or stop making it forever?"

She turned to him and shrugged. "Then you get something else." She pivoted in her seat and waved her arm behind her. "They've got a whole smorgasbord—room after room. You don't need to eat the same thing every time." She turned back to me and gestured toward her plate, which contained a collection of side dishes, none of which was macaroni. "Me? I like a little variety."

"Why mess around?" the man said. "When you find something you like, you stick with it." He turned toward his wife and planted a big kiss on her lips.

She squeezed his shoulder and kissed him back. "Don't worry, baby. I'm stickin'." She turned back to me with a smile. "Fifty-two years with this worrywart. Can you believe it?"

As I watched the couple, something stirred within me—a gnawing in my gut that I couldn't quite put into words.

My first thought was of Maya. This is what I wanted with her. To grow old together. To have our routines together. To have the same conversations, the same worries, the same food. (Except for me, instead of macaroni salad, it would be aloo saag.) This is why I was doing what I was doing. This is why I worked so hard and worried so much. This is why failure was not an option.

But there was more to this feeling than just a vision of a shared life. There was something unsettling—something that stayed with me long after I said goodbye to the old couple, long after I left the buffet—a worrisome half-awareness that kept me up at night and followed me throughout the coming days, even as I went about my daily business at work.

I didn't know exactly what it was, but I still worried about it. I worried about it during our team meetings. I worried about it when I checked in with Kareem. I worried about it when I worked late with Laney. And I especially worried about it whenever we discussed the Pinnacle account.

Then, on the morning before Pinnacle's second payment was scheduled to go through, the feeling intensified until I finally figured out what it was: *worry*.

The feeling wasn't new. It had been floating around my gut all year (and probably longer)—usually as a low-level background sensation, like a refrigerator's hum you don't notice until it stops...or someone points it out to you. But I'd come face to face with this feeling when I met the old couple in the buffet. (I never did get their names, so I just think of them as Mr. and Mrs. Macaroni.)

Yes, on one level their banter was endearing, and Mr. Macaroni's worrying was kind of funny. But on another level, it wasn't funny at all. It was sad. It was sad how his worrying robbed him of what should have been a wonderful experience—eating his favorite food with his favorite person. His worries hounded him for almost the entire week, abating only while he ate his lunch—then attacking once again. Instead of enjoying a routine he loved, he spent the week dreading worst-case scenarios. (Worst-case in his mind, that is—meaning that, for one reason or another, the buffet wouldn't have macaroni salad.) Scenarios that never materialized but hurt him almost as much as if they had. And obviously, all his worrying about the macaroni salad didn't make it more likely that it would be there. And it didn't help protect him from the pain he would've felt if it hadn't been there. It just made him experience all that pain almost all the time, regardless of what actually did or didn't happen.

It was so obvious. And ludicrous. And easily prevented.

And yet I'd been doing the same thing.

Every day I was plagued by worries. What if Pinnacle doesn't pay on time? "They'll be on time," Sofia assured me. "They set up automatic payments."

What if they don't like our software? "They already love it," Kareem said. "They can't stop raving about the prototype."

What if they're unhappy with our service? "They couldn't be happier," Rohan said. "Dave calls every other day to tell me how thrilled they are."

What if something goes wrong and we're held legally responsible? "That's why I put the no-fault clause in the contract," Tamika said. "Nothing to worry about."

But that just made me worry even more. I worried about Pinnacle. I worried about the branch in general. I worried about becoming profitable in time. I worried about my future. I worried about Maya.

"Worrying doesn't help us," Laney often told me. And of course she was right. I knew that. But I didn't *really* know it—didn't *feel* it—until I met Mr. Macaroni. And although I couldn't just flip a switch and turn off my worries (I had too much riding on the outcome), I could do things that actually helped: working harder, staying on top of the Pinnacle account, brainstorming other ways to bring in more revenue, and keeping the team's morale as high as possible.

But worrying didn't do any of this. It just stopped me from enjoying the success we did have. It wasted my time and energy. And it turned me into someone I didn't want to be: Mr. Macaroni.

Lesson #36:
**Worry is not preparation, nor is it productive,
constructive, or beneficial.**

37. GOMO

There was good news and bad news at work.

The good news was that things were going great—ideas were flowing, the Pinnacle project was moving along nicely, and we had a ton of great additional opportunities.

The bad news was that things were going great—ideas were flowing, the Pinnacle project was moving along nicely, and we had a ton of great additional opportunities. Which meant we had some very hard decisions.

We would inevitably have to forego some of those great opportunities. We simply couldn't be everywhere at once, doing everything at once. We couldn't have our tech team focusing on the Pinnacle project while also working on our security upgrade, the new mobile app, and the AR headset all at once. We couldn't send our three-person marketing team to all seven networking conferences they wanted to attend. Yes, we could do *some* of what we wanted to do—maybe one or two tech projects and one conference—but as much as it pained me to admit it, I knew we were going to miss out on a lot.

Don't get me wrong—I'm not complaining. After all our struggles throughout the year, I was thrilled to see everyone coming together as a team, supporting one another, and feeling enthusiastic about their individual contributions. The excitement in the office was palpable. I looked forward to coming to work each day, and it seemed like everyone else did too.

Zoey and Nikhil had finally set aside their quantum-vs.-binary debate to focus on their joint project. Kareem actually seemed energized by all his extra coding. And Laney and I had settled into a comfortable routine that we both enjoyed, even though it meant coming in early, staying late, and working through dinner—usually take-out in the conference room, where we made our way through piles of paperwork and cartons of lo mein.

Somehow, the shared mission seemed to bring us closer together and made me excited to be at work. So I actually had to force myself to step away for the weekend. I knew it was important to find balance—to take time off to rest, handle a few personal matters, and clean my apartment (which had gotten pretty slobbed-out over the past few weeks). And of course, now that the buffet and I were on good terms once again, I was once again looking forward to my weekly lunch date/career-counseling sessions.

I stepped out of my apartment Saturday morning, prepared for my weekly walk (or so I thought), and immediately turned around and went back inside. The weather must have seen the calendar. Autumn had just arrived, and right on schedule, the air had grown chilly. But once I traded my light hoodie for a warm fall jacket, I felt comfortable and ready to roll.

The brisk air and the brisk walk invigorated me, and by the time I reached the buffet, I was feeling enthusiastic about the day, the meal ahead, and the prospect of my weekly inspirational guidance. Truth be told, though, things were going so well that I didn't feel like I needed much guidance. Yes, I'd been through some rough patches, but that was all in the past. From now on, life was presenting me with an amazing array of amazing options—and so was the buffet.

Maybe it was just my optimistic mood, but as I explored the possibilities, everything looked extra delicious. Meals I'd never tried seemed to beckon me: portobello fajitas, stuffed bell peppers, green chili stew, Greek salad, zucchini fritters, breaded avocados…everything looked like it could be my next favorite meal.

At the same time, many of my old favorites were also drawing me back to them like culinary magnets: thali, mushroom risotto, ratatouille…surefire winners that I'd loved before and knew I would love again.

Maybe it was the change in the weather, but it wasn't just the food that seemed to be turned up a notch that day—even the other diners looked lit up by a special spark. They smiled more, moved faster, and seemed to savor their food on a deeper level than I'd ever noticed.

But, fitting for the new season, there was also a hint of melancholia in the air (or at least in me). Even amid all this bounty, all this joy, and all these present-moment possibilities, I had a bittersweet déjà vu. And unlike most of my déjà vus, I was able to place the source of this one almost immediately. No, it wasn't a memory from earlier fall days, it was from the past winter—specifically, my first time at the buffet, when I'd been so overwhelmed by all the options and ended up eating nothing at all. Once again, I felt the surge of regret that had rushed through me on that day. Back then, however, at least there'd been a silver lining: I still had a whole year to come back to the buffet, to sample many of the appealing foods, and to look forward to future meals.

But now, that future was almost done.

In the past, I could've just picked anything that looked good, knowing that I could get to the rest next time. But in a few months, there wouldn't be a next time. If I didn't take them soon, I would likely go my life without ever sampling the buffet's zucchini fritters. Or their artichoke lasagna. Or their walnut-corn tacos. Or their coconut, broccolini, and farfalle soup. Or any of the dozens—or hundreds, perhaps even *thousands*—of other appetizing meals that I simply wouldn't have time to try.

Right in the middle of the room, I stopped and sighed. Fighting back the lump in my throat, I looked wistfully around me, surveying all the foods that would soon be out of reach. Yes, I could take them now, but after one more season, they'd be gone. In the past. As inaccessible as my childhood, as a grade-school kickball game on the playground at recess, as that summer beach holiday when I found the perfect sand dollar. Or my first day of college—or college, period. Or my old apartment. Or my grandmother. Or my first date with Maya. Or yesterday.

I sighed again, heavier this time.

But I didn't allow myself to grow maudlin or despondent. After all, *I* was still here. And there was still time to eat. Not *everything* I wanted, but *something*. And because of the lesson I'd learned during my first visit to the buffet, I knew I couldn't wait much longer. I had to choose.

After one last scan of the options around me, I went for the stuffed bell peppers (one yellow and one red—I wasn't hungry enough for a third, so the green pepper was another food I'd have to forgo). Was this the best meal in the buffet? Probably not. But it looked hot and hearty, smelled delicious, and somehow seemed like a fitting autumn lunch.

After filling my plate, I sat down, took a bite, and felt a wave of joy rush through me. The peppers (and the stuffing inside them—which, as far as I could tell, was a blend of carrots, zucchini, onions, garlic, and diced tomatoes) tasted even better than they looked and smelled. I'd chosen well.

But then I thought of all those other meals—the ones I hadn't chosen. The ones I'd never eaten and probably never would. They might have tasted good too, perhaps even better. Or maybe they were healthier, allowing me to savor the taste and get fit at the same time. Or maybe they'd introduce me to a whole new style of food—something with endless possibilities and endless delights. I could be missing out on the culinary adventure of a lifetime!

I looked down and noticed that my plate was already half empty. How had that happened? I hadn't even realized I'd taken more than a bite or two, yet the yellow pepper was almost gone. I thought I'd already learned the lesson about staying present (thanks to Edith, Edna, and Ellie), but here I was, sleepwalking—or sleep-eating—my way through lunch.

Fortunately, I caught myself in time to stop fretting over all the food I *wasn't* eating and start paying attention to what I actually *was* eating. I took the last bite of the yellow pepper and savored the warmth and the flavor. I couldn't pin down the spice that gave it that extra kick of flavor. Not cilantro, but maybe something like that. I knew it would be pointless to ask the chef—the buffet never gave away their secrets—so I just enjoyed it…whatever it was.

Even as I focused on the food, though, my mind didn't go blank. I still thought about some of the other foods I'd considered taking. But this time, instead of being filled with regret, I just laughed. I laughed at myself for getting so worked up over the choices. And I laughed at myself for falling prey to FOMO. I knew better. For years, I'd been hearing people talk about the fear of missing out. I'd also heard plenty of people talking about JOMO—the joy of missing out—when they were glad to be out of the loop or uninvolved with the endless trivial (or not-so-trivial) concerns that preoccupy so many other people.

But what I was feeling now wasn't quite either of these. It was more of an acceptance. Making peace with the inevitability, the certainty, the guarantee that I *would* miss out. Maybe that should be my new acronym: GOMO—the guarantee of missing out. Yes, I would definitely miss out—on meals, on work opportunities, on life paths not taken…it was endless. I simply couldn't be everywhere and do everything. And that was okay. Because I *could* do one thing, and as long as I didn't miss it (by sleepwalking through it or focusing on regret), that one thing was good enough.

I savored the last bite of the yellow pepper and started in on the red one, trying to stay in the present. Nonetheless, my thoughts drifted into the future—to the decisions I'd have to make next week at work. There too, I knew we'd be missing out on opportunities. But unlike before, this thought no longer tore me up inside. I knew it was okay. And I knew what to do. I'd send the sales team to the conference in Memphis, which they'd been raving about all year long. But that was it. Anything more would be counterproductive and costly.

Meanwhile, back in the office, in addition to the Pinnacle account, we'd focus on the security upgrade. That's what people needed most right now. It's what *we* needed most. If we delayed it, the consequences could be dire. The mobile app, on the other hand, could wait. So could the AR headset. Maybe till next year, maybe forever. We simply couldn't do everything. We had to choose just a few things. But if we did those well, that would be enough.

Lesson #37:
You will miss some opportunities. And that's okay.
The key is to make the most of the ones you do choose.

38. Leave a Tip

When I first started going to the buffet, I was overwhelmed by all the options. I was confused by the layout and, due to the lack of signs and labels, often uncertain about what exactly I was eating. One thing that was never confusing, however, was the price: a reasonable flat fee that you paid once, right when you entered, and that was that. Then you could eat whatever you wanted. You didn't have to pay extra for fancier foods. You didn't have to pay again if you went back for seconds (or thirds or fourths). You didn't even have to leave a tip.

This no-tip policy made sense to me. After all, there were no hosts or wait staff, and you were expected to bus your own table. So you were just paying for the food you ate.

But over the months, I started to feel a bit uncomfortable about not leaving a tip. No, there may not have been servers or bussers, but someone still had to clean the tables, the floor, and the sneeze guards. Someone had to fill the serving trays. Someone had to cook the food. And long before that, someone had to grow it. Someone had to transport it. Someone had to unload it and put it away in the kitchen. Someone had to devise the menu, decide how much to order, manage the staff, and organize the entire operation. And what a massive operation it was! It was mind boggling how many people and how many steps were involved—just so I could eat lunch.

With this in mind, the flat fee seemed almost embarrassingly low. Maybe I should slip them a little extra from time to time.

No sooner had this thought occurred to me then, as if by magic, I started noticing a few tips jars placed discreetly around the buffet. No one ever mentioned them—much less pressured anybody to use them—but I did see customers putting in a few bucks here and there. And on a few occasions, I did the same. But I never understood the full impact of those jars until my last visit in September.

While browsing my lunch options, I saw a woman drop a bill in a tip jar. I asked her if she knew where the tips went, and she told me that, as

I expected, they helped the behind-the-scenes workers: the dishwashers, cooks, and other kitchen workers. But there was more to it than that: a significant portion was contributed to community initiatives to offset food insecurity. She also answered a question I'd been wondering all year: what happened to all the leftover food? Anything that was safe, clean, and edible went to local food banks and soup kitchens.

I thanked the woman for telling me about the tips, and she smiled and walked away. But long after our conversation was over, it echoed in my mind.

Clearly, for the buffet, "feeding the hungry" was about much more than just letting me stuff my face every Saturday. It was a mission. It was built into their daily operations. And it was making a difference.

I wondered if we could do something similar at work. Maybe I could set up a program where employees could decide to have a portion of each paycheck automatically donated to charity (just like some people did for health insurance or retirement plans). It could be 10%—or even just 1% or 2%…anything would help. And if lots of us did that month after month, it would add up.

Maybe there could also be a more service-oriented option. We could do something as a branch, like what the buffet did with their leftovers. No, our contribution most likely wouldn't be centered around food since that wasn't our area of expertise. But what could we do with technology? Quantum computing and IoT were hardly classic charitable causes. But maybe we could do something with what we had, what we knew, and who we were—like offering technology training to underprivileged kids, giving them valuable skills and setting them up for long-term success. We could open the office for one weekend each month and let staff volunteer to teach. It would be an official Youth Technology Mentoring program.

That seemed like a worthwhile endeavor, but how could I contribute? I couldn't teach technology—I needed Nikhil's help just to update my drivers! What did I have that would help anybody? I wasn't a computer programmer or a teacher. I wasn't a chef. I wasn't a doctor, a nurse, or a vet. What could I possibly offer that would make a difference in anyone's life?

This question haunted me throughout the week after I learned about the buffet's charitable initiatives. I thought about it at work. I thought about it at home. And most of all, I thought about it while I was lying in bed, unable to sleep. And every time I failed to come up with an answer—some skill, talent, or anything valuable to offer—I felt even more worthless. I felt powerless. I felt small.

And then it hit me: small was okay. I didn't need to do or be anything huge, grand, or dramatic. There was value in making a small but meaningful difference.

From this perspective, there was lots that I could contribute. For starters, I had the idea. And I knew how to organize events and manage people. I could put the whole operation together. Beyond that, there must be some way I could help, even with my limited skills. But what could I do? No, I couldn't fix computers—or people, or animals, or cars. But I could drive. Maybe I could pick up the kids who needed a ride. I also knew how to read. Maybe I could read stories to the younger kids. And I could throw a ball or a frisbee. Maybe some of them would just want to go out back behind the office and have a catch. Or just talk. Yes, even I could do that.

Even if it wasn't much, it was something. And ultimately, that's what mattered.

Lesson #38:
Pay it back. Pay it forward. Give in whatever way and whatever amount feels right for you. But give something.

39. Details

I wasn't panicking—yet. There was still cause for optimism. Sofia's latest report showed that the Q3 numbers were solid, thanks mainly to Pinnacle. Compared with our abysmal second quarter, we'd pulled off a remarkable turnaround. True, we were still in the hole, but at least we'd stopped digging. At our current growth rate, we'd break even in about eight months. Unfortunately, I didn't have eight months. I had three. I needed results this year—or there wouldn't be a next year. Not for this branch, at least.

But maybe it didn't have to be that way. Maybe I could get an extension or a loan, especially if the company saw that our branch was heading in the right direction. Yes, I'd made a deal, but there had to be a way out of it, right? I just needed to find an escape hatch.

After reading Sofia's Q3 report, I did something I hadn't done in nearly ten months: pulled out the contract I'd signed before leaving the home office. Sure enough, just as I remembered—right there in black and white at the bottom of page two—there was the clause: the new branch had to be profitable by year's end or it would be shut down. The contract seemed pretty ironclad, but if it were really that cut and dried, why would it go on for another seventeen pages? Surely there was a loophole somewhere in there.

I scanned the pages but couldn't make heads or tails of it. It was all "whereas" this, and "indemnify" that, and "in perpetuity throughout the universe." To make it even more incomprehensible, every other paragraph seemed to contain some foreign phrase I'd never noticed: *ad idem, ab initio, bona vacantia, et sequitur, ex parte, inter alia, per quod, sui juris, uberrimae fidei,* and the one that seemed most ominous of all, *sine die.* It may have been Latin, but it was all Greek to me.

After an hour of poring over this impenetrable wall of words, I realized I needed to show the contract to an actual lawyer. Which meant Tamika. Which meant doing the one thing I vowed I would never do: tell someone else in the office about my little wager (which, in light of our current financial situation, didn't seem so little).

It's not that I'd been lying or maliciously withholding information; I just didn't want to worry anyone. I didn't want them to think they might lose their jobs. I didn't want them to focus on failure. And, I might as well admit it, I didn't want them to think I was an idiot.

Which, judging by her reaction, was exactly what Tamika thought when I showed her the contract. No, she didn't come right out and say it—being the consummate professional she is—but you didn't need a PhD in body language to interpret her reaction. Her eyebrows shot up, then she buried her face in her hands, slowly shaking her head and moaning softly. When she finally looked up and managed to formulate actual words, she asked, "Did you show this to a lawyer before signing?"

"Of course I did!"

"Was it their company lawyer?"

I shrugged and looked around the room. "Well, yeah, but…"

She shook her head again, then slid on her reading glasses and flipped through the contract. "This was…" she turned a few more pages and grimaced, "inadvisable." She set down the contract, took off her glasses, and fixed me with a penetrating stare. "But here we are."

Yes, there we were. But were we stuck here, or was there a way out? That was the question that Tamika would get to the bottom of.

I implored her to keep this all between us. Wasn't there some kind of client-confidentiality thing? It turns out there wasn't—not in this case, at least, since I wasn't technically her client—but she promised not to tell. However, she strongly advised me to come clean to the other employees. Not out of legal obligation but simply because it was the right thing to do—to let them know what might happen, so they could decide their next move and, perhaps, start looking for a position with more job security.

I thought this sounded very responsible, mature, and considerate. And there was absolutely no way I was going to do it. Hopefully, though, it wouldn't be necessary. Tamika just had to find that loophole.

So I left her to it, hoping she'd bring back some good news very soon and we'd be able to put this whole thing behind us. Ideally, before lunch—although, at that moment, I felt so queasy I couldn't even imagine eating. It may have been just nerves—being on edge as I waited for Tamika's report—or it may have been left over from my unplanned "trip to Brazil."

Forty-eight hours earlier, I'd had no idea anything out of the ordinary was about to happen. As far as I was concerned, it was a typical Saturday morning. I woke up feeling relaxed and refreshed, had a leisurely start to the day, and then walked to the buffet. Once I was there, things continued to go as they usually did: I browsed around the food options, served myself something that looked appealing, and found a quiet spot where I could enjoy my meal.

As I often did, I selected a meal that was familiar but that I'd never had at the buffet—something filling without being too heavy, flavorful without going overboard on the spices. The couscous pilaf checked all the right boxes—light and fluffy, yet packed with a wide variety of vegetables, dried fruits, nuts, and a sprinkling of fresh herbs.

One bite in, I knew I'd found a winner. The dried fruit made it nice and chewy, while the nuts and lightly steamed vegetables gave it a satisfying crunch. And the tangy lemon-herb sauce brought everything together so perfectly that, after another bite or two, I stopped thinking about the individual ingredients and just enjoyed the meal as a whole. In fact, I enjoyed it so much that I cleaned my plate and went back for seconds.

I knew I was probably overdoing it, but it tasted too good to stop. Even when I started feeling full, I kept taking "just one more bite" until I'd made it about halfway through the second serving. And that's when I realized I wasn't just feeling full; I was feeling…off.

I wasn't sure what exactly was going on, but my stomach felt awful. Was it indigestion? Cramps from overeating? Bloating from all the fruits and veggies? After a while, it wasn't just my stomach that felt bad. My hands were getting clammy, my breathing was short, and my heart was racing. Oh my gosh! Was I having a heart attack?

No, it wasn't that. This was something familiar—something I'd been through before. But when? And what was causing it now? I sifted through the ingredients on my plate, looking for something that might've made me feel this way. Couscous had never given me trouble. What about the dried cranberries and apricots? No, I had those all the time. Ditto for carrots, celery, and broccoli. Nothing I was allergic to. I kept on sifting, and then I saw it—and I knew right away.

Brazil nuts.

Just like I'd had at the holiday party at Maya's office two years ago, when I'd been eating them by the handful…and paid for it by spending Christmas in the bathroom.

So, I knew what I could look forward to for the rest of the weekend. After a hasty visit to the restroom, I staggered out the door and did something I'd never done before: took a cab home from the buffet. I would've loved a leisurely stroll on that crisp fall afternoon, but there was no way I could've made the walk in my condition. As it was, I barely made it back to my bathroom in time. Just as I suspected, my memorable "G.I. Christmas" (as it's been known ever since) now had a sequel. And instead of spending the weekend relaxing, enjoying the beautiful weather, and filling my cup for the week ahead, I spent the weekend filling the toilet.

When I felt it was safe to leave the bathroom, I researched Brazil nuts, which completely freaked me out. I really could be having a heart attack! Or kidney failure or selenium poisoning or nerve damage…but, more likely, just good old-fashioned diarrhea, just like after the Christmas party.

In retrospect, it would've made sense for me to see a doctor, but I couldn't bear the thought of going anywhere more than five steps from my bathroom. Besides, I had Dr. Laptop, who told me more than I needed to know. It turns out that most people handle Brazil nuts with no problem. (In fact, they're actually pretty good for most people: lowering the risk of heart disease and inflammation, improving bone health and thyroid function, and more.) But not me. Not that it made me feel any better, but I'm not the only one who has this type of reaction. And for most of us in this boat, there wasn't much we could do but wait it out.

(By the way, since I've been thinking of all that time spent reviewing legal contracts with Tamika, I feel I should probably mention that I'm not a doctor, so if you think you need medical attention, yada yada yada, in perpetuity throughout the universe.)

But as bad as the gastrointestinal distress felt, what felt even worse was knowing how stupid I'd been. How had I not seen those Brazil nuts? They were all over the plate—hiding in plain sight. It's not like I could've mistaken them for peanuts, almonds, or any other nut—they look and taste totally different: that distinctive smooth, buttery, woodsy flavor that tastes so good…and then goes so wrong. For me, at least. Which I already knew. I'd been through this before. So how could I miss it this time? It was like strolling through a field of poison ivy just after my last bout had finally stopped itching. Why hadn't I learned? And why hadn't I noticed? Why hadn't I paid attention?

By Monday, the intense cramping finally gave way to a general queasiness, mild enough to let me go back to work but bad enough to keep me from eating lunch. So instead, I spent my lunch hour pacing around my office, berating myself, and waiting for Tamika to get back to me with what I prayed would be good news. If I could just get out of this contract somehow, I would gladly suffer through Brazil nut "parties" every weekend for the rest of the year.

But the lunch hour ended, and there was still no word from Tamika. I kept pacing until two o'clock and then two thirty and then three. And even though I said I'd wait until I heard from her, I just couldn't handle the suspense any longer. I barged into her office, determined to learn my fate, no matter what it may be.

She was just hanging up the phone, and I could tell right away from her expression that the news was not good. My heart sank, but I asked anyway. "No loophole?"

She shook her head. "Why don't you pull up a chair," she said. "Take a look at this clause."

When I sat down next to her, she directed my attention to §54B. Like most of the contract, it was a mix of Latin, legalese, and convoluted run-on sentences that I couldn't make heads or tails of. "What does this mean?" I asked.

She took off her reading glasses and stared at me with a look that seemed to combine pity, disappointment, and disgust. "Remember when we talked about limited liability?" I gave a noncommittal shrug, and she continued. "Well, let's just say that this contract does not provide for that."

"Meaning?"

"Meaning that if this branch isn't profitable by the end of the year, it will be shut down, you'll lose your job, and so will the rest of us—and you'll be responsible for the losses."

"I know!" I said, trying to keep the irritation out of my voice.

She shook her head. "I don't think you grasp the full extent of it." Her tone was as slow and measured as a judge's when sentencing a prisoner to life behind bars. "You will be responsible for any losses incurred by the—"

"Yeah, I get it! It's all my fault! Why do you think I'm trying so hard to—"

"Meaning you'll have to pay them back."

I stopped mid-sentence and swallowed. Hard. "Like, from my own money?" She nodded. "But that could take years—decades!" She nodded again and pointed at §54B.

Without another word, I picked up the contract, staggered to my office, shut the door, and collapsed. Lying on my back, staring at the ceiling, I pictured a future buried in debt, my chances of winning back Maya slipping away, and my vision of lifelong happiness going up in flames.

My stomach lurched again—this time not from Brazil nuts but from the bitter taste of realizing that, for the second time in three days, I'd learned an important lesson too late.

Lesson #39:
Details matter.

40. Otherwise Engaged

Time was of the essence. I couldn't afford to wallow in misery, beat myself up over past mistakes, or waste a single minute on regret. I still had an office to run and—if all went well—a profit to make. And it had to happen this year.

No, it wasn't going to be easy. But the year wasn't over yet, so there was still hope. It was just going to take some creativity, dedication, and teamwork.

So I called an emergency meeting of the whole office. Everyone.

"But what about the phones?" Brenda asked. "What if they ring while I'm—"

"Let it go to voicemail," I said. "I want all hands on deck."

Twenty minutes later, all hands were on deck—meaning, in the conference room. It took a few more minutes for everyone to settle into their seats (which required a bit of rearranging—we weren't used to accommodating the whole team in there at once). And then I stood at the head of the table and attempted my best impersonation of an inspiring leader. Or at least a capable one.

"First of all, I want to congratulate everyone on a strong third quarter. We've shown some really positive signs of growth, and I have all of you to thank for that." I applauded the group. A few joined in tentatively, as if unsure whether they were supposed to applaud themselves. I stopped clapping and gestured toward Liam. "I want to give a special shout-out to Liam for landing the Pinnacle deal, which has been a lifesaver for us." Heat rushed to my forehead as I instantly regretted using the word *lifesaver.* Had anyone noticed? Would they read too much into it? (Or not *too much* but exactly the right amount?) In any case, once the smattering of applause died down, I moved on quickly, gesturing to Laney and Kareem. "And also to Laney for managing the account so effectively, and to Kareem, Zoey, and Nikhil for creating top-notch software that'll keep 'em coming back for more. Great job, guys!" More people joined me in applause this time, and I breathed a sigh of relief. Apparently, nothing suspicious had registered.

But then came the hard part.

"But this isn't the time to take our foot off the gas. Let's build on our success! Let's multiply it! Let's end the year strong and profitable!" I stifled a wince as the word left my lips. I really had to stop dropping hints like that—someone might catch on. Again, I raced ahead. "So, how are we going to do this?" I looked around the room—deliberately avoiding eye contact with Tamika. Everyone seemed to be waiting for me to supply the answer. And when I didn't, their expectant expressions turned to looks of impatience.

Just as the silence was growing awkward, Nikhil broke it. "Okay, we give up. How do we do it?"

"That's why I've called this meeting." I gestured toward the whole group. "For all of us to figure that out…together."

So, for the next hour, we brainstormed ways to bring in revenue. Fast.

I tried to stay open to everyone's suggestions—and some had potential—but more than once I broke my own cardinal rule for brainstorming: shooting down ideas on the spot. "Developing a new product line would take too long," I told Kareem. I was even less patient when Rohan suggested expanding our customer-service offerings. "Yes, I know it's easier to keep existing customers, but this session is about getting *new* ones—this year!" And when Yasmin suggested rebranding the company—positioning ourselves as thought leaders through platform building and strategic alliances—I snapped back at her. "No! You're still thinking *long* term. We want results *now!*"

At that point, the bustling room grew suddenly quiet. They all looked at me.

"And why is that, exactly?" Laney asked.

"Um, well…I guess we don't *have* to bring in money immediately, of course. But, uh…" I unclenched my jaw and tried to force a smile. "I just don't want to lose the great momentum we've built. You know, ride the wave."

"Okay…" Laney side-eyed me. "So, how about taking on more subcontracted work on a freelance basis—like we're doing with Pinnacle?"

"Yes! Now we're talking! What else?"

"We could have a holiday sale—like a Black Friday discount," Liam suggested.

"Or give a workshop or training for other businesses—or end users," Zoey said.

"Or how about we sell this conference table and just get a bunch of TV trays?" Brenda said. I joined in with everyone's laughter, but I secretly thought it wasn't such a bad idea. The group tossed around a few other viable possibilities, but one stuck out as a winner:

Expos.

I loved the simplicity of it: You go. You make sales. You get paid. Period.

It was exactly what we needed at exactly the right time. And with the holidays coming up, we had a ton of options to choose from. Brenda pulled up a list and read out some of the most promising ones:

"Let's see…there's the Cybersecurity Expo in Raleigh, XR-Plus in Buffalo, the Green Tech Summit in Portland, the IoT Expo in Minneapolis, the Smart Cities Conference in St. Louis, Robotics in Tampa, and about a thousand AI expos."

Unfortunately, a lot of them were already filled up. And the ones that still had openings were mostly in early to mid December. "That's not gonna work with net-thirty," I blurted out.

"What difference does that make?" asked Sofia.

"Well, if we're not paid till January, we won't be profitable this year," I said.

"Great!" Sofia clapped. "We can apply the NOL to next year's taxes and then take the—"

"No! All the best shows are on Black Friday weekend, so that's what we're targeting."

There were a lot of grumbles in the room, especially about working on Thanksgiving weekend. But I pulled rank—because I knew something that, aside from Tamika, none of them knew: their jobs depended on this.

And at this point, expos seemed like our best bet. It wouldn't take much—just one big fish. Cut a deal. Cut a check. Save the branch.

To increase our odds, I decided to send *everyone* to an expo. Yes, this was well out of the comfort zones (and job descriptions) for many of them—especially Brenda…and Nora and Sofia and…well, at least half the branch. But I tried to find the best fits with the options available. I'd send our sales/marketing team (Liam, Yasmin, and Diego) to the B2B conference in Vegas. Keiko and Rohan could go to the design expo in Seattle. I'd keep an eye on Tamika by joining her and Nikhil at the "Nano-Q" conference in Tampa. (To be honest, I didn't even know what this was, but Nikhil lit up at the mention of nanotechnology and quantum computing, so I figured I'd let him take the lead.) And although I knew that running the booth at the IoT Expo in Minneapolis would be quite a stretch for Nora, Sofia, and Brenda, I thought it was worth a shot. (Hey, ya never know. If nothing else, it increased our odds: five expos were 25% more than four.) But I was saving the A Team for B-town: XR+ in Buffalo. It was the biggest expo and the highest chance of success, so we needed our best, which meant Laney, Kareem, and Zoey.

"How come you get to go to Tampa while I'm freezing my butt off in Buffalo?" Zoey asked.

"Yeah," Brenda said. "You wanna trade? I could bring my grandkids to Disney World while we're—"

"Guys! Guys!" I cut in. "This is not a vacation!"

"Yeah, we know," Sofia said. Half the group laughed while the other half grumbled.

"Trust me," I said. "If things go well, it'll be very worth your while. I have a feeling you'll all be extremely glad you did it…once it's all over."

What I didn't say is that if we didn't make some quick sales—at the expos or through some unforeseen miracle—it really would be all over: the branch, their jobs, and my future. Hopefully, though, the expo plan would work, and by the end of the year, we'd be safely in the black. Then, once the danger had passed, I'd reveal everything and we could all laugh about what a close call it had been. Maybe they'd apologize for grumbling about the expos once they realized what a hero I'd been—saving the branch without them even knowing they were in peril.

And if we couldn't save it, well, they'd all find out soon enough. Why ruin their holiday cheer by telling them now?

But in that moment, I was feeling optimistic. And maybe it rubbed off on the team because pretty soon the grumbling stopped and they seemed to align with the idea that they were doing this. Despite my assertions to the contrary, some of them reframed the expos as paid vacations. A few of them admitted they were actually glad for the true excuse to get out of Thanksgiving with their families. I also heard a rumor—which I swear I didn't start, though I didn't stop it—that there'd be extra-large holiday bonuses for anyone who landed a new client.

Anyway, for whatever reason, it didn't take long for almost everyone to get swept up in the excitement of the actual work: preparing to set up booths, creating handouts, and most of all, planning tech demos that would turn casual visitors into paying customers. And with all the hustle and bustle, the week flew by. In fact, it wasn't until lunch break on Friday that I came up for air and remembered the rest of my life. At first glance, it didn't seem like I'd missed much. I checked my personal email— nothing of great consequence. Ditto for voicemail. Ditto for social media: just some celebrity gossip, political mudslinging, a few cute cat memes, and…

That's when I saw it. And my heart sank. I reread it, and my heart sank even lower. Then, just to be sure, I read it a third time and confirmed it in a few other places. And that's when my heart completely shattered. It really was true.

Maya was engaged.

Not to me. To Bradford. And they both felt the need to share every last superficial detail of their plans. They posted pictures of the floral arrangements. (Who cares? It's a bunch of dumb flowers that'll die soon anyway.) And a poll of which flavor of cake to choose. (Was this wedding by committee? Make your own decision!) And of course, her dress (in which she looked absolutely stunning, I begrudgingly admitted). And pictures of the venue: the Ramparts. (That stupid wannabe castle—how fake! Like he was old-money royalty instead of just some HR lame-o.) But the worst part of all was the date: December 30. Just over twelve short weeks away.

A phrase popped into my head that I hadn't thought of since seventh grade social studies class: *Pyrrhic victory.* Even if I won the branch battle, I'd already lost what really mattered: Maya.

In retrospect, I'd played this all wrong. If only I'd stayed home, maybe I could've found another way to win her back. Or I could've told her about my plan with the branch—how I was becoming the man she wanted me to be, a better man, the right man for her. In any case, I should've fought harder for her. But all the coulda-shoulda-wouldas in the world didn't matter now. It was too late.

Even though it was the middle of a busy workday, I grabbed my coat and headed out the door without telling anybody. I was done.

Once I was back home, I did everything I could think of to avoid looking at more of their wedding plans. (*Their!* Just that word alone made me want to puke. It should've been *our* wedding plans!) Fortunately, I had plenty of distractions. I watched every Christopher Guest movie in order. I ate three bags of microwave popcorn. I played hours of online arcade games. I cleaned my entire apartment. Twice. And I still couldn't stop thinking about Maya. Also, despite the lesson I'd supposedly learned from Chili Man, I couldn't stop myself from checking all her social media accounts, rereading every single post, obsessing over every single detail, and pining over every picture of her alone—doing my best to skip the ones with nauseating Bradford. And no matter how hard I tried, I couldn't fall asleep.

As I lay in bed, futilely trying to turn off my brain, my heart, and my consciousness, my late night eventually became an early morning. And when the sky began to lighten, I realized I'd done something I hadn't done since college: pulled an all-nighter. I wish I could say that the dawn was symbolic—that the worst had passed and I was filled with the first glimmers of new hope—but that was far from the case. As the sun brightened the sky, I felt worse than ever. And I still couldn't sleep.

I looked at the clock and saw 8:19—Maya's birthday. I looked again after what felt like only a few minutes, but the clock said 8:58, so I guess I had drifted off for a bit. Then I blinked and realized that the clock didn't say 8:58; it said 12:58. Ugh! On top of everything else, now it was too late for me to even make it to the buffet in time. The one bit of comfort I had to look forward to this weekend, and now I wouldn't even have that!

Also, not that I was superstitious (well, okay, maybe a little), but this would break my streak. Every Saturday since moving here, I'd eaten lunch at the buffet. If I didn't make it today, what would that mean for the rest of the year? Would I lose Maya *and* the branch? Would some even more calamitous fate befall me? It wasn't just lunch that was riding on this; it was the rest of the year…and possibly my life! But what could I do? The buffet closed in an hour, and it took almost ninety minutes to walk there. I simply couldn't make it there in time.

Unless…

Of course! It was so obvious—*too* obvious! It was staring me right in the face. (Or, at least, it would be once I went out to the parking lot.) I could drive there! Why hadn't I thought of that right away?

Well, because that's just not what I did. I *walked* to the buffet. Every Saturday. Rain or shine. It was my routine, my ritual for almost an entire year.

But this Saturday was different. Oversleeping meant I couldn't walk there. But it wasn't all or nothing. I could still make it if I hurried.

So I washed my face, put on an extra layer of deodorant and a dab of cologne, threw on some clean-enough clothes, and drove as fast as I could while still being somewhat safe (and not adding a speeding ticket to my growing pile of woes). Halfway there, I glanced at the clock—1:20. I wasn't too late after all!

And then it hit me: if there was still time to make it to the buffet, maybe there was still time to win back Maya. The driving solution had been so obvious once I'd thought of it. Maybe it could be that easy with Maya. Maybe I could go forward with my plan after all: save the branch, fly back home before Christmas, and convince her to take me back. Once she saw how much I'd accomplished and how much I'd changed, why wouldn't she take me back, dump Bradford, and call off the wedding? Or better yet, *don't* call off the wedding but go through with it…with *me* as the groom!

Yes! That was the new plan! The better-than-ever plan! Twelve weeks from now, *I* would marry Maya.

I knew I'd be cutting it close, but I could still make it work. It might be hard for my friends and family to make it there on such short notice, but most people would be off work for the holidays. And okay, so the Ramparts wouldn't have been my first choice of venue, but as long as I was with Maya, what difference did it make? Also, I'm sure this whole plan violated some sort of "bro code." But, hey, all's fair. This was Maya, after all. My heart, my life.

I pulled up to the buffet at 1:32—later than I'd ever arrived there—not nearly enough time for a leisurely stroll up and down the aisles, but still plenty of time for a quick meal. I knew exactly what I wanted—something hearty and comforting—and I knew just where to find it. I headed straight for one of my fall favorites: the shepherd's pie.

Just as I'd hoped, it was flavorful and hearty (loaded with fresh herbs, spices, and veggies: mushrooms, carrots, and peas as well as some sort of white bean mixed in with the base of mashed potatoes), and it fully lived up to its reputation as comfort food. Without even rushing, I polished off the last bite by 1:59. No, it wasn't the most sophisticated meal I'd ever had, but I can't remember the last time something tasted so good or filled me with so much hope.

Lesson #40:
As long as there's time, there's hope. Sometimes you just have to find a different way to reach your goal. (And the vehicle for getting there might be more obvious than you think!)

41. Desperate

When I returned to the office on Monday, I was still feeling cautiously optimistic—and with good reason. I knew I had a good team, a good opportunity, and a good plan. But I also knew that the best plan in the world is worthless unless you act on it. And we needed to act *fast*!

The expos were just over a month away, and half of us (myself included) didn't know the first thing about our topics. Yet somehow, we'd have to transform ourselves into instant experts, create dazzling demos, and deliver pitches compelling enough to turn strangers into clients—on the spot.

Yes, it was a tall order, but I hadn't forgotten what I'd learned from driving to the buffet. We could still reach our goal; we just had to pick up the pace. Which meant I'd have to drive the team a little harder than usual. (Okay—a *lot* harder.) No, this wouldn't win me any popularity contests, but it might win me Maya. And it might save the branch, save everyone's jobs, and save my future.

For better or worse, though, the team didn't know any of this. (And even if they had known about Maya, I don't think that would've lit the fire under them in quite the same way it did for me.) So I had to find other ways to motivate them to get more done in less time, to move faster than they thought possible, to achieve greatness—or at least adequate preparation. Which meant I couldn't just cross my fingers and hope for the best. And I couldn't passively stand by while the branch went under and Maya married Bradford.

With so much at stake, this was no time to act like "The Waiter"—I had to be out there on the front lines, rallying the troops and keeping things moving, even if that meant getting in someone's face and cracking the whip. Maybe they'd call me pushy, aggressive, or bossy, but that was okay—after all, I *was* the boss. And I was going to let them know that I was watching and that I expected results.

It wouldn't take lengthy meetings, just a few friendly-but-firm words to make my presence felt. So, taking a deep breath and filling myself with steely resolve, I shut my computer and walked out of my office, determined not to go back until I'd at least touched base with every employee and conveyed a sense of urgency.

As I began making the rounds, I approached the first person I saw and tried out my new get-it-done-now attitude. "Hey, Keiko! How's the design coming along?"

She looked up from her work, startled. "Oh, just sketching out a few ideas for the display, which I thought we could—"

"Hmm…not so sure about that." I pointed to the area of her sketch that still seemed…well, sketchy. "Not quite the quality we need. We've really gotta up our game if we want to lure in the big fish. Next-level stuff. I know you've got it in you. Now let's make it happen, okay?"

She gave me a worried nod as I walked away. I didn't intend to frighten anyone, but maybe it wasn't the worst thing in the world to put a little fear into them. Let 'em feel the heat!

I walked across the room and clamped my hand down on Diego's shoulder. "Hey, buddy. You write your pitch for Vegas yet?"

He spun around, looking confused. "Write?" He shook his head. "I dunno. I was thinking this would be more of a conversational environment. Just go with the flow and see how things—"

"No! No! No! Every word's gotta count! Come on, man—you're the copywriter. This is what I'm paying you for—not just to shoot the breeze for a few hours and then spend the night playing blackjack and pounding free drinks. If you want results, you gotta be prepared—and then you gotta deliver."

He swallowed hard as my cold stare lingered on him for a few extra moments. Then I turned my attention to my sales manager. "So, Liam, what kind of tricks you got planned for Vegas?"

He looked up from his phone. "Tricks?"

"Yeah, you know—something fresh, out-of-the-box, mind-blowing. Something they've never seen. Something that'll get 'em racing to sign those contracts!"

He laughed for a moment, until he realized I was 100% serious. "Look, I've been doing this a long time," he said. "I don't need tricks. I might go to a magic show while I'm there, but I won't be the one on stage." Again, he laughed. Again, I didn't.

"Liam, this is no joke. If we're gonna hit our numbers, we've gotta stand out from the crowd. We've gotta have something flashy, irresistible, hypnotizing…" Suddenly, something clicked in my brain. "Yes, that's it! Hypnotizing! Maybe you can learn from those Vegas hypnotists, like the way they modulate their voice to be more persuasive with—"

"Are you suggesting that I hypnotize prospective clients?" As Liam stepped back, he shot me a look that was one part amusement, one part confusion, and one part revulsion.

"Hmm…probably not. Gotta keep it ethical, everything on the up-and-up, right? But still…" I patted his back. "Now you're thinking. Keep those wheels turning, and tell me what you come up with by the end of the day."

By late morning, I'd already made the rounds. Twice. Except I hadn't seen the most important person of all yet—so, just before lunch, I burst into Laney's office to give her an infusion of inspiration.

"Hey, Laney—glad I caught you. We've got a lot to talk about. Lots of ideas. Lots of irons in the fire. How's it going with the demo? Ready to roll? Ready to dazzle 'em? What about the team? You got everybody else working on their projects? Gotta be perfect, gotta be sharp, gotta be ready for action. Makin' deals, makin' money, makin' dreams come true. That's what we're all about, right? That's the name of the game."

She cocked her head and squinted slightly, as if scrutinizing me before deciding how to respond. "Funny question," she eventually said. "Have you had a lot of coffee today?"

"Nope! Not a drop. Why? You wanna go get some coffee? We could make it a business lunch. Lots of business to handle, lots to talk about, no time to waste. We could start by going over the plans for—"

She held up her finger, silencing me mid-thought, then walked past me, quietly closed the door, and came back and looked deeply into my eyes. "Look, I'm not sure how to tell you this, but…" She sighed. "You're kind of freaking me out. And you're freaking out everyone else too."

I laughed. "What are you talking about?"

"All morning I've had people in my office asking me to get you to back off and chill out—saying you're acting erratic and putting way too much pressure on them."

"Pressure? It's called lighting a fire under them—motivating them to get results!"

She pinched the bridge of her nose and shook her head. "This isn't motivation; it's desperation. And frankly, it's very off-putting."

"Well, I'm sorry to burst your bubble, but we *are* desperate! In case you haven't noticed, it's mid-October and we're still not profitable."

"Relax. It's a process that every—"

"Don't tell me to relax!" I shouted. "We can't afford to relax! We're sinking!"

"No, we're not. We're heading in the right direction. We don't need to make a profit this year or even next—"

"Yes, we do!"

"No we don't!" she yelled. Then she closed her eyes and took a deep breath. "Look, it's okay to operate at a loss for a while. Most businesses do it while they're—"

"Well, we're not most businesses. We need a profit NOW! Which is why you need to stop complaining and start perfecting your Buffalo presentation."

Laney clasped her hands and adopted an ultra-earnest expression. "Of course, I'll get right on that, and it'll be one hundred percent perfect. I'll also make sure the rest of the team is running like a well-oiled machine, doing all their usual work, and also preparing perfectly for their expo presentations, which will land us tons of new clients and make us millions of dollars. Is that right?"

"Yes! Thank you! How hard is it to—"

"I was being facetious! And the fact that you can't even recognize how absurd you're sounding is kind of…" She picked up a thick manila file from the stack on her desk and waved it in my face. "I've got to take care of Pinnacle. They're the only thing that's keeping us afloat right now, and if I neglect them, we're sunk. So just back off!"

"Back off? Maybe *you* need to step up! And everyone else too! I'm sick of carrying the weight of this whole branch by myself!"

"Are you kidding me?!" She slammed the file back on her desk. "Are you seriously kidding me right now? Because from where I'm standing, *I'm* the one who's carrying this branch. I'm the one doing all the work, managing the accounts, managing the team, and keeping things running—without getting a fraction of the credit or the money I deserve—while you get to sit on your butt and reap all the rewards. And now, on top of everything else, I've gotta put out your panic fires!"

I threw my hands in the air. "Well maybe you shouldn't be *putting out* fires! Maybe you should be *starting* them too—trying to get things cooking for once."

She glared at me and made a guttural sound that I'd never heard from a human being before. "For once?! What exactly do you think I've been doing for the last eight months?"

"I don't know, but it's definitely not working, because we're still in the red!"

She glared at me with such intensity that for a moment I thought she might bite me. Her face was inches from mine, but she yelled loud enough to be heard ten miles away. "Because it's a PROCESS!!! Why can't you get that through your thick skull?! It takes time, but we'd get there a lot faster if I didn't have to deal with your INCOMPETENCE, IGNORANCE, and STUPIDITY!!!"

My face tingled, as if she'd just slapped me as hard as she could. But I stood my ground and met her glare…and her volume. "Look, I didn't hire you to insult me, and I certainly didn't hire you to lose money. In case you didn't notice, I'm running a business here. And that means we've gotta profit this year, or else!"

"Or else what?"

"Or else the company'll shut down the branch!"

Laney let out an incredulous guffaw. "No, they won't. Because unlike you, they actually know how to run a—"

"Yes, they will! That's been the deal from day one: no profit, no branch!"

Suddenly, things got very quiet. And then they got very loud. Much louder than before. And much nastier. And much worse.

Before that moment, I'd only heard Laney swear twice (once when she banged her shin on her chair and once when her car got towed). But she must've sworn at least a hundred times in the next ten minutes. And these were not under-the-breath mutterings; these were wall-rattling yells—the kind that, closed door or not, were definitely echoing throughout the office. And they were definitely still echoing in my head that night as I sat on my couch, replaying the argument for the thousandth time, wondering how it had come to this, how I had botched things so badly, how my business and my life had taken such a wrong turn and, in a matter of minutes, gone from being filled with potential to being an epic failure.

I thought of everything Laney said. And everything I said. And everything I could've done better. And then I thought of a seemingly random memory: a weird scene I'd witnessed months earlier at the buffet and had forgotten until that moment.

I'd been having my typical Saturday lunch—relaxed, enjoyable, and delicious. I was just polishing off a bowl of Vietnamese curry and was looking forward to the pecan pie I'd taken for dessert. But before I could finish, about twenty minutes before closing time, a man burst into the room and started yelling to no one in particular—or, rather, to anyone within earshot (which was everyone in the room, since he was shouting at the top of his lungs). "Everybody get out of my way! I need food! I'm starving!" Whether it was because he'd asked or simply because they wanted no part of this guy, everyone moved far away from him. "No, don't get out of my way!" he shouted. "Get me something to eat! And make it good. Make it healthy. Make it perfect. Make it NOW!"

I tried to keep my head down, focus on my pie, and above all, avoid eye contact. But curiosity got the better of me, and I eventually glanced up—and immediately regretted it. From across the room, the man locked eyes with me and headed toward me like a heat-seeking missile.

As he got closer, I saw that his face seemed like a perfect match for his voice and his actions. His hair was a mess, and his eyes bulged halfway out of his head, darting from side to side, even as he walked straight toward me. His tray was filled with a hodgepodge of unrelated foods. I'm not sure whether other people had assembled the meal for him or if he'd hastily grabbed these random items himself, but the odd combination looked less appealing than anything I'd seen before at the buffet.

As luck would have it, just before the man arrived at my table, the woman who'd been sitting directly across from me finished her meal and left. (Or maybe it wasn't luck and she hadn't finished—maybe she was just thinking faster than I was.) In any case, the man plopped down in the vacated seat, shoved a handful of food into his mouth, and stared intently into my eyes. "Hey, man, let's eat lunch together! You can be my lunch buddy." Crumbs—and a few larger chunks—spilled out of his mouth as he chewed, but he kept up his manic monologue. "Gotta eat fast, though. Closing soon. Two o'clock. Gotta finish everything. No time to waste—right, lunch buddy?" He shoved a few more handfuls into his mouth while he talked. "Hey, we should be lunch buddies every week. You wanna be my weekly lunch buddy? You wanna be my friend? My best friend? I need a best friend. Yeah, that's what I need. Friends. Lots of friends! You wanna be friends?"

I cleared my throat and looked around the table for back-up, but none of the remaining diners seemed inclined to bail me out. They were all keeping their heads down—like I would've done if I'd been smarter.

Before I could come up with a credible excuse to avoid ever seeing him again, the man turned his attention to a woman sitting nearby. "You wanna be friends too? You wanna be my girlfriend? I need a girlfriend— bad, really bad. We could go on a date right now, right after lunch. But first I gotta finish lunch—fast! Time's running out! I'm starving! Gotta eat!"

The woman muttered something about meeting her husband, then got up and left—as did everyone else at the table, myself included. I knew enough not to look back, but I could hear the man ranting as I left. "Hey! Where's everyone going? Don't be rude! We still got a few minutes left. I need a friend! I need a girlfriend! I need food. NOW!!!"

Given how strange this scene had been, it's surprising that I hadn't thought about it again until all those months later. But maybe it wasn't that surprising at all. There wasn't much to ponder—it was as clear as day: the man was desperate. And the more desperate he became, the more everybody wanted to get away from him.

It went without saying that I would never act like that. Or so I thought. But that's exactly what I'd done at work. I'd become the desperate man. The one who freaked everybody out. The one who nobody wanted to be around. The one who tried to move so fast that he lost control.

It was so obvious now. I just wished I'd realized it earlier that day, when there was still time to stop myself from making a mess. Before I'd started pressuring everybody. Before I'd yelled at Laney. Before I'd blurted out my secret about my profitability deal with the company. And before she'd said those devastating two words:

"I quit."

Lesson #41:
Desperation pushes people away and causes you to make poor choices.

42. What's Left

The day after the fight, I couldn't even drag myself out of bed, much less get myself to work. I had too many questions I didn't want answered. Was Laney really gone? If so, how would I get by without her? And what about everyone else? How much had they heard? Did they all know about my little wager now? And how mad were they that I'd gambled with their jobs, their office, and their futures—and hadn't even told them? Had everybody else also quit? Was *anyone* left at all? How bad was it, exactly?

I had to admit that the prospects looked bleak, but as long as I stayed in bed, there was still hope. Maybe the office was still running. Maybe everyone else was still there, operating at top capacity. Maybe they'd even stepped up their game, realizing they'd have to make up for Laney. Maybe the expos would still be a success, the branch would still be saved, and in two months I'd be marrying Maya. Wishful thinking, I know, but my wishes could still come true.

Or so I thought—until late that morning when Brenda called and confirmed my worst fears.

Well, maybe not my *worst*, but bad. Very bad. People had heard me and Laney yelling, and now they all knew about my wager. And, not surprisingly, they were livid. And when Laney quit, it triggered a mass exodus.

"I've got an inbox full of resignation letters," Brenda said. "Should I forward them to you?"

I groaned. "No. Just…what's the damage?"

"Well…" I heard her clicking her mouse. "We lost Sofia and Liam and Yasmin and…well, you already know about Laney, and there's also Nora and Kareem, who went to Pinnacle, along with…" She paused for a long sigh. "I guess I should tell you—Pinnacle canceled their account and hired everyone they'd been working with, including Diego and—"

"Enough!" I groaned again. "Just tell me who's left." All at once, my heart plunged into my stomach. "Is *anyone* left?"

Brenda's weak laugh did little to reassure me. "Well, let's see…*I'm* here. And Nikhil and Rohan and…oh, wait. Sorry, Nikhil quit too—joined the Pinnacle crew. Keiko's a maybe, and so is Zoey—she said she wanted to think it over. But Tamika's definitely staying."

"Tamika? Really?"

"Yeah, she said she'd known about the, um…deal. I think she felt guilty for not saying anything sooner."

I let out a bitter laugh. "Well, the way things are going, I might need a good lawyer. To go with my—who is there again?—my customer service manager and maybe a designer and tech VP? Some 'Dream Team.'"

"The Dream Team plus a world-class administrative assistant," Brenda said. "Although, to be honest, I'm only staying because Tamika told me I'd have better luck getting unemployment if I waited until the end of the year when we officially shut down."

I hung up, rolled over in bed, and contemplated Brenda's phrasing: *when* we shut down, not *if*. As much as I hated to admit it, I knew she was right: inevitably, we would shut down. And Laney was also right: I *was* incompetent, ignorant, and stupid. And above all, Maya was right: I wasn't going places.

As if to prove just how right Maya was, for the rest of the week, I didn't even leave the house. Not to go shopping, not to get the mail, and certainly not to go to work. What was the point? Two months from now, the office would be closed, we'd all be unemployed, and Maya would be married. (And not to me.)

There simply wasn't time to make a difference. It had taken us almost the whole year to stop bleeding cash each month. Now we were starting from scratch—except with only about a quarter of the staff and just over two months until my year-end deadline.

It was time to face the facts: I had failed.

The week passed in a blur of self-pity, bad TV, and the occasional frozen meal. I had no recollection of heating or eating them, but the wrappers strewn around my apartment proved I had fed myself—at least enough to stay alive. In a sense. I may have brushed my teeth once or twice, but I never so much as turned on the shower. I'm sure I reeked. I'm sure my breath stank. And I'm sure that every cell of my body exuded the same message: *loser.*

But on Saturday morning, something felt different.

I'd lost track of days, so I'm not even sure how I knew it was Saturday, but somehow my body sensed it, like how it often wakes me up just before my alarm goes off. I felt something shift, like the subtle change in the air when spring arrives. A glimmer of…well, not exactly hope, but something to look forward to. It didn't take long for my mind to figure out what it was: aloo saag.

I looked at the clock: 9:22. In just a few hours, I'd be eating my favorite meal in the whole world. No, I wasn't delusional. I didn't think a bowl of curried spinach and potatoes would solve my problems, save the office, or do anything other than provide a bit of comfort, pleasure, and escape for an hour or so. But right then, that sounded like heaven.

So I did something I hadn't done all week: I took a shower. And then I shaved, brushed my teeth, combed my hair, and put on some clean clothes. I grabbed my keys and my wallet, and then I did something else I hadn't done all week: I opened my apartment door.

The light was almost blinding. I squinted and may have actually recoiled. My first instinct was to scurry back indoors, lock the door behind me, and settle for another frozen meal consumed in my curtains-drawn cave. But the aloo saag was calling to me, drawing me out into the light, toward the buffet. I could almost smell it already, and I had no choice but to follow its beckoning aroma. So I took a moment to let my eyes adjust to the light, locked the door behind me, and started walking.

Despite the abundant sunshine, the air was brisk. But it felt good. Invigorating. And in spite of my circumstances, I felt buoyant. Enlivened. Oddly giddy. Like a condemned prisoner eagerly anticipating his last meal: That first spoonful hitting the tongue. The explosion of flavor. The rush of dopamine.

I quickened my pace.

I must have walked even faster than I realized because I reached the buffet ten minutes before they opened. But that worked out just fine with me. It ensured that I'd be the first person in line, the first one in the door, and the first one to the Indian-food room. When the door opened at noon, I darted in, paid, and then practically sprinted to the spot where they kept the aloo saag, only to find…a loaf of bread.

No, it wasn't the naan they usually offer next to the aloo saag. And it wasn't roti or chapati or puri or dosa or any of the other breads that were supposed to be in this area. It was just plain old white bread.

I looked left: more white bread. I looked right: the same.

I spun around and saw, to my horror, that the other tables in the room were also filled with bread. Not just white bread—the full spectrum: whole wheat, rye, pumpernickel, sourdough, multigrain, soda bread, flatbread, focaccia, and so much more. There were breads for breakfast (English muffins, corn bread, and bagels), breads for dessert (cinnamon rolls, coffee cake, and sticky buns), and breads for snacks and side dishes (garlic bread, dinner rolls, and breadsticks). But no naan. No aloo saag. And no Indian food of any kind.

This could not be happening. They couldn't do this to me. Not today. I knew that the buffet sometimes rearranged their rooms, but now was not the time. I was not in the mood for playing hide and seek or any other game. I was in the mood for aloo saag. Which was supposed to be here…but wasn't.

After rubbing my eyes and verifying one last time that the Indian-food room had indeed been converted into the bread room, I dashed around the corner and into the next room—looking around for where they might have moved the saag to. Nowhere in sight.

My heart raced and my breath grew short—and not just from the mad dash I was making. I was panicking—and with good reason! If I couldn't find the aloo saag, then…

No, I refused to go there. Instead of continuing to spiral, I would calmly collect myself, think clearly, and remember the lesson I'd learned way back at the beginning of the year: it's okay to ask for help. Whew! Yes, that's what I would do. And everything would be fine—just fine.

So I stopped the next person walking by—a man with tortoiseshell glasses, neatly parted hair, casual-Friday attire, and a dad bod that made me think he knew his way around the buffet. "Excuse me, sir. I was looking for the Indian food. It used to be back there." I pointed my thumb toward what was now the bread room. "Do you know where they moved it to?"

He shook his head. Ugh! My instincts were off. I could've sworn this guy would steer me right. But, again, I caught myself before I spiraled. I would simply ask the next person I saw. No biggie.

But then, before I could move on to a more informed, more helpful patron, this unassuming man revealed himself for who he truly was: a khaki-wearing messenger of death. Staring straight into my eyes, he spoke four short, horrible words, each one hitting me like a dagger to my heart—and my stomach: "No more Indian food."

He said it as nonchalantly as if he'd mentioned the weather or the time. "Sorry, pal." He patted my shoulder and strolled off toward the deep fryer.

No. This guy clearly didn't know what he was talking about. The buffet had *every* kind of food! I should know—I'd been there every week for almost a year. And they *definitely* had Indian food—most notably aloo saag. And I was going to find it if it was the last thing I did.

I stopped the next person I saw—a woman in jeans and a loose-fitting floral shirt. She'd been striding across the floor like she was on a mission (perhaps searching for saag as well?), but I stepped in front of her and put my hand up. "Excuse me, do you know where the Indian food is?" I asked with a hopeful smile. But my smile vanished the moment she replied.

"Discontinued."

And then this horrible, heartless woman simply walked away with absolutely no regard for whether she'd just ruined my life. But no, there was still hope. Maybe they'd spread the Indian foods around the buffet instead of putting it all in one room. Yes, that had to be it.

I grabbed the forearm of a young man walking in front of me. "Hey! I'm looking for some Indian food—aloo saag…or anything else: curry or dosas or—"

"They stopped it. Tuesday was the last day. No curries, no naan, not even basmati rice."

I tightened my grip on his forearm. But now I wasn't trying to get his attention; I needed it for support. Nonetheless, he pried my fingers off of him and went on his way, leaving me to reel in the aftermath of his news: the final nail in my culinary coffin.

My head spun, my knees grew weak, and before I realized what I was doing, I let out a wail, collapsed into a heap on the floor, buried my head in my arms, and sobbed.

Within moments, a crowd had formed around me.

"Are you okay?"

"Are you breathing?"

"Did you faint?"

"Do you know what year it is? Who's the president? What's your name?"

"Someone call nine-one-one! He needs a medic!"

I glared up. "No! I don't need a medic! I just need some Indian food!" I buried my head again and kept sobbing as the hovering crowd continued to talk over me.

"He's fine! Somebody bring him some curry."

"No can do. Didn't you hear? The Indian chef quit."

"He didn't quit; he's just on vacation."

"It's not a vacation; he's striking because they won't give him a raise."

"It has nothing to do with the chef. Their curry vendor went out of business. Once they find a new supplier, they'll make Indian food again."

"No they won't. I heard that the owner got sick after eating some Indian food last week, and now he's taking it out on all of us by banning it from the buffet forever."

"You guys don't know what you're talking about! This is pure speculation, hearsay, rumors. Nobody knows why this happened."

But as I sat on the floor sobbing, I realized that they were all wrong—especially the last guy. Someone did know why this happened. *I* knew. This was happening because the buffet was tormenting me. It didn't think I'd suffered enough. Clearly, it wasn't bad enough that I'd lost my girlfriend and she was about to marry someone else, that I'd lost my assistant and most of the staff, and that soon I'd lose my job, my house, my car, my office, my remaining employees, my career, and all hope for my future. Now, on top of all that, the buffet decided to play a cruel joke on me—to take away my last shred of dignity and my last source of comfort. It wanted to reduce me to what I really was: nothing.

Well done, buffet. You made your point. I could see it. And everyone around me could see it too. The secret was out. I was nothing—a big fat zero. Or worse than that, actually: a negative. A hopeless case. A pathetic loser.

Someone reached down and grabbed my arm. "Here. Lemme help you up."

I pushed their hand off me. "Leave me alone," I blubbered. "All of you!"

The crowd grew silent. Nobody moved. And then everyone moved—granting my wish: leaving me alone. Except for one little girl who stood in front of me, revealed only when the rest of the group had dispersed. Standing up straight, she was the same height as I was at the moment—hunched over on the floor. Her big eyes looked right into mine with curiosity, innocence, and timeless wisdom seen only in children. I attempted a smile and stretched out my hand to her, but she recoiled, turned her back on me, and ran off into the crowd.

I'm not sure how long I stayed on the floor, but at some point I heard another person clearly addressing me in an unmistakably official tone: "Excuse me sir, we're going to need you to—"

"Okay! Okay!" I wiped away my tears, hauled myself off the floor, and glared at the man (who was either a plainclothes security guard or a self-appointed enforcer of unwritten rules). And before I could get kicked out (or permanently banned—not that it would matter at this point), I wandered off—drifting from room to room in a daze, not even knowing what I was seeing. I just knew what I *wasn't* seeing: aloo saag. Or any Indian food. Room after room, table after table, bowl after bowl, tray after tray—and not a dollop of curry in sight.

I must have walked through a dozen rooms or more—twenty, thirty, who knows?—a fool on a fool's errand. I knew it was hopeless, but it gave me a sort of bitter satisfaction to prove myself right: Ya see? No saag in this room! Ya see? No saag here either. Ya see? I am a loser, and the buffet is heartless, and the universe is a cold, cruel place where everything good always goes bad and all hopes are dashed sooner or later—usually sooner. So why bother?

Yet I continued trudging through saagless room after saagless room. And at some point, I noticed something (other than the lack of saag, that is): a tray of pad Thai that didn't look half bad. But it still wasn't aloo saag, so I walked on. And a while later, I noticed a display of falafel, hummus, and pita that seemed somewhat appetizing. And then in the next room, I passed by some tacos that almost made me double back and grab a few. But no, it wasn't aloo saag, so I kept walking into the next room.

And then the next and then the next and then the next.

And each of these rooms was lined with food of all kinds. There was spicy food, mild food, hot food, chilled food, common food, unusual food, healthy food, junk food, appetizers, entrées, side dishes, and desserts…and it just went on and on.

Just like it always had.

And no, there wasn't aloo saag or any other Indian food. Clearly, that wasn't here now and likely wouldn't be here for the foreseeable future, if ever. But there was still a lot of other food. More than I could eat in a lifetime. And a lot of it looked good—*really* good!

I glanced at my watch: 1:37. I'd wasted over an hour and a half! But I wasn't out of time yet.

I looked up and, from the midst of this mind-boggling bounty, one dish in particular drew me in: green chile stew that smelled amazing and looked mouthwatering. Without pausing to think about what I was doing, I served myself a bowlful, took it to the nearest table, and dug in.

No, it wasn't aloo saag. But it was delicious. And it was comforting. And it taught me exactly what I needed to know.

Lesson #42:
Even if your first choice feels like the best by far,
it's rarely the only path to success.

43. Sorry

Aside from discontinuing Indian food, the buffet didn't make many mistakes. Sure, every now and then a meal didn't taste that great. A few times their baked goods were a bit burnt around the edges, and once or twice they were badly undercooked. For the most part, though, their food was fantastic and the imperfections were few, far between, and relatively minor.

With one notable exception.

One day in late spring (when, if I remember correctly, it felt hot enough to be mid-summer), I had one of the worst meals of my life. It was partly my fault because I was lost in thought—stewing over the latest updates on Maya and Bradford's budding romance—so I wasn't paying attention to my food selections; I just assembled a meal on autopilot, not even noticing what I'd taken until I sat down and had my first bite of salad.

Yuck!

I looked down at my bowl and was horrified by the sight: slimy cucumbers and rotten tomatoes on a pile of wilted lettuce, topped with what I'd thought was ranch dressing but turned out to be rancid dressing.

I cleansed my mouth with a few gulps of water, pushed the bowl aside, and hoped I'd have better luck with my entrée, sweet and sour tofu—but it turned out to be all sour and no sweet. And the veggies mixed in reminded me of a science experiment gone wrong—unidentifiable greens (including some that were clearly not supposed to be green) that looked like they'd been forgotten in the back of the fridge for months. I couldn't even bring myself to take a bite. As I held the fork in front of my mouth, the smell alone turned my stomach. I could only imagine how bad it would taste—but decided not to find out.

Hoping the third food would be the charm, I put down my fork and moved straight to dessert: strawberry shortcake. This had always been one of my favorites, but not this time around. One bite told me that the "fresh" strawberries were quite the opposite. I gagged. Not caring who saw me or how disgusting it looked, I spit out the food (and I use the term loosely). When I examined the uneaten strawberries, I saw the problem: they were covered in mold.

At that point, I got up, brought my almost-full tray to the cleaning station, and headed for the exit. I briefly considered starting over with a different meal, but the other foods I glanced at on my way out looked like they'd also gone south. With my stomach already gurgling ominously, I didn't want to push my luck. Hunched over in discomfort, I staggered home and ate nothing for the rest of the day (unless you count multiple servings of antacid).

If that had been my first experience at the buffet, it definitely would've been my last. However, by that point, I'd eaten so many good meals there that I figured this bad experience was an anomaly. And that turned out to be the case. I kept going back, kept getting excellent food, and would have forgotten all about that rotten food if it hadn't been for the way the buffet handled it.

Apparently, I wasn't the only one who'd had a negative experience, because when I returned to the buffet the following Saturday, the cashier greeted me with the news that today's meal would be free—as would my next two meals after that. She handed me two vouchers and a photocopied letter:

> Dear Valued Customer,
>
> Last week, The Buffet accidentally served numerous meals that contained spoiled ingredients. As a result, many of you ate unpalatable food that, in some cases, caused nausea or other illnesses. I sincerely apologize for these terrible experiences— including the physical distress we caused and the violation of the trust you put in us. As The Buffet's manager, it is my responsibility to prevent issues like this from arising, so the blame falls squarely on me for this oversight.
>
> While there is never any excuse for a mistake of this magnitude, we did belatedly discover what caused it: unbeknownst to us at the time, a blown fuse cut power to four refrigerators (all of which shared a single outlet). Although it is too late to undo last week's

fiasco, we have taken steps to prevent anything like this from happening again. We separated our refrigerators so each one gets its own outlet. Furthermore, we now check our fuse box at the beginning and end of each day. We also bought a generator, which will keep our power on in the event of an outage. In addition, we hired a QC specialist to conduct quality-control inspections of every food item before it is offered to our customers. Lastly, all staff members have now been trained to spot potential issues with food—ranging from spoilage to problems with sanitation—to assure that everything we serve is of the highest quality possible.

We hope these steps will help earn back your trust in The Buffet and improve our food and service for the future. For now, however, to apologize for the problems we caused last week and to thank you for giving us another chance, we would like to offer you three free meals.

Please let me know if there is anything else I can do to improve your experience at The Buffet. Feel free to call me any time. I am here for you, and I welcome your feedback.

Then the manager signed the letter and gave his phone number. And I know it really was his number because, out of curiosity, I called—then hung up as soon as he answered and identified himself. Juvenile of me, I know, but I doubted he'd give it out to so many people, many of whom were likely irate.

(And by the way, in case you're wondering how I remember this letter verbatim, I saved it. Yes, it's a sad reflection of my life at the time, which consisted of little more than going to work during the week, eating at the buffet on Saturdays, and writing down lessons in my journal, which is where I kept this letter.)

In any case, I enjoyed the free meals—and many subsequent paid meals thereafter. And I didn't give the incident or the apology letter another thought for many months. However, after the blow-up at work—with Laney and so many others quitting because of how I'd mishandled my high-stakes "wager" with the company—I realized I owed my remaining employees a big apology. And the buffet's letter seemed like a perfect model to use when I spoke to everyone on Monday.

So I went back through my journal, found the letter, and reread it. Actually, I didn't just reread it; I studied it. I thought about the principles it embodied. And I considered how I could apply them to my situation.

As I reviewed the letter, I pinpointed seven key elements:

1. *Actually saying "I'm sorry"* (or similar words, such as "I apologize") – not being indirect, cagey, or ambiguous in a way that makes people wonder whether this actually is an apology.

2. *Saying precisely what you're sorry for* – not keeping it general or vague (e.g., saying, "I'm sorry for whatever I might have done" or "Mistakes were made").

3. *Acknowledging how the wronged party feels and how they've been affected* – not making it all about yourself (e.g., going on and on about how terrible you feel, to the point where it feels like a calculated cry to be comforted by the person you wronged, rather than vice versa).

4. *Taking ownership* – not blaming others—especially not the person you're apologizing to (e.g., by saying something like, "I'm sorry you're so oversensitive that you couldn't take a joke and got offended").

5. Describing what you'll do to improve and to avoid similar situations in the future – not leaving the person wondering if this is just going to keep happening.

6. *Being open to feedback and letting people decide if, when, and how they want to respond* – not assuming that just because you apologized, the situation is now resolved—or assuming that people won't still be upset (e.g., saying, "Gosh! What's your problem? I said I'm sorry—why can't you just let it go and move on?").

7. *Knowing when to stop* – not undoing whatever reparative steps you've taken by following up your apology with excuses or turning it back on the other person (e.g., by saying, "Okay, I messed up—I'm human! But it's not like you're perfect either. There was that time when you…").

I wrote these elements in my journal and contemplated them until I'd internalized them. And I thought about how I could apply them to my own situation. (And then I thought about it some more, and some more, and some more.)

Then, on Monday morning, I asked my remaining employees if they'd join me in the conference room. Once we'd all gathered there, I looked around at the group—still surprised that there were so few of us left: only Brenda, Rohan, Tamika, Zoey, and me. But regardless of the size of the team, I had something I needed to say to all of them on an individual level. So I stood up, looked from one face to the next, and, with my heart in my hand (and in my throat), addressed them:

"First of all, I want to apologize for not telling you about my profitability deal with the company. I realize that by keeping this from you, I've violated your trust, jeopardized your future, and, as several of you have already told me, hurt your feelings. It was wrong of me, and I fully accept the blame for creating this difficult situation."

As much as I wanted to run back to my office and hide under the desk—or, at the very least, avoid eye contact—I forced myself to keep facing the people I'd wronged. Taking a deep breath, I continued:

"If I'm fortunate enough to continue working with you, I promise that from this day on, I'll be completely transparent. No secrets. No backroom deals. All cards on the table. And I promise to work together as a team, keeping everyone fully informed so you can make the decisions that feel right to you."

As I paused, I again made eye contact with each person there, one by one, forcing myself to feel their hurt and their disappointment in me. Quietly, I concluded my apology: "Please know that I'm one hundred percent open to hearing your thoughts and feelings. If you want to talk, I'm here to listen. Or if you need a while to think it over, please take as much time as you want. And whatever you decide to do, know that I'll honor and support you."

There was so much more I wanted to say. I wanted to tell them that we still had a great team, that there was still time to turn things around and become profitable by the end of the year, and that I still wanted to give it our best shot at an expo or two. But I remembered the buffet's letter and the importance of knowing when to stop—giving them time and space to process everything in their own way, even if it wasn't what I would've chosen.

While mentally rehearsing my apology, I'd feared the worst: raised voices, spiteful name-calling, perhaps even threats (legal or otherwise). I imagined them interrupting me before I could even get my words out—telling me I was the worst boss ever (or *ex*-boss) and walking out en masse (not that there was much of a "mass" left at that point), leaving me in the conference room, utterly alone and utterly defeated.

But in optimistic moments, I allowed myself to consider my ideal outcome: hugs, expressions of gratitude, and assurances that everything was okay and that, yes, of course we'd be able to move forward together—reaching our shared goals, growing even closer, learning from the past, and emerging stronger than ever as individuals and as a team. The whole situation might even turn out to be a blessing in disguise.

Or so I'd hoped.

In reality, the team's reaction was, in many ways, even worse than what I'd imagined: stony silence. They just sat and stared at me without a word. Eventually, when it became clear that I was done speaking—and that none of them wanted to say anything just then—they filed out of the conference room and returned to their workstations. No, they didn't leave the office, but in some ways that would've been preferable. Everyone staying only prolonged the awkwardness, the negative energy, and the uncertainty.

Throughout the day, the gnawing in my gut was worse than anything I would've felt from eating Brazil nuts, raw dough, and moldy strawberry shortcake combined. But I knew it was my own doing. And now there was nothing to do but wait, stay open to hearing from them (if or when they wanted to reach out), and hope for the best.

That afternoon, we agreed that everyone would take the week off (with pay) and then let me know if or how they wanted to move forward.

It was the worst and the longest week of my life. I continued to come to the office every day, just in case someone showed up and wanted to talk. But no one did. And no one called. Or wrote.

Left alone, I didn't know what to do with myself. Should I plan for the Buffalo expo? Should I look into liquidating our assets? Should I contact an employment agency…or a bankruptcy attorney?

Instead, I just paced the floors, berated myself, and repeatedly checked my phone for messages. Nothing. Not a single word from any of them. No sign of whether there was hope or whether we were done for. Until Friday afternoon at 4:45, when a message came in, signed by all of them. It consisted merely of three short sentences: *Don't let it happen again. We trust you. Let's do this thing.*

Lesson #43:
When you make mistakes, don't make excuses.
Instead, make a sincere apology, make things right,
make sure it won't happen again, and make
yourself better.

44. Behind the Scenes

I called them "The Faithful Four." Despite the jam I'd put them in, how much I'd messed up, and the long odds against us, they stuck with me. And, true to their word, the remaining team members—Brenda, Rohan, Tamika, and Zoey—were in the office Monday morning, ready to move on and move forward.

But it's one thing to be *ready* to move forward—and another to actually do it. Especially when you have no idea which way "forward" is. There was no yellow brick road laid out for us (and I no longer had my "good witch" Laney at my side to point the way), so we had to find the best path on our own. But with so many options and no clear-cut right choice, which one should we pick? Should we proceed with our plan of attending five expos? (After all, there were still five of us, so it was technically possible.) Should we pick one or two to focus on? Should we stay in the office and contact some of our previous clients or pursue the few lukewarm leads we still had? Or should we move in an entirely new direction?

Even though I didn't know *what* we should do, I knew *how* I wanted to do it: with teamwork and transparency. So, unlike before, I laid everything out on the table—figuratively and literally. Brenda printed all our notes and records, which she spread out on the conference table. Then, after brewing a pot of coffee and filling the biggest mugs we could find, the five of us met in the conference room, pulled up our chairs around the now-oversized table, and examined the printouts, starting with our financial statements.

As expected, they were not pretty.

In fact, the situation was even more dire than any of us had realized. Even when we'd had the Pinnacle account, we hadn't been on pace to make a profit that year. Without Pinnacle, we weren't even close. If we still had our full staff, digging our way out of debt in the next six weeks would have been a daunting task. With just the five of us, it seemed almost impossible.

Almost. But not completely.

After all, we were "how" people. We didn't dwell on why it couldn't be done. Because it could. (At least in theory.) We just had to get down to the business of figuring out how. And then do it.

We'd already taken the first step—in many ways, the most important one of all: taking a clear-eyed look at the current situation. No sugar-coating. No vague generalities. Hard, cold specifics, right in front of us in black and white, in all their gruesome, grisly yuckiness. It was enough to make us recoil in horror. Give up. Run away. Hide under the table. Or spend the rest of the day watching funny cat videos and pretending the situation didn't exist. But that certainly wasn't going to fix it.

But what would?

That was the million-dollar question. And yes, to get us into the black, the answer would have to generate somewhere in the ballpark of a million dollars—which is what I would owe if we didn't turn this thing around...*fast!*

So, we spent the morning discussing the situation, weighing the pros and cons of possible paths, and, with varying levels of success, trying not to freak out.

By noon, we still hadn't decided on a path. But we did agree on several points:

1. The expos were a good idea. (There was a reason we'd decided on this path in the first place.)
2. We should only do shows in November. (This way, even with our net-30 terms, we'd be paid by the end of the year—which, as the Faithful Four now understood, was essential to our branch's survival.)
3. We shouldn't do every show we'd signed up for. (As much as I hated to forfeit the non-refundable deposits, attempting Tampa's Nano-Q Conference without Nikhil was hopeless. Ditto for Seattle's Design Expo without Keiko. And IoT had never really been our strong suit. Which left us with our next point...)

4. Our two best possibilities were the Vegas B2B show and XR+ in Buffalo.

5. Whatever we chose, we needed to make a decision soon because we had a *lot* of work to do and not a lot of time to do it in. (Hence our self-imposed deadline of deciding before lunch.)

Five people, five points of agreement—not a bad start. But after that, our opinions diverged.

"Let's do both," Rohan said. "Double our chances."

"No, we're stronger together." Brenda clasped her hands. "All of us in Buffalo."

Tamika shook her head. "That makes me very nervous—putting all our eggs in one basket."

Rohan looked at Zoey. "Whaddya say, Z? Party in Vegas?"

Zoey laughed. "Sounds like fun, but I'm with Brenda. We're better off going all in with one show—all of us together. And Buffalo's clearly the best fit. We could pitch the AR headset—it's perfect for small businesses."

The more we discussed it, the more the Faithful Four remained faithful to their original positions. And it soon became clear that I would have to cast the deciding vote. But unlike the others, I was torn. Both sides seemed to have their merits and their drawbacks. Would our motto be *Divide and conquer*…or *Divided we fall*? Should we go for a unified front…or a diversified portfolio? Saturday night on the Strip sounded like fun (and it would probably be about thirty degrees warmer than Buffalo)…but Zoey was right about XR+ being a better fit. The only thing I knew for sure was that, whether we went to Vegas or not, either way would be a gamble.

I suddenly realized that while I'd been lost in thought, everyone else had grown silent. All eyes were on me. I had to make a decision. And it had to be now. (We were already twenty minutes past our usual lunchtime.) It was time for me to step up and be a leader.

"Okay, guys," I said. "There's only one fair and sensible way to decide this." I reached into my wallet and pulled out a quarter. "Heads, we all go to Buffalo. Tails, we split up and do both shows." Although Tamika shook her head and Zoey groaned, I went ahead with my plan. Clearing the space in front of me, I balanced the quarter between my index finger and the conference table, gave the coin a flick, and watched it spin.

In those few seconds while our fate was yet to be determined, scenes of the two possible outcomes flashed through my mind: Imagining myself in Vegas with Rohan felt fun but somehow...*off*. I shifted myself to Buffalo with Zoey. A bit better, but I still felt insubstantial, nervous with only one person for backup. I added Tamika—a bit better, a bit stronger. I thought of Rohan and Brenda taking on the Vegas expo by themselves. Then I mentally brought the whole group together in Buffalo. Yes. That's when it all clicked. We were one unit, one team. All working together toward a common goal. We'd fill the double-sized booth with our complementary roles, personalities, and areas of expertise. And, at least in my mind and in my gut, it worked.

The quarter was spinning slower. Within a few moments I would know whether I got my newly formed wish of having all of us together in Buffalo...or if we'd be split up on almost-opposite sides of the country. *Come on, heads!* The coin wobbled, about to fall when, without planning to, I reached out and grabbed it.

"Hey!" yelled Rohan. "What are you doing?"

"I thought you were gonna decide where we were going," said Brenda.

"I did." I glanced from side to side, grinning at the confusion on my teammates' faces. "We're going to Buffalo. All of us."

Rohan let out a groan, and Tamika shook her head. Brenda, on the other hand, grinned broadly while Zoey nodded and gave me a thumbs up. However, even the partial approval evaporated the moment I explained the next part of the plan: "Because the expo is Saturday, we've gotta set up on Friday. So I want us all to get to Buffalo on Thursday so we can—"

"NOOOOO!" the four of them shouted in unison, shooting looks of horror at me.

"Not on Thanksgiving!" Brenda said. "My whole family's flying in."

Tamika shook her head more vehemently than before. "Not doin' it. Not a chance."

"I can live with missing Vegas," Rohan said, "but I gotta draw the line here. I don't work on Thanksgiving, Christmas, or Super Bowl Sunday." His throat-slash hand gesture—which presumably indicated *It ain't gonna happen*—looked uncomfortably close to *Off with his head!*

Zoey, meanwhile, remained ominously quiet, but her glare told me everything I needed to know…and then some: if I didn't back down on this one, I'd have a riot on my hands.

"On second thought," I said, "maybe I'll go alone on Thursday—just to sign in and get situated in the conference center. Then you guys can join me Friday to set everything up. How's that sound?"

They still didn't look thrilled as they did the math and realized they'd have to catch a red-eye late Thursday or early Friday morning. But they would have Thanksgiving at home. Not an ideal holiday weekend, but they could live with it. And at least we now had a plan and could officially break for lunch.

As we made our way out of the conference room, there were more than a few grumbles all around. But by the time we reconvened, everyone was fully on board with the new plan. Or, if they weren't, at least they acted as if they were—projecting confidence, enthusiasm, and optimism. More importantly, they quickly began generating ideas, coming up with ways to bring them to life, and taking the first steps to make it all happen.

We agreed that our best bet was to pitch the AR headsets—Kareem's very first idea, which had seemed so off-base when he'd proposed it. Since then, Zoey had developed it into a viable product, and although we'd never marketed it, it seemed like a perfect fit for the XR+ expo.

Over the next few hours, Zoey dug up the old prototype, familiarized us all with the features, discussed some of its applications, and whipped us into a near-frenzy of enthusiasm for this little gadget's potential. By the end of the day, there was no denying it—this really was happening.

Although the "Profitability Plan" had felt daunting at first, it didn't seem so far-fetched once we took the "watermelon-eating" approach and broke it down into smaller steps. To prepare for the expo, we just needed to do three things:

1. Make signs and pamphlets to hand out to prospects.
2. Write and practice our sales pitches.
3. Create a demo to show potential clients how the headset worked.

Then we had to go to the convention center, set up our booth, and get one big client at the expo (or a few medium-sized ones or a bunch of small ones). If we could do this, one day after Black Friday we could actually find ourselves in the black.

Although I'd opted for the "united we stand" approach, our preparation was a "divide and conquer" operation. Zoey was in charge of the tech demo, with Rohan assisting. Tamika wrote the pamphlets. And because Brenda had taken a few art classes in college, she became our de facto designer, working on the signs and laying out pamphlets. That left it up to me to come up with our sales pitch, practice it, and make sure the team could deliver on my promises.

I'm the first to admit that I'm not a natural-born salesman. If Liam had still been around, I gladly would have delegated this role to him. Or Yasmin or Diego. But they were all gone. Maybe it would work out, though. After all, one big benefit of doing an expo on Small Business Saturday is that clients knew they wouldn't get lost in a big-business maze of bureaucracy and red tape—they could go right to the top. And as uncomfortable as it felt to say it—even after nearly a year in this role—I was "the top."

And at that moment, despite all the challenges we faced, I had to admit that the view from the top didn't look that bad. Sure, we only had until next Wednesday to get everything ready, but when you broke it down, "everything" wasn't really that much. Tamika was writing a few hundred words about our offerings, Brenda was making them look good, Zoey and Rohan were demoing one product, and I was tying it all together and closing the deals. If we'd needed to, we could've been ready by the end of the day.

But we weren't.

That was fine, though. We weren't in *that* big a rush. Better to do a careful job—make sure we dotted every *i* and crossed every *t*. And, above all, make sure the tech demo worked properly. But after a few days, I started to wonder what was taking so long. I mean, Zoey had said the demo would be under five minutes—ideally, just two or three. "People make up their mind *fast*," she'd told me. So why was she dragging her feet with this? A two-minute demo shouldn't take weeks to make, right? Maybe they'd be done by now if Rohan didn't insist on color coding his notes—or if Zoey would just eat lunch at her desk instead of going out to "get her steps in."

And the others were taking their sweet old time too. Brenda was supposedly waiting to use images from the final product, and Tamika was trying out different marketing angles in online split tests. "But we don't need different angles," I told her. "Just one."

"Exactly," she said. "That's why I want to get the *right* one."

"Well, just make sure you've got *something* ready in time," I said, exhaling a little more forcefully than I'd meant to before I retreated to my office to practice my sales pitches (a dozen variations, all of which I'd written and memorized in less than a day, thank you very much).

Over the next few days, I experienced a whole gamut of emotions: nervous (Are we gonna get this done in time?) and then angry (What is everybody's problem?) and then confused (Seriously, what is everybody's problem? Why is this taking so long?). By the end of the week, I was simply deflated.

The cloud that descended on me on Friday afternoon still hadn't lifted when I went to the buffet on Saturday. I'm sure the food looked and smelled as good as ever, but I couldn't honestly tell you. I just wandered through the rooms in a stupor, consumed by doubts about work. Was there something fundamentally wrong with this project? With this team? With me? After all, *I'd* hired these people, approved the plan, and organized the operation. And it wasn't working. A one-day project centered around a two-minute demo had ballooned into an all-week ordeal. And we *still* weren't done! Seriously, what was the problem?

I barely noticed what I was eating—a sandwich of some kind, maybe with a fruit salad on the side—but I must have scarfed it down because I finished just before 12:30. I'd been at the buffet for less than half an hour! When you subtracted the time it took to wait in the entrance line, pay, get my tray, serve my food, and get situated at a table, I'd probably eaten an entire meal in about ten minutes.

This thought made me absolutely furious—not at the buffet or at myself but at my team. An entire meal in ten minutes—that wasn't much longer than the demo was supposed to be. Yet the buffet didn't take weeks to prepare it. They would've been out of business long ago! No, they managed to have everything ready before noon. So why couldn't my team do the same? Why couldn't they prepare a simple experience—something that, like my lunch, would only take a few minutes—and have it ready in a day, just like the buffet?

Right before my anger reached a boiling point, my mind came to a screeching halt—and then backed up and reconsidered my recent thoughts: *Just like the buffet?* Really? Did they really prepare an entire meal in one morning? Or was there more to it than meets the eye? Sure, they might have heated the food and brought it out that morning, but didn't a lot of steps need to happen before that?

I didn't know their behind-the-scenes process, but I could guess some of the steps involved: menu planning, food purchasing, ingredient preparation, staff coordination…and that's not even getting into everything involved with the equipment: buying, setting up, and testing the various cooking devices and appliances, farming equipment, and trucks that transported everything. It was already a multi-month operation. And then there were all the years of training and experience people went through before they were even ready for this stage. Sure, my meal might have taken me ten minutes to eat, but countless hours had gone into that ten-minute experience. The food on my plate wasn't even the tip of the iceberg; it was a single snowflake on its tip.

There was nothing wrong with the buffet, their staff, or the other people they worked with. They weren't slow; that's just how long it took. And there was nothing wrong with my team. They weren't being inefficient. They weren't incompetent. And, despite the paranoid thoughts that had occasionally flashed through my mind over the past few days, they weren't trying to sabotage the operation in order to get revenge. They were simply doing their jobs—thoroughly and professionally. They were creating products and experiences that customers would see, appreciate, and hopefully buy. But those customers would never see 99% of what the team did—everything that formed the foundation for the visible tip. And, despite my misgivings and repeated requests for reassurance, that foundation was coming along just fine. They had guaranteed me that it would all be ready in time, and I trusted them.

Lesson #44:
Visible results may get the most attention, but the work that no one sees makes up the vast majority of any project.

45. The Out-of-Towner

Just as we'd hoped, the team finished their prep in time, and my trip couldn't have gone smoother. By all rights, I should have been thrilled. However, I felt distinctly unthrilled as I stared out the hotel window at the Erie Basin. The photo on the hotel website had been so picturesque—warm and inviting, with a caption claiming that locals call it the "Cheery Basin." But on this cold, dismal afternoon, it looked more like the "Dreary Basin."

The sky was several stages beyond cloudy—an all-encompassing gray that smothered everything below. And the substance falling from that gray sky couldn't rightly be called snow. It looked like a sadistic weather committee had combined the worst traits of sleet, slush, hail, and semi-frozen rain into a single, joy-sapping precipitation. Well, their diabolical plan was working.

I was alone on Thanksgiving, and I'd never felt less thankful in all my life.

For the third time that afternoon, I called my parents. Again, no answer. They must've turned off their phones so as not to be interrupted during their big holiday get-together, as they did each year. But still, I thought maybe they'd make an exception, seeing as I wasn't with them.

Even from this distance, I knew exactly what they were doing at that moment: devouring pumpkin pie while sharing all they had to be thankful for from that year. If I had been there with them, what could I have shared? Let's see…we were coming up on the one-year anniversary (or "antiversary") of Maya breaking up with me. And suspiciously soon after that, she'd started dating Bradford the HR lame-o. But no, just dating him wouldn't have been cruel enough—she had to get engaged. Ah, yes, so much to be thankful for in my love(less) life.

What else? How about the hollow-gut loneliness of being a stranger in a new town, the nerve-racking stress of working without a safety net, and the bitter knowledge that I was a bad impersonator of a manager who had been ignominiously unmasked. And then there were the joys of life in the office: the burst pipe, the week without air conditioning (during a heat wave, of course), and that memorable moment when the server crashed in the middle of our demo to what would have been our biggest client of the year. But of course, all of that paled in comparison to the coup de grâce: Laney's betrayal and the ensuing exodus of employees and Pinnacle (who I'd mentally dubbed "Pit-acle").

So yes, it had been quite a year.

Maybe it was for the best that I couldn't be with my parents or even get ahold of them. The last thing they needed was Captain Downer raining on their Thanksgiving parade. Nonetheless, as an exercise in futility—and because I had nothing else to do—I called again. For a fourth time, the rings went unanswered.

I couldn't stand the view anymore, so I closed the curtains and slumped into the world's least comfortable armchair. Then, not because I was hungry but simply for something to break the monotony, I grabbed my plastic bag of food off the table beside me, reached inside, and pulled out the meal I'd brought specially for the occasion. I could've ordered room service—or simply waited until five, when the hotel restaurant reopened—but somehow my homemade meal seemed more appropriate for the circumstances. So I unwrapped it and sank my teeth into my very own personalized Thanksgiving dinner: a half-stale peanut butter and jelly sandwich.

What did that singer say just before he died—enjoy every sandwich? Well, he'd obviously never tried this one. Never before had I so missed the buffet. I thought back to my most recent lunch there—an assortment of mouth-watering dim sum that I'd been enjoying just five days earlier, although in some ways it felt like a lifetime. Ah, what I wouldn't give to be surrounded by that bounty of culinary delights right now!

But even that would-be happy memory was marred by an unwanted guest: the out-of-towner.

As soon as I'd sat down with my delicacy-packed tray, he'd approached me and asked if the seat across from me was taken. I told him no and invited him to sit down, which I instantly regretted. He plopped down with a world-weary sigh and immediately launched into an account of the traumatic journey he'd just completed. He'd been driving for almost twenty-four hours straight, during which time he'd experienced almost every imaginable mishap: he'd gotten a flat tire in the middle of nowhere, he'd gotten lost three times (once seriously enough to add several hours to his drive), and while he was asking directions at a convenience store, his car had been towed. Even when he was on the road, heading the right way, the journey had been harrowing—driving through hailstorms, over black ice, and through fender-deep slush. And worst of all, he hadn't had a bite to eat the whole time.

"Then why aren't you eating now?" asked the man sitting diagonally from me (who, like me, couldn't avoid being dragged into the out-of-towner's top-volume tale). "They've got everything you could possibly want here, and as you know, it's all you can eat. I bet you'll get your money's worth!" The man laughed, but the out-of-towner simply shook his head in disgust.

"You don't understand—this trip was an absolute nightmare! Everything that could've gone wrong went wrong. I'm exhausted, frazzled, and starving."

"Well then chow down, my friend! Clearly you've already paid, or they wouldn't have let you in here. So eat! Drink! Be merry! The nightmare is over; you can finally—"

"No!" The out-of-towner stood up and banged on the table. "You're not hearing me!" The whole area grew quiet; we were certainly hearing him now. "My whole journey here was terrible! Nothing to eat! Dangerous weather! Car trouble! It was one big…" He stopped midsentence and slumped back into his chair. "Never mind. You just don't get it."

After exchanging baffled glances with several other people at the table, I picked up my tray, muttered an excuse about being late to an appointment, and got as far away as I could from the out-of-towner.

And now, less than a week later, *I* was "the out-of-towner"—over a thousand miles from anything I could even remotely consider my home.

But suddenly I realized I was also the out-of-towner in another sense: just like the man from the buffet, I'd spent the entire afternoon recounting my past woes—all the mishaps, setbacks, and heartaches I'd experienced on the way to this place. Yes, it was all true, just like I assume his tale of woe had been true. Yes, Maya had dumped me, Laney had quit (and stolen my most crucial team members along with our star account), and the server had crashed at the worst time possible. But it was all in the past. In this moment, I was safe, warm, and dry—just like the out-of-towner had been. And like him, I could've chosen to eat almost anything I wanted. Also like him, I had reason to believe that things were looking up.

I didn't know the details of his situation (aside from his recent dreadful drive), but I did know that my own life gave me reason for hope. The next day, I'd be joined by my faithful, brilliant colleagues. We'd prepare for the expo, which could very well be the positive turning point I'd been waiting for. And even if it didn't go as well as I hoped, even a modest success could push us into the black and guarantee me a raise and at least one more year of gainful employment.

No, it wasn't my first choice of how to spend the holiday. But there were worse things in life than being alone on Thanksgiving. There were worse things in life than losing some employees. And, come to think of it, there were worse things in life than peanut butter and jelly sandwiches.

Lesson #45:
Constantly reliving the past can keep you from
living in the present or planning for a brighter
future.

46. The Expo

When I woke up, it felt like I'd stepped into a new world—one where my imagined brighter future had already begun. Granted, the sky was as gray as ever and that mysterious precipitation was still falling, but my mood couldn't have been sunnier. I was just where I needed to be: poised on the brink of a breakthrough.

After I showered, got dressed, and had a hot cup of surprisingly good hotel-room coffee, it was 8:50—still over an hour until the Faithful Four arrived. I'd told them I'd stay in my room until they got here so we could go down to the conference center and set up together, but I was too excited to wait any more. Clearly, I wasn't the only one. By 9:05, the place was already hopping.

The event itself was only on "Small Business Saturday," but vendors (or "presenters," as the events organizers encouraged us to call ourselves) were allowed to set up the day before. So that's what they were doing—and what I'd be doing soon. But for now, I was grateful for this chance to take it all in (and, truth be told, scope out the competition).

At the moment, it all seemed a bit chaotic—hordes of people unpacking equipment, setting up displays, pushing dollies, and, for the most part, managing not to crash into other people's dollies, displays, and equipment. Everyone was dressed as casually as possible: sweatshirts, sweatpants, unfashionably ripped jeans, dirty sneakers, rumpled t-shirts, messy hair, and not an ounce of beauty product to be found. But I knew that tomorrow would be a totally different scene: power suits, slick displays, slick hairdos, and everybody bringing their A game.

And I would be among them: the A team, the slick, the powerful, and, if all went well, the profitable. If only Maya could see me now—well, twenty-four hours from now, when I too would be wearing a power suit, wowing my soon-to-be clients with a dazzling tech display, and captivating the steadily swelling crowd as I addressed them through my headset microphone. Yes, the vision was finally becoming real. I was the man Maya wanted me to be. The go-getter. The world-beater. The husband she deserved. And so much more.

But first things first: we had our own booth to set up, which we'd do as soon as the Four arrived. I checked my watch: 9:52—I should be hearing from them any minute now.

They must have read my mind—mere moments later, my phone rang. "Zoey! I was just thinking of you. Where are you?"

"Hey! I'm at the airport with Tamika, Brenda, and Rohan."

"Great! So I'll probably see you in, what, twenty minutes? Half an hour? You're renting a car, right?"

"Actually, there's been a change of plans."

"That's okay. Do you want me to come pick you up? I've got a rental, so I can be there in—"

"No," she said. "We're not in Buffalo." She paused for a prolonged moment before answering my unspoken question. "We're in Des Moines."

My stomach sank and my mind reeled as I stammered. "You're...what? In...like, Iowa?" I checked the phone number. This was Zoey from the office, right? "What are you...I thought you had a direct flight?"

"We did, but we got rerouted because of the snowstorm." Panic's icy fingers closed around my throat. Before they could finish the job, though, Zoey continued. "But there's supposedly another flight this afternoon, so we can be there in a few hours."

I didn't like the sound of that "supposedly," but for the moment, that's all we had. Two hours later, however, we didn't even have that. Zoey called back to say that, due to the storms, all would-be connecting flights had been postponed or canceled.

For the next few minutes, I was only vaguely aware of Zoey's voice as she kept talking—something about layovers, standby, and rerouting— but I knew what she was really saying: *You're screwed.*

I couldn't do this alone. I didn't have the displays. I didn't have the demo. And even if I did, I had no idea how to operate it.

I couldn't believe it. Just a few hours earlier, I'd been on top of the world, and now I had no choice but to throw in the towel. I had to face reality: I was done. Dream shattered. Game over. World: one; me: zero.

When my mind finally quieted down enough to let me hear Zoey's actual words again, however, I realized that this wasn't what she was saying at all. She wasn't ready to give up. We could still make it work, she said. There was always a Plan B, right? (Or Plan C or whatever we were on by now.) Knowing it was a long shot, I joined her for a quick brainstorm: "Can you run the demo remotely?" I asked. No luck—all the equipment was in her check-in luggage, which had been loaded onto a different flight before the storm shut everything down. "Could someone else do it?" Kareem was the only other person who knew how, but he no longer worked for us (and even if he did, he wouldn't be able to get to Buffalo in time—and besides, everything he'd need was in those stupid bags).

After a few more rejected suggestions, we settled on Plan D for *Drive*: they would rent a car in Des Moines. It would be quite a haul (we looked it up: 855 miles—oof), but if they left now, they could get to the Buffalo airport around midnight, pick up their bags, and set everything up before the expo opened tomorrow morning. Not ideal, but at this point, that's all we had. We were going on a wing and a prayer—except without the wing.

In a stupor, I staggered back to my hotel room, paced the floor, and prayed that the snow would stop. (Perhaps the diabolical weather committee was finally done toying with us, and the Faithful Four would have clear roads and a safe, easy, and fast ride.) As we'd planned, Zoey checked in with progress reports every two hours. Because of the conditions, it was slow going, but at least they were heading in the right direction. Aside from a little scare east of Davenport, when they lost reception and didn't call for almost four hours, things seemed to be going okay. Except it was clearly going to be a much later night (or, rather, early morning) than we'd anticipated. So, figuring that at least one of us should be well rested for the expo, I went to sleep at ten.

Or at least I tried to. Thanks to my whirling thoughts, it was probably more like two or three when I finally drifted off, but I still woke up feeling rested and raring to go by seven. Before I even got out of bed, I called Zoey. She was probably exhausted, but at least she was here. Or so I assumed. My call went straight to voicemail. Ditto for Tamika, Brenda, and Rohan.

Okay, now I was nervous. But those four were nothing if not responsible. They'd probably just turned off their ringers to get some sleep—set an alarm for 7:30 or something like that. Nothing to worry about. They said they'd be there, and they would.

But still.

Anyway, for the time being, I did the only thing I could do—what I'd been doing (or trying to do) for years: focus on what I could control. I got up, showered, shaved, put on extra antiperspirant, ironed my power suit, and transformed myself into the perfect picture of a confident, skillful, and successful business leader. Someone who people could trust. Someone they'd want to work with. Someone Maya would want to marry. A go-getter.

My moment had arrived. Even under these less-than-ideal conditions, I had to rise to the occasion. It was time for the go-getter to go get 'er.

When the transformation was complete, I headed downstairs, flashed my presenter's badge to the woman at the check-in booth, walked through the conference center's grand double doors, and awaited my destiny. Unfortunately, I also awaited the Four, who *still* weren't there. I know they said they could set up in half an hour, but the doors were opening in forty minutes. This was too close for comfort.

I called Zoey again. Still no answer. Ditto for the other three. Come on, people. Unacceptable. Even with all that extra antiperspirant, I was sweating bullets.

I didn't want to stray too far from our booth (or booth *area*, seeing as it was still empty), but even from there, I could see that everyone else was ready to go: Professionally printed signs and banners hanging straight. Tables and displays fully stocked with products and literature. Demos in full swing—flashing graphics, scrolling words, and functional technology. Just like ours would have been if the Four had just gotten there when they said they would.

At 8:45 I left another round of voicemails—my most emphatic yet: "The doors are officially opening in fifteen minutes. I don't care what's going on; just get here—NOW!" Clearly, I hadn't been emphatic enough—by 8:55 they were still nowhere in sight.

The event coordinator came by and asked if everything was okay. "Sure," I said, trying to force a smile. "Just waiting for my team. They'll be here any minute." She looked at my empty booth, looked at her watch, rolled her eyes, marked something on her clipboard, and walked away.

When the doors opened, I still hadn't heard from the Four, so I did the only thing I could: face the crowds alone.

For better or worse, there wasn't much of a crowd. At least not at first. Maybe the weather had kept some people away—or simply delayed them. Nonetheless, the people who were there were potential clients. Faithful Four or not, I had to bring my A game. Such as it was.

A few minutes after the doors opened, a man in a pinstripe suit approached my booth. Okay, it was show time! I made eye contact, smiled confidently, and delivered the line I'd mentally rehearsed so many times: "Are you ready to empower your business with cutting-edge solutions for a brighter future?"

Clearly, he wasn't ready—he simply looked down at his phone, picked up his pace, and moved on to the next booth. Maybe he just hadn't heard me. If only I had that headset mic! Well, I would as soon as the Four arrived—any minute now. Right?

In the meantime, I just had to project, connect, and exude a winning attitude. And maybe try out a few different lines. As the next potential client approached, I greeted her with another well-polished gem: "Would you like to experience seamless integration for unparalleled performance?" I thought I delivered the line convincingly, but her reaction was similar to the pinstripe man's (except instead of looking at her phone, she suddenly seemed very interested in a pamphlet she was holding). I wasn't about to quit, though. Each new person was a new opportunity to succeed and to experiment with other greetings. "Are you ready to revolutionize the way you work?" Again, not ready. "Can we help you simplify complexity with our innovative approach?" Not interested in innovation. "Would you like to build a better tomorrow with today's technology?" Clearly, still stuck in yesterday.

I would've loved to land a new client before the Four arrived—to show them how self-sufficient I was, how I could turn passersby into customers. But so far, the passersby were just passing me by.

That was okay, though. It didn't matter how many people said no—or, in most cases, didn't say anything at all. It would only take one yes to turn things around. I just needed to keep reaching out. Like Liam always said, it was just a numbers game. At the moment, though, my number was still zero.

But another number was bothering me even more: thirty-three—the number of minutes the Four were late. How many of these passersby would have become paying customers if only I'd had that headset? If only I'd had the booth set up. If only I'd had the demo. If only I'd had backup. If only the Four had done the one thing they had to do: *show up!*

Ignoring the gradually growing crowd for a moment, I pulled out my phone and called Zoey yet again. And this time—miracle of miracles!—I actually got through.

"Hello?"

"Zoey! What's going on?! Why aren't you here?!"

"I've been trying to call all morning. We lost service."

"Where are you?!"

"Hold on. Ro, where are we?" I couldn't make out the voices in the background, but a few moments later, Zoey got back on the phone. "I think Kendalville?"

"Is that close? When are you getting here?"

"It's south of ninety, just outside Fort Wayne."

"I don't…what are you saying?"

"We're still in Indiana."

I've heard people describe blacking out, seeing red, feeling their head spin, going weak in the knees, being unable to breathe, and even having their heart stop. In that moment, I felt like I was experiencing all of these simultaneously. It was like time stopped, like *I* stopped. Yet somehow I must have remained conscious and functioning because I could hear my voice shouting: "Indiana! Why are you in Indiana?! You're supposed to be HERE!"

And I could hear Zoey's tinny, staticky voice shouting back: "We're trying! We've been driving all night through a freaking blizzard! It's bumper-to-bumper! And then they closed the highway after Joliet, so we had to—"

"Who cares?! Just shut up and drive! I need you here! I need that demo!"

"Look, I'm trying to help, but we're like four hundred miles away. And they rerouted our bags to Harrisburg. The whole area is under like three feet of—"

"Zoey, you're talking gibberish! This doesn't make any sense. You and the bags and the equipment and…OW! Watch it, jerk!" It took me a moment to realize what had happened: some idiot had spilled his scalding-hot coffee all over me. My torso felt like it was on fire. Worse yet, my shirt and suit were drenched.

The man backed away without so much as an apology—not that it would've mattered. It was too late. My shirt was ruined. My suit was ruined. The expo was ruined. My life was ruined.

Although I could hear Zoey's voice mid-sentence, I hung up, walked away from the booth (probably a business taboo, but it's not like there was anything to steal—or like I was doing any business anyway), and went back to my room to assess the damage. It was worse than I'd thought: my once-white shirt was stained a disgusting shade of blotchy brown, and my once-glorious power suit was drained of every ounce of power it once possessed. As was I.

I couldn't go back down there. What would be the point? The Four weren't there. I didn't have a demo. And I didn't have any other business clothes. Why didn't Liam tell me to bring a backup suit? Why didn't the Four set up a remote demo? Why did it have to be snowing (or whatever that diabolical precipitation was called)?

Aaaauuuggghhh!

I punched the mattress about a hundred times. Then, when my anger gave way to despair, I peeled off my soaking suit and put on the fanciest clean clothes I had: jeans and a sweatshirt. Collapsing on the bed, I contemplated my bleak situation and weighed my unappealing options.

I could pack up my bags, head for the airport, and catch the first flight out of here. But, given the weather, that might not be for days. And where would I go anyway? What was the point of heading home? The office was closed for the weekend, and thanks to this epic fail, it would soon be closed forever. In any case, a few weeks from now, my home wouldn't be my home. My home would be…where exactly?

I had nowhere to go and no way to get there. But just staying in my hotel room felt like the most depressing option imaginable. I had to get out or I'd explode. Or rot. Or worse.

I could go back down to the conference center and try to run the booth on my own. It wouldn't be ideal—no display, no demo, and almost no idea what I was talking about. Plus, I'd need a new suit. Maybe I could dash out and buy one in town. Yeah, right—in the middle of a snowstorm on one of the busiest shopping days of the year? The expo was only open for another six hours or so; by the time I went shopping, got a suit, got back, and got changed, it would be almost over.

In theory, I could go exactly as I was, but in these clothes, who would take me seriously? I couldn't do that. On the other hand, it's not like they were taking me all that seriously in my suit. And at this point, what did I have to lose? Worst-case scenario, I wouldn't get clients I already didn't have—clients I certainly wouldn't get if I stayed in my room.

So, before I could talk myself out of it, I grabbed my presenter's badge, walked out the door, went back down to the conference center, walked to my booth (or, rather, designated area), and stood there in all my jeans-and-sweatshirted glory, praying that my imagined worst-case scenario wouldn't come true.

It didn't. The reality was far worse. Twice I was mistaken for a repairman. And I counted over a dozen people who openly laughed at me. And that's not counting the smirks while people pointed at my sign, which I suppose was understandable, given that I'd made it with a poster board and black marker I'd borrowed from the event coordinator—a far cry from my neighbors' professionally printed, full-color masterpieces. And it probably goes without saying, but I'll say it anyway: I didn't get any clients.

Disaster wasn't nearly a strong enough word for this situation. I humiliated myself. I made the world's-worst first impression and ruined all chances of ever doing business with these people. And I irreparably tarnished our company's brand. (Could I be sued for that? Probably, but I'd worry about that when the time came.)

Then, just when I thought things couldn't get any worse, who should come walking toward me but the person who'd caused all my problems to begin with: no, not the Four (though they weren't exactly on my "Nice" list at the moment); it was the guy who'd spilled coffee on me. And here he was again, holding…you guessed it: a fresh cup of coffee. As if preparing for a repeat performance, he was striding with dogged determination straight toward my rumpled-but-at-least-clean sweatshirt. Somehow I would have to restrain myself from assaulting him. Although if I got thrown in jail, at least I'd have a place to live. But still.

"Hey there!" The Coffee Man came to a halt right in front of me. He must have sensed my irritation (as I will euphemistically call it) because a worried look flashed over his face as he took a step back. "I come in peace." He raised his hand, palm out, and then extended it toward me. After a few moments, I reluctantly shook it, and he smiled and exhaled. "I felt so terrible about spilling on you. I've been looking for you ever since. I thought maybe I could pay for the dry cleaning. It's the least I—"

"No, no. It's fine," I said. "Don't worry about it." Coordinating payments and cleaning seemed like a logistical nightmare, and the thought of prolonging my interaction with this buffoon was more than I could handle.

"Well, at least accept my humble peace offering." He handed me his cup. "It might be the last thing you want right now, but I thought you could use a coffee."

I let out a mirthless laugh. "I could use something a lot stronger than that." Nonetheless, the steaming cup of joe did look extremely appealing.

"But for now, I'll take what I can get." He handed me the cup, and I took a sip, which tasted even better than the coffee in my hotel room—probably the same brand, but the man had been right: never had I needed a taste of comfort more than I did just then.

He smiled and nodded as he watched me savor another sip. "One of those days?"

I let out another short laugh, this one even more mirthless than the last. "More like one of those years."

"Tell me about it."

I knew he was speaking rhetorically, but for some reason, I took his offer at face value. "Well, let's see…" I began. "It was one year ago, almost to the day, that the love of my life dumped me. So, there's that." His compassionate nod encouraged me to continue. "And then I got transferred to a town I'd never heard of and tasked with creating a whole new branch and, with absolutely no guidance or support, making it profitable within a year. Or else."

"Or else what?"

"Or else I'd get shut down, lose my job, and lose all my employees' jobs too. Which at the moment seems inevitable."

He looked half intrigued and half horrified. "Is this some kind of reality show or something?"

"I wish! Nope, just boring old reality." I took another sip of coffee. "Although, it wasn't all boring. And it wasn't all bad. We did build a pretty good team, and things were hoppin' for a while. It's just…well, we lost a few key members, and now that year-end goal is pretty much out of reach. I thought this expo might turn it around, but, as you can see…" I gestured toward the empty booth and my handmade sign, which I'd propped against the partition.

"Still," the Coffee Man said, "that rapid growth is pretty impressive. Most businesses take years just to—"

"Hey, Bill." A woman in a dark suit tapped his shoulder.

"Oh, hi, Janice. Do we have to go?"

"No, Fred's still talking to that acquisitions guy. I said we'd meet him here." She looked at me. "Hi, I'm Janice. I see you've met Buffalo Bill."

"Yes, I am local," Bill told me, rolling his eyes. "So…ha-ha. Joke never gets old."

We shook hands and I introduced myself to them both. Then Bill turned back to Janice. "He was just telling me about this new branch he's built up this year. It's actually rather extraordinary."

"Really?" Janice looked curious.

I shook my head. "Bill's giving me way more credit than I deserve. To tell you the truth…" I stopped myself just before I blurted it all out. Why lose the tiny shred of dignity I still had? If they knew the truth…then what? They'd know I wasn't some power-leading, world-beating go-getter. They'd know I was just a guy who was in way over his head. They'd know I was a failure. And so would anyone else within earshot. No way. I couldn't tell them that.

But what if I did? What if I just came clean, dropped the act (which, in any case, had failed miserably), and just told the truth? For the second time that day, I asked myself, *What's the worst that could happen?*

I took a deep breath, looked into Janice's eyes, and jumped off the honesty cliff. "I really had no idea what I was doing. And in a lot of ways, I still don't. I didn't have any training or experience doing this sort of thing. Honestly, most of what I learned came from a buffet."

Bill looked confused. "A buffet? Like, a cafeteria?"

I laughed, realizing how crazy this must sound. But it was too late to turn back now. "Yeah, I went there every weekend and…" I looked at my watch: 12:06. "Actually, this is the first Saturday all year that I haven't had lunch there."

"So, what happened?" Janice asked. "Did you meet some business guru there—or get a bunch of good fortune cookies?"

I laughed again. "No, not exactly, but…hmm, where should I even start?" I started at the beginning, telling them about my first time at the buffet—how blown away I'd been by the sheer quantity, how overwhelmed I'd been by the number of options, and how I'd left with an empty stomach but a valuable lesson.

I told them about the characters I'd seen there: Chili Man, Matcha Man, and the Pasta Guru—not technically business gurus, although they'd all indirectly helped me with my business. I told them about the watermelon-eating contest, the bread-making demo, and even my fiasco with the Brazil nuts. I told them about how I'd learned to ask for help, how I'd learned to find balance, and how I'd learned to break down big projects into bite-sized tasks.

As I talked, other people came and listened. Great—now even more people would know my pathetic truth. But at this point, who was I fooling? Anyone could plainly see I was no power executive. And anyone could plainly see I wasn't about to get any customers, so I might as well enjoy myself and tell my strange little story. At least this way I managed to get a few chuckles from the crowd every now and then. Even if it was at my own expense, I could live with that.

At one point, Bill waved to someone in the crowd and was soon joined by a man in a green checkered tie. "Hey, Fred! You gotta hear this guy!" Bill turned back to me. "Tell him about Matcha Man—he sounds just like a guy Fred used to work with."

I obliged, and within minutes, the four of us were sharing another laugh, as were several other people who'd stopped to listen. I might not have been making sales, but it was nice to be smiling for a change. I felt better than I had all day. Yet a little voice inside me kept telling me to shut up—to stop talking about the buffet, to stop telling embarrassing stories, to either get down to business or get out.

Usually, that voice was inside me, but sometimes it came from the outside—as with the man who pulled me aside, put his arm around my shoulder, and told me, "Look, son" (even though he was barely older than me), "I'll give you a little free advice. You seem like a nice enough guy, and you've got a funny story—but people don't want a nice guy with a funny story: they want *results*! They don't care about your lunch; they care about themselves. They wanna know *what's in it for me?*"

His criticism may have been the most condescending, but at least it wasn't nearly as barbed as some of the others I received that day: "You should've spent less time learning about food and more time learning how to run a business!" "Maybe when your company goes under, you can work in a cafeteria." "News flash: this isn't a buffet; it's a technology expo—and you don't have any technology."

At first I pushed back. I *did* learn business skills from the buffet. We *do* have technology. And it happens to be brilliant! But I gave up trying to argue my points after one man said, "I guess your technology's so brilliant, you figured out how to make it invisible." He gestured at the empty booth. Several other people laughed…and then left.

Fine. Let them go. At that point, I'd given up on doing business; I was just trying to enjoy my swan song. If people didn't feel like sticking around, who needed 'em?

But many people did stick around—to talk, laugh, and listen to my stories about the year. Stories about working my way through setbacks and challenges. Stories about building a branch from the ground up…only to watch it crumble. Stories about the lessons I'd learned in the process. And most of all, stories about the buffet.

Many of the people who stayed seemed genuinely interested, compassionate about what I'd gone through, and even inspired by some of my temporary triumphs. These people listened politely. They asked questions. They laughed *with* me instead of at me. And some of them stayed for hours.

But nobody stuck around longer than my coffee buddy, Buffalo Bill. He spent almost the whole afternoon chatting, swapping stories, and encouraging others to come join us. And never once did I get the sense that he was judging me or getting ready to launch into a "Here's what you're doing wrong" lecture. Or so I thought. But, sure enough, late in the afternoon, he pulled me aside and asked if we could chat for a moment in private. Oh boy, here we go. The pit in my stomach told me what was coming: *Look, you're a nice enough guy, but…* Et tu, Billy?

He started off gently, as people often do in these situations…just before pulling out the blade. "Hey, I'm sorry again about your suit."

"Forget about it," I said. "It happens. You don't have to feel bad, and you didn't have to stick around to make it up to me or anything."

"That's not why I came back." He flashed a sheepish grin. "Well, to be honest, that is why I came back—out of guilt. And a bit of pity, when I saw your sad-sack booth."

I sighed. Okay, let's just get this over with. He must have sensed my growing annoyance because he rushed forward with a conciliatory tone. "But that's not why I stayed. I really enjoyed hearing about your business…and the buffet."

He extended his hand, and when I went to shake it, I saw he was holding a business card.

"Give me a call when you get back to the office. I'd love to talk about possibilities for doing business together."

I held back, not taking the card. Was he making fun of me? Botching the expo was one thing, but having him mock my incompetence was just cruel. Especially after I thought we'd actually bonded. Maybe my initial reaction had been correct all along—he *was* a jerk!

But he looked sincere as he pressed the card into my hand. "No promises, but I'll put in a good word for you."

I took the card but still wasn't convinced that he wasn't pulling my leg. "Why would you do that after…" I gestured toward the empty booth.

"Your tech's gotta be good, of course. And it sounds like it is." He shrugged and offered a half smile. "But so are a lot of people's. So who do I want to work with? A guy who keeps going in the face of adversity. A guy whose team drives all night through a blizzard to get the job done—or at least give it their best shot. A guy who sees lessons and opportunities for growth where others see only a bowl of spaghetti."

After we shook hands, he started to walk off, but after a few steps, he turned around. "One more thing." He shook his head. "You don't need the suit."

I smiled, slipped his business card into my jeans pocket, and walked back to my empty booth. But, on second thought, it wasn't actually empty. No, there weren't any fancy signs, demos, or displays, but there were over a dozen people still hanging out—talking, laughing, and trading contact information.

And by the end of the day, Bill's wasn't the only business card I had; I'd collected over a dozen others from people who wanted to talk more—not just to exchange funny stories but to discuss business. No, they weren't paying customers. And they certainly weren't guaranteed clients. But they were hot leads. They were personal connections. They were glimmers of hope. Which is a lot more than I'd had that morning.

Lesson #46:
No matter how sophisticated your products are, authentic human connection is a company's most valuable resource.

47. The Side Door

Exactly one week after the expo, I found myself back at the buffet—stuffing my face with veg tempura and processing everything that had happened over the past seven days. And there was certainly a lot to process, starting with the expo itself: resigning myself to failure when the team couldn't make it, but ending the afternoon with a handful of prospects.

In retrospect, it would've been fitting if the sun had returned at the same moment my hope returned, but the storm hung around until Monday. And because of all the other stranded travelers, I couldn't get a flight home before Tuesday. Unfortunately, though, I couldn't go straight home. I had to go to Harrisburg, PA, where the all-important luggage with the all-important demo equipment had been rerouted and was now being held in the airport's storage room. "*Temporary* storage room," the customer-service rep emphasized, which meant I'd have to pick it up by the end of the week or it would be classified as relinquished.

"Relinquished?" I asked.

"Surrendered," the rep said. "Permanently impounded. Most likely destroyed."

"Meaning, even though it's only there because of your mistake—and the storm—I have to get it back by Friday or I won't be able to get it back at all?"

"That is correct, sir. Is there anything else we can assist you with today?"

The next available flight to Harrisburg wasn't until Wednesday, but at least I made it there without further incident or delay. Within minutes of arriving at the airport, I managed to find the temporary storage room, locate the luggage, and fill out all the paperwork—all of which went remarkably smoothly…until I signed the release form. The manager winced.

"Is there a problem?" I asked.

There was. Because the luggage wasn't registered in my name (it was Zoey's), I wasn't able to claim it. Even when we called Zoey, and she told the manager it was okay. Even when she got on video and, to prove it really was her, held up her driver's license and her plane ticket (which, due to the storm, she hadn't been able to use). Even when she told them she'd write the nicest five-star review they'd ever seen.

"I'm sorry, ma'am. It would be a violation of company policy and aviation regulations."

"Isn't there *something* we can do?" I asked.

There was. They could send the luggage back to the point of origin, where the registered ticket-holder could claim it. Meaning Zoey could pick it up at our local airport tomorrow. No additional charge. Why they couldn't have told me this three days ago—*before* I'd booked my flight here instead of going straight home—was beyond me (and apparently beyond the manager, who just shrugged when I asked). I had every reason to be irate, but I was just relieved that within twenty-four hours, the luggage and I would both be safely home.

But the relief didn't last long. Because once I got my ticket home, got my boarding pass, and got on the plane, I remembered what I was going home to.

It would be like New Year's Eve in reverse: instead of counting down to a celebration, I'd be counting down to failure—unless I could stop it in time. But time was quickly running out. I'd get home late Thursday and go back to the office Friday. Which was December 1. Which meant that, because of our net-30 terms, in order to receive payment by the end of the year, I'd have to finalize a deal by the end of the day or else…well, by this point everyone knew what was at stake.

Fortunately, the rest of my return trip was straightforward. I made it home on Thursday night, went to the office early Friday morning, and held a quick meeting with the team. After I'd apologized once again for my long-distance freak-out—and thanked them once again for doing everything in their power to try to get to Buffalo—we reviewed the situation, came up with a plan, and then hit the phones. I called every prospect, connection, or lead I could think of, no matter how far-fetched, distant, or cold a lead they might be. At this point, what did I have to lose? Well, *everything*, I guess. But I wasn't going down without a fight—or at least a call.

I started with Buffalo Bill, but he was out of the office until Monday. Ditto for a couple of other people I'd met at the expo. And the ones I did get through to either needed more time or approval from decision-makers who weren't available just then. So I moved on to former clients who we'd done short-term jobs for earlier that year. But they were all…well, I'll spare you the blow-by-blow and just say that the next day's meal at the buffet was a time of processing, not of celebrating.

Given the situation, I should've felt distraught. After all, time had just run out on my business, my team, and my future. Everything I'd been working toward all year—and everything I'd planned for the rest of my career and the rest of my life—had been resting on this. But I'd failed. The deadline had passed. And we still weren't profitable. Which meant that in just under a month, I'd lose my job, lose the branch, and lose Maya—forever. So why was I feeling so calm? Was I in denial? Resigned to failure? Or just too exhausted to care? Possibly, but I don't think so. I think that, despite what the numbers said, part of me wasn't ready to give up.

The problem was, I didn't have any more options—at least none that I could think of. And I'd been thinking long and hard. In fact, I'd been so lost in thought that I'd forgotten where I was and nearly jumped out of my skin when I heard the buffet's PA: "Attention buffet diners: the buffet is now closed."

Closed?! It felt like I'd just gotten there! I hadn't even finished eating. Where did the two hours go? Where did the *year* go?

I quickly polished off the last of the tempura, gulped down the rest of my green tea, brought my tray to the return station, and made my way to the exit. I must have been the last person out because the cashier locked the door behind me. As I stepped outside, though, I literally bumped into a small group of people trying to get in.

The older man in front pulled on the door, but it was locked. He knocked and then waved to get the cashier's attention. She shook her head. "Sorry, we're closed."

"Please," the man said. "My family's visiting from out of town, and I wanted them to see this place." He pointed back at a middle-aged couple and their two kids.

"Come back Monday," the cashier said.

"They're leaving tomorrow." The man clasped his hands and for a moment I got the sense that he was about to drop to his knees and beg. He didn't, but his pleading tone of voice made it sound as if he had. "Please, just for a few minutes. We don't even have to eat—I just want to show them around."

A woman behind the man stepped toward the door. "He's been talking about this place for months. We'd really love to see it with our own eyes. We'll pay you double."

The cashier's resolve seemed shaken, but it wasn't crumbling. She shook her head again, though it seemed to pain her to do so. "I'm really sorry. There's a closed-circuit camera here." She pointed to a small surveillance camera mounted just above the door. "If my boss saw me let people in after two, I could get in big trouble, especially when…" Her voice trailed off as she looked down and to the right. After a few moments, she looked back at the family and said, "You know what, I can let you in the service entrance. Just go down the alley to your left and take the second door."

"Thank you so much!" the man said. "I can pay cash so you don't have to—"

"No worries," the cashier said. "And if you're quick, you can still get some Middle Eastern food. They always clear that room last."

"Thank you! Thank you! Thank you!" the man said, joined by the entire family.

Out of curiosity, I followed the family as they walked to the alley. Sure enough, a few moments later, the cashier opened the side door and ushered the family inside.

As the door swung shut, I felt like another door swung open in my mind. Of course, the family could have pounded and tugged on the front door all day long, and it would've stayed locked. But even though it was slightly out of the way and not visible at first, this side door got them to the same place.

Did I also have a "side door"?

Sure, the "front door" of my business plan was now locked—I'd missed the chance for a standard net-30 contract to come through in time. But maybe that wasn't the only way to get where I wanted to go. After all, I'm the one who came up with the net-30 policy; I could also change it. Why not net 21? Or net 30 but with the first installment upfront? Or the "big head, long tail" approach that Yasmin used to talk about—where the client makes a large initial payment followed by a small monthly retainer.

I didn't have the definitive answer in that moment, but I had something just as important: hope. And I had a new perspective. I'd seen it with my own eyes: just because one door was locked, that didn't necessarily mean they all were. I just had to look around and maybe get a little creative. And I was more than willing to do that.

Lesson #47:
There's almost always another way to reach your goal.

48. Shared

I could hardly wait to tell the Faithful Four about my "side door" idea—to let them know that all hope wasn't lost, that we could save the branch, that one month from now we might still have jobs. Eager to work out the details before telling anyone, I got to the office bright and early—before we technically opened—only to find everyone else already there.

Not just *there*, but as bustling and busy as I'd ever seen them. Brenda was in the middle of an animated phone conversation. Tamika was so immersed in her speed-typing that she didn't even notice me walk right past her. And Zoey and Rohan were tinkering with the AR headset—wires, laptops, and complex-looking tech equipment strewn all around them.

Once Brenda hung up the phone, I managed to get everyone's attention and ask the question that had been running through my head since the moment I walked in the door: "What is going on?"

"Plan B," Zoey said. "Since we couldn't do the demos live, we'll send people the equipment and walk them through the process."

"And if they like it, they can license the technology," Tamika added. "I'm drawing up the contracts right now so we'll be ready."

"But the timeline," I said. "What about the—"

"Don't worry about net-thirty," Tamika said. "We'll have them pay upfront with the option of a monthly retainer after that for ongoing support."

I couldn't suppress the smile of joyful amazement spreading across my face. "It's like you guys were reading my mind…and then some. When did you come up with this?"

"We talked about it last week," Rohan said. The other three nodded.

"Why didn't you say anything to me?"

Rohan shrugged. "No point going to Plan B before we tried Plan A, right?"

So, Plan B it was. And by the looks of things, it was already much more than just a plan. Zoey and Rohan had already installed the demo's software into two additional headsets. Tamika's contract was almost finished. And Brenda had already taken messages from three prospects. "Kendra from Helix is free anytime. Jocelyn from Cornerstone wants to talk, but she's out of the office till three. Let's see…" She flipped through her notes. "Then there was some guy who called himself Buffalo Bill."

The rest of the week felt surreal—partly because it was so mundane, so easy, so ho-hum…in the best possible way. After worrying, agonizing, and stressing out for an entire year—culminating in the last few weeks of frenzied activity and frequent panic—the solution turned out to be no big deal at all. We didn't need to revolutionize the industry. We didn't need to unveil a groundbreaking discovery. We didn't need to set the world on fire. We just needed to get a few clients who paid us more than our expenses (which were considerably lower now that our staff had been reduced by roughly two-thirds).

I was reminded of the lesson I'd learned way back in March, when I'd seen the confused newbie at the buffet: don't overcomplicate it! We didn't have to travel to Buffalo or anywhere else. We didn't even have to leave the office. We just overnighted the AR equipment to any interested prospects, then had video conferences so they could experience it firsthand. Zoey and Rohan walked them through the setup and showed them how to use the various features (all of which were customizable for their business). I discussed options and closed the deals. Tamika finalized the contracts. And Brenda set up payment schedules, using the "big head, long tail" approach: a large payment upfront to license the software, followed by a monthly retainer for maintenance, support, and updates. I'd been worried about pushback on this arrangement, but the companies all preferred it since they had budgets they needed to use up by the end of the year. They also preferred meeting via video since they didn't want to travel (snowstorm or not), and this gave them a better sense of how we'd be interacting throughout the year (or, if all went well, for many years to come). So, in a weird way, it worked out better that the Faithful Four never made it to Buffalo.

During the week, we had five video conferences and got three new clients. None of them was as big as Pinnacle, but they added up. The

Helix account got us almost 30% to where we needed to be. Cornerstone added another 35%. And on Friday afternoon, good old Buffalo Bill's company, Omni, brought in over 55%. It was official. Over the course of a single week, we'd gone from massive debt to substantial profit. And just like that, we were in the black.

Success!

Then, shortly after we'd finalized the deal that put us over the top, we said goodbye and headed home, just like any other week. And just like any other weekend, I had my typical Saturday lunch at the buffet. Except it wasn't like any other weekend—because every other time I'd been to the buffet, I hadn't known whether the branch would make it. But now, after eleven months of uncertainty (and a fair bit of stress and anguish), the results were in: we'd done it!

To celebrate, I treated myself to the massive Buddha Bowl I'd heard people raving about all year. Getting through all those beans, nuts, and veggies would give me plenty of time to think. And I certainly had a lot to think about and a lot to feel good about. And yes, I did feel good as I savored the meal (which, by the way, surpassed the hype) and reflected on everything I'd just been through: the expo, the video conferences, the deals, the profit—the culmination of a yearlong dream. I thought about the crisis I'd averted by not failing (losing the branch, losing my job, losing any hope of winning back Maya, and most likely losing my entire life savings from having to pay off seven-figure debt). But most of all, I thought of everything this meant for the future: job security for the team, career advancement for me, and most of all, the possibility of winning back Maya, getting married, and building a life together…starting in just a few weeks! I couldn't remember the last time I felt so optimistic, so relieved, so happy.

But there was something else.

Something was lurking at the back of my mind. It wasn't worry that the deals would fall through; even if everyone canceled their accounts, their upfront payments were so big that we'd end the year in the black. It wasn't worry about the branch's future; it was already profitable, and we now had a very scalable business model and many more hot leads. And it wasn't cold feet about Maya; I'd never been so sure about anything—and once she heard about my success, that would eliminate the one concern she'd had about me.

So what was it? Why did I feel…whatever this was? Not quite empty or hollow, not exactly let down, and certainly not depressed. Just…something missing. (And no, it wasn't hunger—by this point, I'd already finished most of my meal. And despite Buddhism's emphasis on emptiness, the Buddha Bowl left me feeling very full!)

I put down my fork and looked around the buffet. I didn't see anything funny, but I couldn't help but laugh at the strangeness of it all—strange because it was so ordinary. Here I was, in the midst of the biggest turning point of my life, yet everyone around me was just going about their everyday lives. At the table across from me, an older couple sipped hot drinks and talked quietly, seemingly encased in their own private world, just like I'd been until I started looking around. The table next to theirs was packed with what looked like a family reunion: three generations of people who bore a striking resemblance to one another. Their lively conversation seemed to flow easily, and they all looked happy. Even when one of the youngest children spilled his soup and started to cry, the woman next to him (his mother, I assume, judging by their matching red hair) kissed and comforted him, helped him wipe up the spill, and soon had him smiling, laughing, and enjoying his dessert (which, as far as I could tell, looked like a big, gooey brownie). Next to the family was a table of four boisterous young men who looked like they'd just walked off the football field—and sounded like they hadn't yet transitioned to their indoor voices. But their good-natured energy was contagious, so no one seemed to mind. I certainly didn't. In fact, it boosted my spirits a bit and helped me realize what was missing in my seemingly good-and-getting-better life: other people.

Yes, I could celebrate on my own—make it a "party of one," as the cashier often called it when I paid—but a party of one didn't feel like much of a party. And as much as I enjoyed savoring my recent success by myself—alone in a crowd—it didn't feel complete without the people who'd made it possible: the Faithful Four. They're the ones who'd gotten me through the difficult times, they're the ones who'd made success even sweeter, and they're the ones I wanted to be sharing this moment with.

No, I wasn't going to call them in to the office over the weekend, but I did the next best thing: *I* went to the office. But not before I made a stop at the local all-in-one party store, where I bought all the supplies I'd need for an office party on Monday: I got balloons. I got streamers. I got a tablecloth big enough for the conference table. I got snacks. I got drinks. I got paper plates and cups. I got games. I got prizes. I got a karaoke machine.

I also got a ton of ideas for speeches I wanted to make—things I wanted to tell the four amazing people who'd stuck by me and made success possible. I wanted to honor them, to recognize their talent and creativity. I wanted to commemorate their dedication and perseverance. But above all, I wanted to say one thing—the two words written on the huge sign I bought at the party store: *Thank You!*

Lesson #48:
Success is sweeter when it's shared.

49. You Can't Take It with You

The thank-you party went even better than I'd hoped. I somehow managed to keep it a secret until just before lunchtime, when I called everybody into the conference room for an "urgent matter." I wasn't completely lying. After all, what's more urgent than telling people you appreciate them?

Anyone glancing in wouldn't have known that the non-alcoholic sparkling cider I'd gotten wasn't actual champagne. Let's just say it didn't take much for these four to let their hair down. They all hit the "dance floor" (aka the area around the conference table, which I'd pushed against the wall) the moment I put on my customized "Dance Party" playlist. They also weren't shy about going back for thirds, fourths, and beyond of the "gourmet" pizza (delivered from the shop down the street) or the equally "gourmet" cake (from the local supermarket). And the karaoke machine kept things lively well past the lunch hour. (Who knew that Tamika could do such a spot-on Aretha impression? Zoey's voice, on the other hand…well, at least she was enjoying herself.) I think we all had more pent-up anxiety than we'd realized until then, when we finally had an outlet to express our relief—and our joy.

But more than the food, the decorations, or the singing and dancing, I could tell they appreciated my appreciation. My thank-you speech actually brought Rohan to tears (although he claimed it was allergies—despite the fact that it was December and we were indoors). Unlike my overly prepared expo pitches, this time I just spoke from the heart, telling them the unadorned truth. I told them I couldn't have done it without them. I told them they were four of the most extraordinary people I'd ever met. I told them I was in awe of their intelligence, their talent, their creativity, their determination, their perseverance, their loyalty, and the positive spirit they brought to everything they did. I told them I learned from them every day. I told them I was a better person because of them. I told them they'd changed my life, and I was forever grateful.

Even with all my gushing, I don't think I managed to convey the full depth of my gratitude, but I hope that even a fraction of it got across. And I think it did. After all, everyone hugged me afterward—even Zoey, the self-proclaimed "non-hugger." And then we got back to partying.

Before we knew it, the lunch party had extended until the end of the day. And because we still had leftover cake, we decided that the Monday thank-you party should morph into a Tuesday holiday party. On Wednesday morning, we tried doing a bit of work but couldn't get any traction. The new clients didn't want to launch anything on their end until the new year, and the remaining prospects we contacted claimed they weren't available to meet (even online) for the next few weeks. This may have been true, but I got the distinct impression that they were just in holiday mode and didn't feel like increasing their workload just then. And who could blame them? We were in the same place ourselves. So by lunchtime, we stopped fighting it and declared that the holiday party would continue. After all, there are multiple holidays this time of year, so it seemed fitting that our party extend for multiple days.

We restocked the food and drinks (including some actual champagne, along with three more cakes) and declared Thursday an open-house holiday party. At the height of it, we had more people than could fit into the conference room because everyone had brought their friends and family. Everyone except me, that is. But I was fine with that. After all, the Faithful Four felt like my friends and family.

The party continued through the end of the week, although by Friday it was back to just the five of us. Also, there was an unexpected twist (unexpected to me, that is): the others declared that Friday wasn't a holiday party; it was another thank-you party. But this time, they were saying thank you to me.

As I'd done for them on Monday, each of them made an impromptu speech expressing their gratitude for me. And this time, I was the one who had a sudden attack of "allergies." The four of them even got me a gift: a small plastic replica of a slot machine, displaying three repeating words—*Jackpot Jackpot Jackpot*—along with a handwritten card that said, *Never stop betting on yourself—it's the safest bet there is!*

As Zoey handed it to me, she said, "May you never stop growing, never stop being courageous, and never stop taking risks."

Tamika winced slightly. "*Calculated* risks."

I laughed, hugged them all (again, even Zoey, at her initiation), and thanked everyone profusely—until Rohan cut me off and declared, "Enough with the sap. We've got more cake to polish off. Let's keep this party going!" So that's just what we did—straight through till the end of the day.

As the festivities were wrapping up, Tamika said she wanted to sing one last karaoke song: "Chain of Fools," which she dedicated to all the former employees who'd left. I laughed along with them but felt a bit uncomfortable doing so. After all, I harbored no ill will toward Laney, Kareem, or any of the others. They were good people doing what they felt was right for them. Besides, it had clearly worked out fine for the five of us. Still, I admit it felt good when we all joined together for one last rousing chorus.

After the week of constant revelry and companionship, it felt odd to be alone for a quiet weekend. But I cherished the time for reflection—both at home and at the buffet.

With all the activities, festivities, and drama at work, I'd hardly had time to think about the buffet. But as I walked through its food-laden rooms that Saturday, it hit me: the following week would be my last time there—definitely this year, and possibly *ever*.

It was hard to imagine not going to the buffet every Saturday. By this point it wasn't just part of my weekly routine, it had become an integral part of my life. I'd learned so much there, I'd encountered people I would remember forever, and I'd had some absolutely amazing food.

As I looked at the food displays, I saw dozens of mouthwatering meals that I wished I could pack up and take with me. But of course I couldn't. Right from the start, the buffet had made it clear—they didn't have many rules, but this one was ironclad: *no takeout!* You can eat as much as you wanted while you were there, but you couldn't take it with you. (No paying for one meal and then stuffing a doggie bag with enough to last all week.)

I thought of how my company had the same principle. My apartment, my car, and everything at the office belonged not to me but to the company. And just like the buffet's food, I could enjoy it while I was there, but I couldn't take it with me.

In exactly one week, I'd be leaving town with the same two suitcases and one carry-on bag I'd come with. So, if I couldn't take anything with me when I left, what would I have to show for the past year? What was the point of all that time, effort, and stress? What had I actually gained?

No sooner had I asked the question than the answer came to me: I'd gained a *lot!* No, it wasn't tangible (aside from the plastic slot machine), but it was far more valuable than anything material. I'd gained wisdom and lessons—from the buffet and from work. I'd gained confidence. I'd gained skills. And, by helping the branch become profitable, I'd gained job security for the Faithful Four and myself. Plus, I'd gained evidence that I was a worthy leader—worthy of success and worthy of Maya.

On top of all this, I'd also be taking a year's worth of memories with me. But this meant I had to actually remember the things I did. Which meant I had to fully experience them. Which meant I had to stop spacing out, getting lost in my thoughts, and drifting through my life. Which, at the moment, meant drifting through the buffet's endless aisles. I needed to stop, pay attention, and be present.

So, starting immediately, that's what I tried to do. I looked closely at all the food around me. I weighed my options, considered what looked the best, and chose carefully. Then I savored every bite I took. And to this day, I still remember almost every detail of that meal: a spicy Greek moussaka packed with breaded eggplant and zucchini, sauteed potatoes, and a fragrant sauce of tomato, onion, and garlic. I'm not sure whether it really was one of the best meals I'd had all year or it just felt that way because I was paying extra close attention, but in either case, I loved it.

I tried to do something similar during the following week at work: to be fully present and savor every moment with my coworkers, no matter what we were doing—going through mundane paperwork, tying up loose ends, planning for the branch's future (including the Youth Tech-Mentoring program, which they were 100% on board with), or just chatting in the break room. But unlike my experience with the moussaka, I found that I was only half present at work. While part of me was living in the moment, the other half felt like I was recollecting a distant memory. Even the happiest moments felt tinged with the sadness of knowing I'd be leaving soon.

But did I really have to leave?

Why couldn't I stay on—turn the Faithful Four into the Faithful Five? After all, we'd built a profitable branch together, why not keep growing it throughout the coming years and turn it into something even more amazing? I had a good thing going—why walk away?

I knew the answer in a single word: Maya.

But why couldn't Maya come here? We could build a life together in this town: Go to the buffet together every Saturday. Maybe put down roots and start a family. She could even work with me at the branch—turn the Faithful Five into the Faithful Six. Or she could work somewhere else. As long as we were together, that's what mattered.

On the other hand, I thought of what my coworkers had encouraged me to do: keep moving forward, betting on myself, taking risks. Staying here would be staying with the known. And I hadn't come this far just to play it safe—to give up on a bigger dream. Besides, they assured me they'd be fine on their own. Which I guess is good. After all, the best managers make sure they're *not* indispensable. I'd already done my part: I'd brought them together, encouraged them to connect and use their individual and collective talents, and helped them find a path that allowed them to do that—profitably. It felt natural to step away now. After all, that was the plan.

But still.

As I pondered my options throughout the week, I kept coming back to the buffet's policy: *You can't take it with you.* If I walked away from the branch, what would I take with me? And where would it all end? Would I just keep walking away forever? Or would I ever allow myself to put down roots and grow?

I still hadn't answered these questions when the week came to an end. Fittingly, it was on the shortest day of the year, so it was already pitch dark by closing time. We'd all said our goodbyes earlier, agreeing to stay in touch—and not to make a big deal of this parting. So at the end of the workday, it was just me. And just like any other night, I turned off the lights, set the alarm, and locked the door behind me. But there was one big difference: before I left, I would slip the key under the door.

Supposedly.

But was I really ready to walk away forever—taking nothing with me but memories, confidence, lessons, and perhaps a year-end bonus? I never did figure out the answer, but I realized something more important: I'd been asking the wrong question. The important thing wasn't what I was taking for myself, but what I was leaving for others—in other words, *What had I given?*

On a practical level, I'd given them a branch, a career, an already-lucrative business that was poised to grow. And even if I didn't stick around to share in that growth, I could savor the knowledge that I'd helped set four people up on a fulfilling path. I'd also helped other businesses reach more people and improve their lives in innovative ways. Like the man who plants a tree he never sits under, I'd helped create a legacy for others to enjoy. And that was more than enough satisfaction for me.

Before I could talk myself out of it, I slid the key under the door and walked away.

Lesson #49:
What matters most isn't what you take—it's what
you give.

50. Goodbye and Hello

As my time in this town came to an end, I found myself in a position similar to where I'd been a year ago: I had to sell, donate, throw out, or recycle everything I wouldn't be bringing with me—which, like the previous year, was only as much as I could fit in two suitcases and one carry-on bag. Fortunately, the process was much easier this time around since almost everything in the apartment belonged to the company, as did the car.

By Saturday morning, I was ready to take off—quite literally: my flight was leaving in less than three hours. This didn't give me much time, but I didn't need much time. I finished packing my three bags, checked the apartment one last time to make sure I wasn't forgetting anything, and left the keys on the kitchen counter before I locked and closed the door behind me. And then, on my way to the airport, I made one more quick stop: a final trip to the buffet. After all, it was Saturday, and I wasn't about to leave without saying goodbye to my maybe-magical mentor.

Like my first visit, I wandered from room to room without taking any food. But this time, it was intentional. I didn't want to eat. I just wanted to see it all one more time before I left: the salad bar that had seemed so bland at first but soon revealed a huge variety of wonderful options. The Italian-food section where, with the Pasta Guru's help, I'd learned that there's more to pasta than just spaghetti and tomato sauce. The five-alarm chili that Chili Man ate week after week, despite the pain it caused him. The Belgian waffles that inspired me to ask for help. The matcha that wasn't everyone's cup of tea. The sourdough bread that took so long to make yet was worth every minute. The chocolate cake that could be my best friend or my worst enemy, depending on how much I ate. And the seemingly endless rows of food in the buffet's numerous rooms, offering nearly limitless choices—which, like the cake, could be a blessing or a challenge depending on how I approached them.

But today I wasn't choosing anything. Or rather, I was choosing not to choose. I was choosing to say goodbye and walk away. For now, at least. I didn't know when I'd be back, but I promised myself that someday I would return.

I looked at my watch: 1:15—still plenty of time to eat something before my flight, but for some reason, I wanted to make this visit just about reminiscences and goodbyes, not about food. Somehow, it felt more pure. I even left a tip, although I hadn't eaten a bite. I'd taken plenty from the buffet throughout the year, so it only seemed right to give a little back.

On the way out, however, I did bend (or, who am I kidding, *break*) one of the buffet's only rules. I hadn't planned to, but I got swept up in the moment. As I walked through the Chinese food section, I spotted something I'd never seen at the buffet—an assortment of fortune cookies. I figured that if ever I needed good fortune, it was now. So, when no one was looking, I shoved one of them into my coat pocket. Call it a souvenir. Then I walked out the front door and moved on to the pressing business at hand: flying back home and winning back Maya.

I hardly remember anything about the check-in process, the airport, or the flight itself. In my mind, I was already back on the ground, already moving on to the next chapter of life, already with Maya.

We'd arranged to meet at a coffee shop the next day: December 24, which seemed fitting. Perhaps Christmas magic would be in the air, and our rekindled love would be the ultimate present.

I felt like she was already as good as mine. Once she heard about my success and saw how I'd changed over the past year, it seemed inevitable. After all, I'd addressed all her old objections: Ambition? Check. Career on the rise? Check. Going places? Figuratively and literally. And if everything went according to plan, she'd be coming with me!

Seriously, how could Bradford compete? No disrespect to HR, but it's hardly a position for movers and shakers. I, on the other hand, had just built an entire office from the ground up and, within a year, turned it into a thriving enterprise. While he'd done what—meet with new hires to go over the employee handbook? I almost felt sorry for the guy, but, you know, all's fair.

The plane was actually a bit early, so I could've met with Maya that night, but I stuck with our plan. I checked into my hotel (which felt pretty weird, given that this had been my hometown for so long), picked out tomorrow's outfit (carefully planned so as not to look carefully planned), and rehearsed my lines (enough to make them sound confident, convincing, and impromptu). And then, to make sure I was well rested for the big day, I went to bed early—and proceeded to check the bedside clock every five minutes for the next five hours.

Around 3:45, I gave up any hope of falling asleep. At some point, though, I must have dozed off, because I opened my eyes and saw light pouring through the blinds. It was time. After a year of hard work, struggles, victories, losses, lessons, and growth, my big day had finally arrived. I had earned it. And I was ready—except for one last detail.

I showered, shaved, put on my careful/casual outfit, paced around the hotel room for a few hours, and then tidied up (in case Maya wanted to come back with me—not to get ahead of myself, but, you know, better to be prepared). And then I drove straight to the nearest jewelry store.

I'd been imagining this moment all year, so I knew just what I wanted—and thanks to my imminent raise, I spared no expense. It only took a few minutes to pick out the perfect ring: a simple gold band with a marquise-cut diamond—rare, enduring, and impossible to overlook, just like our love.

With the jewelry box settled in my pocket, I drove to the coffee shop and—despite my detour—arrived forty-five minutes early. The shop was pleasant enough, although the lack of options was appalling. (Yes, I'd been spoiled by the buffet.) You could choose from a few muffins, bagels, and croissants (none of which looked fresh or appealing) as well as a meager selection of beverages: bottled orange juice, overpriced water, and the requisite tea or coffee (which, granted, was offered in over a dozen varieties). Despite my lack of sleep, I was jittery, so I ordered a decaf coffee, secured the best table (the one with the most privacy), and waited.

Two decafs later, at 2:55—just minutes before our scheduled meeting time—I had to use the bathroom. And when I came out, there she was.

I noticed her before she noticed me. Even from across the room, she looked more beautiful than I remembered. With her long black hair flowing down over her cream cable-knit sweater, she was a vision of casual elegance—a vision of our shared future. And just from her voice and demeanor as she stood at the counter, ordering a decaf latte, I could tell she was excited to see me. The decaf was also a good sign—not only did it prove we were on the same wavelength, but it suggested that she also had jitters about our reunion.

She paid, put her change into the tip jar (another good sign), and turned around to scan the room. The moment our eyes met, any doubt I might've harbored about the outcome of this meeting completely vanished. She was positively glowing, and the smile that swept across her face was worth a thousand words of love—or at least the only word that ultimately mattered: *yes.*

Holding her coffee in one hand, she gave me a one-armed hug as we both started talking at the same time: "So good to…" "How long have you…?" "You look…" "Do you wanna…?" We laughed, and I gestured toward our table. "Let's sit down. I have so much to tell you!"

"Me too." She smiled encouragingly as I held the chair out for her.

When I sat across from her and we locked eyes, it was like the past year had never happened. Or, rather, like it had happened in a flash but still managed to turn me into a new man—the man who was finally ready for her, deserved her, could give her the life she wanted. And despite the recent twists and turns, that life was starting now.

"So, how have you been?" she asked.

"You first, please."

"Well." She sighed. "I guess I'll start with the most important part…" She stared into her coffee, as if searching for the words that would convey what we were both clearly feeling. After a few moments, she looked up and smiled coquettishly as she met my eyes. "I'm pregnant."

The moment she spoke that word, my heart broke.

It didn't just break—it *stopped.* Literally. I know that because what happened next was just like the accounts I've read of near-death experiences: I floated out of my body, high above the table, above the coffee shop's roof, above the trees and buildings around the shop. Looking down from that vantage point, I managed to hear enough of Maya's words to realize why my heart had stopped: "trimester… moving… nursery… family… happy… wedding… Bradford."

Then the scene split into two. Instead of the current heart-stopping nightmare, the second scene showed me what was *supposed* to happen: the scene where I told Maya about the last year. The one where I described the lessons and the growth that made me ready for her, for us. The one where she couldn't help but notice my newfound confidence, couldn't help but be impressed by my profound wisdom, and couldn't help but take the next inevitable step: to admit that she'd been wrong to let me go, confess that she'd never stopped loving me, and tell me she wanted to spend her life with me, starting now. The one where I got down on one knee, pulled out the ring, and slipped it onto her finger—after which we left the coffee shop hand in hand, stepping into a shared eternity of loving bliss.

But as perfect as that scene should have seemed—everything I'd dreamed of and worked toward for the whole year—something about it felt off. Hollow. Wrong. It wasn't based on Maya loving me; it was based on her loving my success.

And then, while I looked on from above, a third scene emerged. In this one, we had never broken up and I had never left—the best scenario of all. Or so I thought. But as I watched this scene, I noticed that Maya wasn't glowing the way she'd been just minutes earlier. We weren't connecting. And even though I looked like myself, it wasn't really me— the person I'd become. In this version, I'd never taken a chance—going away, gaining a year's worth of experience, a year's worth of confidence, and a year's worth of lessons. I'd never run a business. I'd never even been to the buffet. Was this really what I wanted?

As I watched these three scenes playing out concurrently, all three versions of Maya spoke the same words at the same time: "It's your choice."

Immediately, with an unceremonious *kerthunk!*, I was dropped back into my chair, my body, the coffee shop where the original scene was taking place—the one where Maya was still talking about loving bliss and planning to share her life…with someone else. In this scene, despite my heart-stopping, out-of-body experience, I was managing to nod, smile, and periodically make appropriate responses: "Really? Great! Congratulations!"

I must have been sufficiently convincing because she wasn't giving me odd looks, calling for a doctor, or storming out of the shop. She just kept talking as if everything was exactly as it should be: "…with Bradford's parents for a while after the baby is born."

She paused, smiled, and took a sip of coffee. And then something shocking happened. More shocking than her pregnancy. More shocking than my out-of-body experience. More shocking than anything that had happened to me over the past year—perhaps ever. I heard myself say five shocking words:

"I'm so happy for you."

No, that wasn't the shocking part. I'd already spent the past few minutes (or however long it had been) making similar positive remarks. What made this statement shocking was what I realized immediately afterward:

I meant it.

I truly was happy for her. I was genuinely pleased that she was building a life, a marriage, a family—everything she wanted, whether or not it was with me. She was happy, and that made me happy too. In fact, what I felt was more than ordinary happiness. I felt like all was right in the world, everything was exactly as it should be. We were both moving forward, not backward. We had both grown and changed. We had both forged new paths. And now it was time to let go, move on, and walk those paths separately. No second guessing. No regrets. Just gratitude. And love. A different kind of love than what I'd imagined, but love nonetheless.

She put down her coffee and asked, "So, how about you?"

"Me?" I just smiled. What could I say?

"Did you have a good year with…was it a new company?"

"Sort of—same company, new office. It was…" I shrugged. "It was good. I got to work with some great people. Went to an expo. And I found a nice lunch place—all you can eat."

She gave me a look of good-natured bemusement. "You mean, like, a cafeteria?"

"Sort of, I guess." We both laughed. "But enough about me. What's next for you?"

She glanced at her watch. "Actually, I have to meet Bradford pretty soon. We're going to his parents for Christmas. Then they're going to help us get ready for the wedding—just six days away." She offered a conciliatory smile. "I know this seems a bit weird, but—"

"No, no," I said. "I really couldn't be happier for you." I squeezed her hand and smiled. "For both of us."

Twenty minutes later, I was back in my hotel room. Alone.

I'd already paid for another night, but I was ready to hit the road. Before I checked out, though, I rummaged in my coat pocket and pulled out the smuggled cookie. I cracked it open, pulled out the fortune, and read the buffet's final lesson for me.

Lesson #50:
Know when to move on.

Epilogue

After that fateful meeting with Maya, I immediately headed off to celebrate the holidays with my family. One night after dinner, I tried to tell them about what I'd been through over the past year, including my new job, the new town, and even the buffet and everything I'd learned there. They seemed interested, but I don't think they really understood how much it had changed me. Frankly, I felt a little silly waxing poetic about the deep significance of an all-you-can-eat lunch place, so I let it go. Mainly, they were just glad I was there—ultimately, that's all that really mattered to them and, in a way, to me too.

They also comforted me about Maya—even though I assured them I didn't need comforting—and convinced me to pawn the ring (which I did, albeit for less than half the retail price). In any case, it was nice to be surrounded by loved ones, especially on the night of her wedding (which I did not attend, for numerous reasons—mainly because I wasn't invited). Surprisingly, it didn't sting—and I even offered up a silent toast to the happy couple. I wished the best for them. For all of us.

A few days later, it was time to get back to work.

My first step was to meet with my boss to review last year's numbers, get my next assignment, and perhaps discuss the lessons I'd sent—or so I thought. It turns out, she never got the lessons because by that time, she'd already left the company, leaving no contact information. This means I never got to ask her the question I'd been wondering all year: *Why had she chosen me?*

When I asked her replacement (who was now technically my boss), he peered deeply into my eyes and offered an inscrutable nod. "She saw something in you," he said. Then he handed me the folder of information for my next assignment, shook my hand, and disappeared into his office.

And before I knew it, I was on another flight—heading to another new town, which, like the last one, I'd never even heard of. Within a few hours, I'd be landing, heading to my new home—this time I'd been upgraded to a townhouse (hoo-ha!)—and getting ready to scope out the new office that I would hopefully be turning into another thriving, profitable branch of the company within twelve months.

The process was starting all over again. But would it be the same? Could it be? Time would tell.

True to their word, the company did give me a raise and a promotion. The promotion was simply a change in job title. Instead of being Assistant Manager of Internal Operations, I was now Director of Non-local Operations. Not to sound ungrateful, but I liked my old title better. Even the initials sounded friendlier: AMIO. Like *amiable, amicable, amigo.* DNO was like…*dunno.* I'm sure a more evolved person wouldn't care about stuff like this, but I wanted a title that said, *You're a big-wig.* Director of Non-local Operations just says, *We don't want you in our office—go away.*

But, like I said, the new title did come with more money, and that was certainly welcome. Granted, it was just 10% (not much more than inflation), but as they say, it's better than a slap in the face. And it would eventually build up pretty significantly because I got the raise every year, as long as I opened a new office and got it up and running profitably within twelve months. Which I did…six more times.

Each time was different, and each time was challenging. But it did get easier, mainly thanks to the lessons I'd learned during that first year. The second time around, I hired an assistant right away. And we didn't waste any time while setting up the office. Yes, we researched our options, studied best practices, and turned to third-party experts when helpful. But we didn't obsess over each little step; we learned, considered, decided, and moved on.

Throughout the year, I made a habit of reaching out to others for their ideas rather than waiting for them to come to me (as "The Waiter" at the buffet had done). I encouraged everyone to consider other points of view, rather than thinking that their perspective was the total picture (like those old nearsighted brothers). When we were faced with a project that felt overwhelming, I remembered the watermelon-eating contest and broke the project down into bite-sized chunks. And although I wasn't quick to give up just because something didn't work perfectly right away, I did recognize when it was time to pull the plug on a project and move on to something with greater potential—rather than doing the work equivalent of eating food that was rotten, too spicy, or just plain bad.

And of course, I remembered to express gratitude and give back something each week.

For a while, this job suited me fine. I finally knew what I was doing, but I still faced new challenges and situations that forced me to learn and grow. In addition to the managerial challenges, the new technology developments kept things interesting. (Looking back now, our creations during that first year seem a bit passé, even though they were cutting edge at the time.)

Also, like I said, the money was nice. The 10% raise that didn't seem like much the first year started to build up—the magic of compound growth! I ran the numbers: The second year, I made 110% of my first-year salary. The third year was 121% of my first year. The fourth was 133%, the fifth was 146%, the sixth was 161%, and the seventh was 177%. If I stuck around another year, I'd be making almost double my original salary. By the fifteenth year, it would be almost double again.

So, yes, the money was good. It was enough. Actually, it was more than enough. But after a while, it wasn't enough. I wanted something more. I don't mean a bigger raise, a bigger house, or a fancier car. I mean…

I don't know what I mean, exactly. But I do know that something was calling to me. Something else. And I wanted to find out what it was.

So, after seven years, seven new towns, and seven new offices, I put in my notice.

Everyone at the company thought I was crazy. So did my friends. "Have you done the math?!" they asked. Yes, I'd done the math. "Do you realize what you're giving up?!" Yes, I realized—I'd been doing it for the past seven years. "What are you going to do next?" I had no idea. But I was going to find out.

Call me superstitious, call me sentimental, but right after I quit, I did something I hadn't done for seven years: I went back to where it all began—the first new town, the first new office, and of course, the buffet. I wanted to see it all again—to close this chapter before I began the next one. And besides, I had a little something up my sleeve—or, rather, in my pocket—that I knew would make people very happy. For now, it was my little secret, but I was itching to share it.

When I got into town, I drove straight to my old office. "Good afternoon, sir. How can I help you?" asked the woman at the front desk. I introduced myself, and she said to make myself at home. I didn't recognize the receptionist—or any of the other twenty-odd people there. I learned that of the Faithful Four, only Rohan remained, and he was out for the holidays. Tamika had retired. Brenda had moved to be closer to her grandkids. And Zoey was now freelancing.

Even without my old work buddies, the office looked so familiar—but it felt so different, like returning to my old high school. Amazing that I could feel so removed from a place that had played such a big part of my life. Being there felt like having one foot in the present and one in the past. And that's not where I really wanted to be. I was looking toward the future.

After leaving the office, I drove to my old apartment. I got out of the car and looked from the outside, but I didn't feel called to do more than that—no tug to knock on the door, ask the current resident if I could come in and look around, or even linger for more than a moment outside. It didn't feel like part of my life—more like a place I'd seen in a movie long ago. But I was grateful that it had played a role in getting me to where I was now and where I was heading next—which was the one place I most wanted to go—the main reason for this whole trip: the buffet.

Yes, it was partly a sentimental gesture, but it wasn't just a way of revisiting the past. This was my way of moving forward. This is where I would receive the guidance I needed for the next stage of my life. After all, this is where I'd learned the most important lessons for that first year in my new position. Surely its magic could help me now. And this time, I could also help the buffet—by sharing my big secret.

Thanks to my success, I could now do something I hadn't been in a position to do seven years ago: leave a massive tip. And I do mean massive. It would be truly epic—colossal, gigantic, gargantuan, ginormous. Bigger than anything they'd ever seen. Enough to keep their trays stocked for many meals to come.

I planned to slip it into the tip jar anonymously, so I would never know for sure how it was received, but I could just imagine the look on people's faces—the awe, the amazement, and (once the shock wore off) the gratitude. It would be the stuff of legends. But for all that the buffet had added to my life (and to so many others), they deserved every dollar.

As I'd done almost every Saturday when I'd lived there, I left my car near my old apartment and walked. Even after all these years, I could've made that walk in my sleep. Like the office, much of it was the same—familiar houses, businesses, and other restaurants—but a lot of places had changed or were completely new since I'd last been there.

Although I was walking faster than usual, it seemed to take longer than I'd remembered until I reached the buffet. Or rather, the site where it had once stood. Now, instead of a buffet, it was vacant.

The buffet was gone.

In its place was an empty space between the same old nail salon and the discount shoe store that had been there seven years earlier. But now, instead of the world's greatest all-you-can-eat place, there was just a path leading to the other buildings in the strip mall (none of which I had any interest in visiting).

I walked back to my car in a daze, half disbelieving what I'd seen—or *hadn't* seen. Somehow I made it back to my hotel, where I went to bed without eating dinner. (It seemed like the right thing to do—like eating at a time like this would somehow be disrespecting the buffet.)

Lying in my hotel bed that night, my stomach turned. I couldn't believe it. The buffet was gone! Demolished! Destroyed! Like it had never existed, except in my own mind—which, for a few hours there, I was starting to question.

By the light of morning, though, I saw things differently. Of course the buffet was real. Even though its physical structure was gone, its spirit and its lessons would live on. By knocking down the walls, they hadn't destroyed the buffet; they had freed it. Now it wasn't just in one place.

It was everywhere.

Appendix A: Lessons

Lessons from Chapters 1–50

1. You have almost endless options but limited time. Choose something, or you'll be left unsatisfied.

2. Guidance can help—but first and foremost, trust your senses, trust your gut, trust yourself.

3. You find what you look for, so look for what you want to find.

4. You don't have to go it alone. Help is available; you just have to ask.

5. Structure and hierarchies reduce chaos, confusion, and waste.

6. When you're faced with a problem, it doesn't matter how many bad options there are. You just need one viable solution.

7. No single person needs to have every quality and fill every role. But together, a team can be balanced, complementary, and stronger than the sum of its parts.

8. Rejections don't mean there's anything wrong with you, but they can provide opportunities for growth.

9. Make a decision and align with it.

10. Don't overcomplicate it.

11. Set healthy boundaries.

12. Not every decision is either/or.

13. Look for guidance in unexpected places.

14. Sometimes there isn't a catch.

15. It's not what you *could* do that matters; it's what you actually *do*.

16. Start small.

17. Everything you try is either a success or a learning experience.

18. Sometimes less is more.

19. Trust the process. What looks imperfect is often just unfinished.

20. Don't keep doing what you know will hurt you and help no one.

21. There's not usually one "right" answer to every question. The best guidance may be different for each person and each situation.

22. Find the sweet spot between not enough and too much.

23. Be present.

24. Winners know when to keep going, when to try something different, and when to quit.

25. If you want something, don't wait for someone to give it to you. Speak up, take action, and invite others to do the same.

26. No matter how good things seem in theory, if the reality falls short, it might be time to change.

27. You can learn from others, but ultimately you have to do what feels right to you.

28. A great trend won't help unless it's the right fit for you.

29. Advice can be helpful, but you can't please everyone. Ultimately, you have to do what feels right to you.

30. Obvious ideas can work. But for true innovation, you have to dig deeper, pass up the low-hanging fruit, and reach beyond the front row.

31. Your perspective is valid, but it's just one piece of the puzzle.

32. If you don't like something, that doesn't necessarily mean it's bad—or that the people who make it, offer it, or like it are bad. It's just not your cup of tea.

33. Instead of running the same race as everyone else, carve out your own lane…and win.

34. Perseverance doesn't guarantee success, but it does make it possible.

35. Even the biggest task is manageable if you break it into bite-sized pieces.

36. Worry is not preparation, nor is it productive, constructive, or beneficial.

37. You *will* miss some opportunities. And that's okay. The key is to make the most of the ones you do choose.

38. Pay it back. Pay it forward. Give in whatever way and whatever amount feels right for you. But give something.

39. Details matter.

40. As long as there's time, there's hope. Sometimes you just have to find a different way to reach your goal. (And the vehicle for getting there might be more obvious than you think!)

41. Desperation pushes people away and causes you to make poor choices.

42. Even if your first choice feels like the best by far, it's rarely the only path to success.

43. When you make mistakes, don't make excuses. Instead, make a sincere apology, make things right, make sure it won't happen again, and make yourself better.

44. Visible results may get the most attention, but the work that no one sees makes up the vast majority of any project.

45. Constantly reliving the past can keep you from living in the present or planning for a brighter future.

46. No matter how sophisticated your products are, authentic human connection is a company's most valuable resource.

47. There's almost always another way to reach your goal.

48. Success is sweeter when it's shared.

49. What matters most isn't what you take—it's what you give.

50. Know when to move on.

Bonus Lessons

Introduction: Seize opportunities when you can. You never know if or when they'll arise again.

Epilogue: Wherever you are, wherever you look, you can find the lessons you need.

Entire Book: Life is filled with nearly boundless possibilities. Engage with the ones that draw you in. Experience them fully. Appreciate them. Share them. Celebrate them. Then give something back. In other words, *live*.

Appendix B: Questions

Use these questions as conversation starters with coworkers, reading groups, or anyone else who's also read this book, or you can simply reflect and answer them on your own.

1. What part(s) of this book do you most relate to?

2. What's one lesson that particularly resonates with you, and how might you apply it to your work or other areas of your life?

3. In the book's opening scene, the narrator is presented with a tremendous opportunity that also carries tremendous risk. Have you ever had to make a similar choice—between taking a risk vs. playing it safe? If so, what did you choose—and how do you feel about that choice? If you were faced with a similar opportunity now, what would you choose—and why?

4. In the buffet, the abundance of choices presents both a blessing and a challenge. When in your life have you been in a similar situation?

5. While trying to find waffles at the buffet (and do everything himself at work), the narrator learns that it's okay to ask for help. Are you ever reluctant to ask for help or support? If so, how might it benefit you to do so?

6. When things go wrong, the narrator often focuses on negatives. Have you ever found yourself doing this? What helped you shift your focus?

7. A man eating at the buffet for the first time overcomplicates their very straightforward policy (one flat fee for all you can eat). When have you overcomplicated a situation (at work or elsewhere)? In what ways is a simpler approach sometimes more effective?

8. The narrator quickly learns that his open-door policy hinders his productivity. Where in your life could you benefit from clearer boundaries?

9. When the buffet makes a mistake, the manager offers a model apology. Have you ever received a pseudo-apology (or non-apology) that left out some of the key elements of the buffet's letter? If so, how did it make you feel? When you are the one who needs to apologize, how can you do so in a way that mends fences and improves the situation rather than making things worse?

10. One recurring theme is that a helpful approach for large projects is to start small, break them into manageable tasks, and understand that any process takes time to develop. When might a similar approach benefit you?

11. "Chili Man" keeps eating five-alarm chili even though it hurts him. Have you ever done anything that you knew was painful and/or counterproductive? If so, how did you break that habit? Or, if you still do this, how might you be able to break that habit?

12. After observing "The Waiter" at the buffet, the narrator begins to mentally divide people into two categories: Waiters (who passively wait for others to provide guidance or direction) and Self-Servers (who proactively take the lead in projects and other areas of their lives). What category do you tend to lean toward, and how does this affect your life?

13. The narrator wrestles with how closely to watch the competition. How do you balance learning from others with staying true to your own approach?

14. After receiving mixed (and sometimes contradictory) advice at work and at the buffet, the narrator learns that you can't please everyone. When have you experienced this lesson firsthand, and how did you handle the situation?

15. Rather than focusing on the present, the narrator often finds himself regretting the past or anticipating the future (either with eagerness or with worry). Do you tend to focus most on the past, the present, or the future, and how does this affect you?

16. Learning about the buffet's charitable actions inspires the narrator to consider ways in which he might be able to give back (or pay it forward). In what ways do you—or *could* you—contribute to others?

17. At several points in the book, the narrator suffers major setbacks. What setbacks have you faced in your career (and/or other areas)? Did they force you to shift to "Plan B" (as sometimes happens to the narrator)? What helped you move forward and regain your footing?

18. At the expo, rather than hiding behind slick demos or technology, the narrator takes an unexpectedly vulnerable and authentically human approach. Have you ever shown similar vulnerability? How was it received by others, and how did it feel for you?

19. What did you think of the book's final sentence? How might this apply to your own life?

20. What was your biggest takeaway from this book? How might you apply it to your life?

About the Author

Dan Teck is the bestselling author of *Rewrite Your Story* and co-author/creator of *Soul Biz*, the 365 Book Series, and the Soulful Journals Series. Drawing from his experience managing a technology-training company and an independent bookstore, he brings a unique perspective to the challenges and opportunities explored in *The Buffet*. A full-time entrepreneur since 2005, he now leads the Your Soulful Book community (co-founded with his wife, Jodi), which helps aspiring authors write, publish, and market books that share positive messages and inspire readers—as he hopes this book does for you!

Learn more at www.danteckauthor.com.

A Note from the Author

If this book inspired you, I'd love if you'd leave a quick Amazon review—it helps other readers find it too. Thank you!

I'd also like to thank the people who helped bring this book into the world—especially the ever-supportive members of my writing group, my thoughtful early readers (Bianca, Christine, Jordan, and Marci), and the many mentors who've shaped my work over the years. And most of all, thank you to my wife, Jodi, whose inspiration, wisdom, and steady encouragement mean more than I can say.